The States and Public Higher Education Policy

THE STATES
AND PUBLIC
HIGHER EDUCATION
POLICY

Affordability, Access, and Accountability

Edited by Donald E. Heller

The Johns Hopkins University Press
Baltimore and London

© 2001 The Johns Hopkins University Press
All rights reserved. Published 2001
Printed in the United States of America on acid-free paper
9 8 7 6 5 4 3 2 1

The Johns Hopkins University Press
2715 North Charles Street
Baltimore, Maryland 21218–4363
www.press.jhu.edu

A catalog record for this book is available
from the British Library.

Library of Congress Cataloging-in-Publication Data

The States and public higher education policy : affordability,
access, and accountability / edited by Donald E. Heller.
    p.   cm.
Results partly from a conference held in Ann Arbor, Mich.,
in June 1998.
Includes bibliographical references and index.
   ISBN 0-8018-6494-1 (hardcover : alk. paper)
    1. Higher education and state—United States—Congresses.   2.
State universities and colleges—United States—Administration—
Congresses.   I. Heller, Donald E.
  LC173.S65 2001
  378.73—dc21

00-008878

Contents

III   ACCOUNTABILITY

Foreword

The contributors to this volume argue convincingly that affordability, access, and accountability are the three key policy issues facing public higher education in the opening years of the new century. I believe they are correct in this judgment, but it is worth considering briefly whether these issues are new or surprising. What, for example, might one have picked as the key issues in 1950, or in subsequent decades? A thorough answer to this question would take us far beyond the scope of this Foreword, but let me suggest that affordability and accountability are relatively recent issues, whereas access clearly has roots as far back as the World War II GI Bill and the Truman Commission Report of 1947 (President's Commission on Higher Education, *Higher Education for American Democracy* [New York: Harper & Bros, 1947]). That access remains on the view screen is a testament both to its continuing importance and to our failure to truly achieve it, despite decades of effort and expenditure.

It is also worth noting that each of these terms is a type of code word, with definite political connotations. In the early 1970s, *access* was often contrasted with *choice*, with *access* being a code word for enrollment in a low-priced public university or community college and *choice* signifying the opportunity to enroll in a higher-priced, private college or university. In that era, these terms signaled policy positions that favored either public or private institutions. Today, *access* entangles one in the complexities of affirmative action and the process of selective admission to undergraduate and professional programs at prestigious institutions. To a lamentable degree, the political emphasis on access, equity, and opportunity that gave rise to need-based financial aid programs such as federal Pell Grants seems to have waned in recent years as the focus has shifted to merit awards and the concerns of middle- and upper-income families about how to pay for college.

Indeed, *affordability* has now become a code word for policies that help middle- and upper-income families pay for higher education, as opposed to the more common definition, which refers to families at all income levels. Rapidly rising tuition charges in recent years have sent a chill through many relatively high-income families as they contemplate future expenses for higher education. The myth abounds that students from middle-income families are being squeezed out of college by low-income students who receive a free ride through grants and by wealthy students who can afford to pay.* Regardless of the facts, perceptions are powerful inducements to political action, and politicians at both the state and federal levels have been falling over themselves in recent years to enact programs to help the beleaguered middle- and upper-income groups finance college costs. Examples of such programs are the federal tuition tax credit, the HOPE program of merit scholarships begun in Georgia and copied elsewhere, tax-favored college savings plans, prepaid tuition programs, and the reduction of public tuition charges made possible by state budget surpluses. One of the clear challenges facing public policy at this moment is to sort out the legitimate from the dubious claims regarding affordability that are casually tossed around in these debates. The economic—as opposed to political—fact is that true *affordability* remains a problem primarily for students from low-income families, which simply means that the promise of access has not yet been met. Ironically, achieving *affordability* in its current political definition means competing for resources that might otherwise increase access, rather than being in harmony with it—a situation that cries out for correction.

The third of our issues, accountability, can now be brought into play. It, too, is a code word, focused on the need to curb the increasing escalation of college costs and to ensure that the quality of the programs offered is high. That the three issues under review are clearly linked should now be clear, in that rising college costs—all else being equal—will reduce both access and affordability. Because politicians are concerned with families' views on both the cost and the quality of higher education, trends in those measures are particularly sensitive. Given that college prices have been increasing rapidly and that complaints about college quality are increasingly being heard, one can readily see why political demands for accountability on the part of colleges and universities have been escalating. Tensions between governors and public college presidents are apparent in many states, with politically appointed boards of trustees often placed in the middle, with divided loyalties. Two intellectual dilemmas confound this problem: (1) the economics of cost, price, and production in higher education is messy and poorly understood, even by those within the industry, and (2) the measurement or assessment of

---

*College participation in the United States is strongly and positively correlated with income. While all income groups made gains in their college participation rates between 1970 and 1996, the largest gains were made by middle-income students (College Board, *Trends in college pricing* [Washington, DC, 1999]).

outcomes from higher education is rudimentary at best. The upshot of these dilemmas is that, in an atmosphere increasingly devoid of trust, it is difficult to define and implement a meaningful system of accountability.

The cost dilemma can be traced to the multiple sources of funding (tuition, state and federal support, gifts, endowment earnings, research grants, and auxiliary income) and the multiple and joint activities of colleges and universities. Furthermore, the politically sensitive price that parents pay—tuition—is influenced by the other revenue sources, so that if state appropriations drop, tuition may rise as an offset, even if costs have not changed. Thus, in the early 1990s, when states reduced support for public higher education, tuition rose at double-digit rates two years in a row, contributing to family worries about affordability. Explaining these factors, and trying to control them, is a daunting task, which gives rise to much frustration for all participants. No easy solution seems apparent.

While much work has been done on defining and measuring educational outcomes, it is still fair to say that we do not have any established system for codifying such outcomes and relating them clearly to the various inputs. Indeed, one of the complexities of educational production is that a critical input (the student) plays a key role in the educational outcomes of others—that is, some of the best education is produced by a student's peers, which is part of the appeal of a selective college or university. When we add in the complexities of joint production of undergraduate education, graduate education, and research, the conceptual problems increase geometrically. Even with the best will in the world, developing useful accountability systems for educational outcomes remains a difficult and challenging task.

In complex human activities such as higher education, one is drawn back to the necessity of trust as an alternative to regulation, but trust must be deserved and, once lost, is difficult to recapture. It is my hope that the thoughtful chapters in this book will contribute to a better understanding of the central policy issues confronting higher education, and to our ability to work together, across political lines, to ensure access to higher education for future generations and to make sure that quality higher education is affordable to all who seek it. If we meet those goals, then we may also succeed in reestablishing trust among families, politicians, and our institutions of higher education. That may prove to be the best form of accountability.

DAVID W. BRENEMAN

Acknowledgments

This book results partly from a conference held in Ann Arbor, Michigan, in June 1998. The conference, sponsored by the Center for the Study of Higher and Postsecondary Education at the University of Michigan School of Education and co-sponsored by the State Higher Education Executive Officers (SHEEO), brought together policymakers, college and university administrators, and academics to examine three key issues facing public higher education at the end of the twentieth century: affordability, access, and accountability. Many of the contributors to this volume were participants in the conference, and they helped to make it a lively and valuable gathering.

In addition to these contributors, I would like to thank others who spoke at the conference: Gordon Davies, president of the Council on Postsecondary Education in Kentucky; Elizabeth Lanier, former chairperson of the Ohio Board of Regents; Jerry Martin, president of the American Council of Alumni and Trustees; Rebecca McGowan, regent of the University of Michigan; Aims McGuinness, senior associate at the National Center for Higher Education Management Systems; James Mingle, executive director of SHEEO; Candace de Russy, trustee of the State University of New York; and Michigan State Senator John J. H. Schwarz. Michael McLendon, formerly a research assistant in the Center for the Study of Higher and Postsecondary Education, provided invaluable assistance in helping to organize and manage the conference, and the Office of the Dean of the School of Education provided financial support for the conference.

Jacqueline Wehmueller, editor-in-chief at the Johns Hopkins University Press, was instrumental in helping to shape the original manuscript proposal that evolved into this book. Linda Strange provided excellent assistance as copy editor, helping bring together and make consistent the work of fourteen authors with different writing styles. Managing editor Barbara B. Lamb and senior production editor Carol Zimmerman also provided valuable assistance to the project. Barbara E. Cohen produced the index.

I want to acknowledge the assistance and encouragement of my colleagues in the Center for the Study of Higher and Postsecondary Education at the University of Michigan. My work on this volume benefited from numerous discussions with and suggestions from them.

Finally, I thank my wife, Anne Simon, and my daughters, Rose and Lena Heller, for their support and patience while I worked on this book. Much of the time and energy that went into this project would otherwise have been spent on familial pursuits.

The States and Public Higher Education Policy

INTRODUCTION: The Changing Dynamics
of Affordability, Access, and Accountability
in Public Higher Education

DONALD E. HELLER

Affordability, access, and accountability are the three key issues facing public higher education at the start of the new millennium. With more than 80 percent of all undergraduates in the United States attending public colleges and universities, very few discussions on higher education take place without one or more of these issues being central to the debate. In an era when education at all levels is receiving increasing attention from policymakers, parents, students, and the media alike, colleges and universities are under increasing scrutiny. What do these various parties expect from public institutions of higher education? In this volume we attempt to address this question by examining affordability, access, and accountability from a variety of perspectives.

Concerns about the affordability of college have existed for some time.[1] The President's Commission on Higher Education (1947), appointed by President Truman after the close of World War II, expressed its concern about the impact of affordability on the opportunity to attend college:

> It is the responsibility of the community, at the local, State, and National levels, to guarantee that financial barriers do not prevent any able and otherwise qualified young person from receiving the opportunity for higher education. There must be developed in this country the widespread realization that money expended for education is the wisest and soundest of investments in the national interest. The democratic community cannot tolerate a society based upon education for the well-to-do alone. If college opportunities are restricted to those in the higher income brackets, the way is open to the creation and perpetuation of a class society which has no place in the American way of life. (vol. 2, p. 23)

Among the commission's recommendations was that "in publicly controlled institutions there be no tuition or other required fees for the thirteenth and fourteenth school years, irrespective of whether they are offered by a two-year or a four-year college; and that fees above the fourteenth school year be reduced at the earliest possible moment to the level prevailing in 1939" (vol. 2, p. 22). Because the federal government did not directly control any colleges or universities (with the exception of the military academies), it had no authority to implement this recommendation. Almost twenty years passed before the federal government implemented the Higher Education Act of 1965, the nation's first broad-based financial aid program for college, and another nine years before the cornerstone of the Act, the Educational Opportunity Grant program (now called Pell Grants), was funded at a level that had any measurable impact on students.[2]

The states have historically relied on the general state subsidy, in the form of direct state appropriations to public colleges and universities, to maintain affordability. Through this subsidy of all or most of the cost of instruction, institutions could keep tuition rates very low and, in many cases, could adhere to the 1947 recommendations of the President's Commission by making the first two years of college free. Until the last two decades, such major public institutions as the City College of New York and the California community colleges charged no tuition, and public institutions with tuition charged well below comparable private institutions and required a relatively small proportion of family income. Over the last three decades, however, tuition prices at public colleges and universities have skyrocketed, increasing more than 700 percent, while the median family income has grown at less than half that rate.

The concern about college affordability expressed by the President's Commission in 1947 can also be interpreted as a warning about access. As David W. Breneman points out in the Foreword to this volume, in the context of higher education, *access* has had different meanings. Historically, definitions of accessibility have included such components as

- *Financial accessibility:* Does the student have the financial resources necessary to attend college?
- *Geographic accessibility:* How far does a potential student have to travel to attend college?
- *Programmatic accessibility:* Is the academic program that the student wants available?
- *Academic accessibility:* Has the student had the proper academic preparation in her or his precollegiate years?
- *Cultural/social/physical accessibility:* Do precollege students receive the necessary encouragement and support to attend college from parents, families, peers, schools, and others? Do some policies (either de jure or de facto) prohibit or encourage the enrollment of students from particular groups, such as racial minorities, or older, nontraditional college students? Are there physical barriers to attendance, especially for students with a disability that limits their mobility?

Access to college is particularly critical in today's economy; some form of higher education is increasingly required to obtain a job that supports a middle-class lifestyle.

The accountability movement in public higher education is the most recent of the three issues addressed in this book. Although higher education institutions have long been considered stewards of the public trust, in recent years attention has focused not only on what colleges and universities do, but also on how well they do it and what resources they use. This attention has come from (1) legislators, governors, and coordinating boards, responsible for allocating state budget expenditures to the institutions; (2) students and their families, who are paying an increasing share of higher education costs; (3) businesses and other employers, which hire the college and university graduates; and (4) accrediting and other oversight bodies, which provide quality assurance for education.

The reasons for this increased scrutiny are numerous. Because the funding of higher education is increasingly seen as a discretionary portion of state budgets, colleges and universities are expected to justify their receipt of state funds. News media attention to what happens on college campuses makes policymakers and the public aware of such less-than-flattering topics as campus crime, drug and alcohol abuse by students, poor graduation rates of athletes, work habits and productivity of faculty members, and million-dollar-a-year athletic coaches.[3] And, as tuition charges increase, students and their parents expect more value for their dollar.

The contributors to this book address the issues of affordability, access, and accountability by going beyond the headlines to examine how public colleges and universities are affected by and are responding to the current societal pressures. While we do not provide all the answers, we do identify the key questions facing these institutions and suggest some implications for students, parents, campus leaders, faculty, and policymakers.

Overview of the Book

The volume is organized in three parts paralleling the themes of affordability, access, and accountability, with a concluding essay on the role of technology in helping to chart the future of these issues. Although the themes are addressed specifically in the three parts, the connections between the three issues will be apparent. Affordability is a key determinant of access to college, particularly when considering students of different background characteristics (such as income and race). As concerns about affordability and access have grown among policymakers, parents, and others, calls have increased for higher education institutions to be more accountable. Clearly, none of these issues can be analyzed in isolation but must be examined in the larger context of the societal forces shaping all three.

In Chapter 1, I provide an overview of the rise in college prices in recent years and how this can be reconciled with increasing college enrollments. Data on tuition prices, financial aid availability, and family incomes are used to construct measures of affordability based on the ability of students and their families to pay for college. The chapter includes an examination of how affordability has changed for students in different income groups and different racial and ethnic groups. I also explain why undergraduate enrollments have continued to rise in the face of rapid increases in tuition prices.

In Chapter 2, Michael Mumper analyzes the reasons for tuition increases. After reviewing the literature on this topic, he describes the results of his visits to eleven states where he talked to policymakers about why public college prices have risen so much in recent years. Policymakers have the tools and the authority to set tuition prices at any level they desire, so recent increases did not occur accidentally. Mumper groups the stories he heard into five major categories. He describes the stories and draws conclusions about why policymakers allowed such large price increases, given what they knew about the potential impact on students and the institutions.

In the final chapter of Part I, Arthur M. Hauptman describes the three key policy levers that states use to finance public higher education: direct state appropriations to institutions, the setting of tuition policies, and state financial aid programs. He relates how the use of these mechanisms has evolved over the last fifty years, analyzes the problems with the structure and use of these mechanisms in the current policy environment, and suggests some ways in which states can better coordinate these policies to ensure that public higher education is both affordable and accessible.

Part II addresses access to public higher education, beginning with a chapter by Patrick M. Callan that examines the interaction between state and federal policies on access to colleges and universities. States do not operate in a policy vacuum; what occurs at the federal level affects the higher education policies implemented by the states. Callan provides an overview of how the states and federal government worked to ensure access to college over the last half-century and how that interaction broke down in the 1990s. He identifies six elements that may help policymakers reframe and revitalize access to higher education.

Sylvia Hurtado and Heather Wathington Cade (Chapter 5) and Brian Pusser (Chapter 6) examine one of the key access issues now being addressed by policymakers both on and off public campuses: affirmative action. Recent legal challenges and referenda in a number of states have dealt a blow to three decades of efforts to reverse the effects of centuries of discrimination against minority students. Hurtado and Wathington Cade examine the elimination of affirmative action from the perspective of a major public university in Texas, where a federal court decision in the case of *Hopwood v. State of Texas* forced public institutions (in Texas and other states of the federal Fifth Circuit) to stop using race and ethnicity in the admissions process. They describe how the decision affected minority students' access to the institution, as well as the views of students, faculty, and staff members about race.

Pusser examines another setting where affirmative action was challenged, California, but does so from the broader perspective of state policy. He describes the 1995 decision by the regents of the University of California to eliminate the use of affirmative action on the university's nine campuses and the impact of Proposition 209, the 1996 ballot measure that eliminated the use of race in hiring and determining admissions to public higher education. He analyzes how these changes affected access to California's public colleges and universities and examines the resulting tensions between institutional autonomy and state policy.

The final part of the book addresses the issue of accountability, opening with a chapter in which William Zumeta provides an overview of states' attempts to impose accountability standards on public colleges and universities. Zumeta describes in detail how four states (Tennessee, Missouri, South Carolina, and Washington) implemented the standards and considers the institutional implications. In Chapter 8, Michael Nettles and John Cole examine a particular form of accountability: assessment. They analyze the literature on and history of state efforts to assess the performance of public colleges and universities and describe their own research on the current condition of assessment efforts nationwide.

Part III closes with an essay by Edward P. St. John, Kimberly A. Kline, and Eric H. Asker drawing links between accountability and student outcomes. The authors review the literature on how college affects students, focusing on persistence and graduation, and examine how two states (Florida and New York) have wrestled with holding institutions accountable for improving student outcomes. They conclude by offering an alternative way of looking at student outcomes and the role of public accountability.

In the Conclusion, I explore what the future may hold for the issues of affordability, access, and accountability in public higher education, with a focus on the role of technology. Virtual learning and computer-based distance education have exploded onto the scene in recent years and have opened up both new opportunities and challenges for institutions and policymakers alike. I examine how technology has been reshaping public higher education and how it may affect it in the future.

Howard Bowen (1977), in his classic treatise *Investment in Learning*, outlined the value of higher education for individuals and for society as a whole. The book was written toward the end of an era in the United States in which policymakers and the public recognized that investments in higher education served society as a whole, not just the individuals who attended colleges and universities. Since the late 1970s we have seen the focus shift to how higher education benefits individuals, with less recognition and analysis of how it furthers broader public interests. This has been accompanied by a change in attitudes toward paying for college, with the responsibility shifting from society (in the form of state appropriations for public institutions and scholarships for students) to individuals and their families (in the form of tuition and loans).

From the 1960s through the 1980s, the question of access to higher education was focused on populations traditionally underrepresented on college and university campuses. This included students from lower-income families, who benefited from the student aid provisions of the Higher Education Act of 1965 and its subsequent reauthorizations and from the historically low tuition allowed by direct state appropriations, and minority students, who benefited also from the changes engendered by the Civil Rights Act of 1964. Access to higher education also improved for women, whose college participation has outstripped that of men, and older students, who benefited from the expansion of part-time and non-degree programs.[4] The access gains made by lower-income and minority students in particular are now threatened by changes in college financing policies and attacks on affirmative action, as outlined in Parts I and II of this volume. While states and institutions have responded in a variety of ways to these threats, evidence is only now becoming available to judge the effectiveness of those responses.[5]

The accountability movement in higher education holds great potential for influencing how colleges and universities respond to changes in affordability and access. If the performance-based funding and related policies described in Part III are used to encourage particular behavior by institutions, it is logical to assume institutions will respond by altering their policies in accord with the stated goals. For example, funding formulas that reward institutions for achieving broader racial and ethnic diversity among their students will encourage colleges to find mechanisms for improving access for minority students, despite the declining ability to use race-based affirmative action practices. Such formulas, however, may put additional pressures on affordability, because African American, Hispanic, and Native American students come from families that, on average, have lower incomes than white and Asian American families. On the other hand, performance-based funding mechanisms that reward institutions for increasing their graduation rates may work against the goal of access for minority and lower-income students, who often are at more risk of dropping out and staying out of college.

Notes

1. This volume focuses primarily on undergraduate education. For recent analyses of access to and affordability of graduate education, see Bakst (1997), Bowen and Rudenstine (1992), and Choy and Moskovitz (1998).

2. Two major pieces of legislation before 1965 provided financial aid for college. The Servicemen's Readjustment Act (popularly known as the GI Bill of Rights), passed and signed into law in 1944, provided educational, housing, unemployment, and other assistance to returning veterans. However, as Mumper (1996) points out, "The G.I. Bill . . . was not viewed as a student-aid program. To its many supporters, it was a benefit program for military service that was merely disguised as college aid" (p. 75). This view supports that of Eleanor Roosevelt; following passage of the bill she wrote, "There is one great fear in the heart of any serviceman, and it is not that he will be killed or maimed but that when he is finally allowed to go home and piece together what he can of life, he will be made to feel he has been a sucker for the sacrifice he has made" (quoted in Goodwin, 1994, p. 512).

The National Defense Education Act, passed in 1958 in response to launching of the Sputnik satellite by the Soviet Union, focused primarily on elementary and secondary education and on training in the sciences and foreign languages. It contained provisions for a campus-based loan program for college students but did little to address the overall affordability of higher education (Mumper, 1996).

3. See, e.g., "Drug and alcohol arrests increase" (1999), Funk (1994), Haworth (1998), May (1999), Weiss (1998), and Chapter 2 of this volume.

4. The gain in women's college participation has been one of the most astounding stories in access to higher education in recent years. In 1960, 54 percent of all men enrolled in college within a year of high school graduation, compared with 38 percent of women (National Center for Education Statistics, 1999). In the same year, 63 percent of all college students were male. By 1996, only 44 percent of college students were male, and although male college enrollment rates had increased to 60 percent of high school graduates (a gain of six percentage points), the female enrollment rate increased to 70 percent (a gain of thirty-two percentage points). For more on this gender shift, see Gose (1999) and Lewin (1998).

5. The Texas "top 10 percent" and California "top 4 percent" plans outlined in Chapters 5 and 6, respectively, have been the most visible policy responses to the affirmative action prohibitions in those states. A similar plan has been enacted by

the board of regents of the State University System of Florida. Other efforts by higher education institutions faced with the demise of affirmative action include more outreach to and linkages with school districts that enroll large numbers of minority students (Selingo, 1999).

References

Bakst, D. (1997). The federal government's role in providing access to graduate education. *College and University, 72*(3), 25–27.

Bowen, H. R. (1977). *Investment in learning: The individual and social value of American higher education.* San Francisco: Jossey-Bass; reprint ed., Baltimore: Johns Hopkins University Press, 1997.

Bowen, W. G., & Rudenstine, N. L. (1992). *In pursuit of the Ph.D.* Princeton: Princeton University Press.

Choy, S. P., & Moskovitz, R. (1998). *Student financing of graduate and first-professional education, 1995–96.* Washington, DC: National Center for Education Statistics.

Drug and alcohol arrests increase at colleges. (1999, May 23). *New York Times*, p. 26.

Funk, J. (1994, February 18). Regents to send profs back to class; new regulation would require 10 percent more teaching time. *Cleveland Plain Dealer*, p. 5B.

Goodwin, D. K. (1994). *No ordinary time: Franklin and Eleanor Roosevelt: The home front in World War II.* New York: Simon & Schuster.

Gose, B. (1999, November 26). Colleges look for ways to reverse a decline in enrollment of men. *Chronicle of Higher Education*, p. A73.

Haworth, K. (1998, November 20). Graduation rates fall for athletes. *Chronicle of Higher Education*, p. A41.

Lewin, T. (1998, December 6). American colleges begin to ask, where have all the men gone? *New York Times*, p. 1.

May, T. (1999, February 28). Looking like a million dollars. *Columbus Dispatch*, p. 1E.

Mumper, M. (1996). *Removing college price barriers: What government has done and why it hasn't worked.* Albany: State University of New York Press.

National Center for Education Statistics. (1999). *Digest of education statistics, 1998.* Washington, DC: U.S. Department of Education.

President's Commission on Higher Education. (1947). *Higher education for American democracy* (Vols. 1–6). New York: Harper & Bros.

Selingo, J. (1999, November 19). Why minority recruiting is alive and well in Texas. *Chronicle of Higher Education*, p. A34.

Weiss, K. R. (1998, September 21). Universities, students are learning the facts of life in a dangerous world; crime statistics, investigations put campuses under a cloud, but the need for honesty is being addressed by officials. *Los Angeles Times*, p. B2.

I AFFORDABILITY

1 Trends in the Affordability of Public Colleges and Universities: The Contradiction of Increasing Prices and Increasing Enrollment

DONALD E. HELLER

Concerns about paying for college are prevalent throughout U.S. society. Media reports regularly trumpet the rising cost of higher education, including one article that proclaimed the arrival of the "$1,000-a-week price tag" for college. Recent books have focused on the rising cost of college and what can be done about it. And the federal government has formed two blue-ribbon panels in the last decade to examine the issue of college affordability.[1]

Much of the attention has focused on the country's most expensive private institutions, those that charge more than $30,000 per year for tuition, room, and board. More than 80 percent of all undergraduate students, however, attend public colleges and universities, with an average cost well below that of the elite private institutions.

A recent study by the College Board (1999a) found that the average student in a public four-year institution paid $8,000 in tuition, room, and board, and the average community college student paid $1,600 for tuition. Nevertheless, a recent poll conducted for the American Council on Education found that 65 percent of all Americans were worried about paying for college—exceeding the proportion concerned about the quality of kindergarten through twelfth grade (K–12) education or worried about becoming victims of violent crime (Ikenberry & Hartle, 1998). Other surveys reveal a silver lining to the public's anxiety about college costs, however. A study conducted for the National Center for Public Policy and Higher Education found that although people were concerned about paying for college, the level of concern had declined from that expressed five years earlier (Immerwahr, 1998).

Both surveys reveal the public's recognition of the importance of a college education, as is confirmed by recent college enrollment trends. As the tail end of the baby-boom cohort reached high school age in the late 1970s, many higher education leaders and observers predicted that colleges and universities would face a major crisis in the 1980s as the pool of eligible students dried up. Based on this prediction, combined with pronouncements by

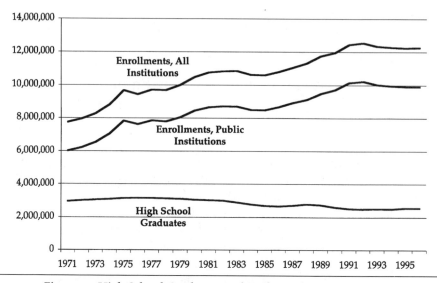

Figure 1.1. High School Graduates and Undergraduate Enrollment, 1971–1995.

Each year represents the end of the high school year and beginning of the college academic year, so "1971" indicates spring high school graduates and fall college enrollments in 1971. Data from National Center for Education Statistics (1999), Tables 101 and 172.

many economists (most notably Richard Freeman (1976) in his book *The Overeducated American*) about a surplus of college-educated people in the United States, college leaders feared that hundreds of institutions would close by the end of the 1980s.

Despite the analysts' predictions, college enrollment grew in the 1980s. Figure 1.1 illustrates the relationship between the demographics of the college-eligible pool and undergraduate enrollments. In 1971 the United States had 2.9 million high school graduates; the number peaked at 3.2 million in 1977 with the tail end of the baby boom, then declined to a low of 2.5 million in 1994, 22 percent below the peak of seventeen years earlier. The number of undergraduates (at public and private institutions), however, continued to grow during the 1970s and 1980s, with only small dips during this period, and reached 12.4 million in 1991 before leveling off. This peak was 61 percent higher than the 1971 level (7.7 million students) and 24 percent higher than the level reached at the close of the 1970s (10.0 million). The enrollment growth in public colleges and universities (also shown in Figure 1.1) was even

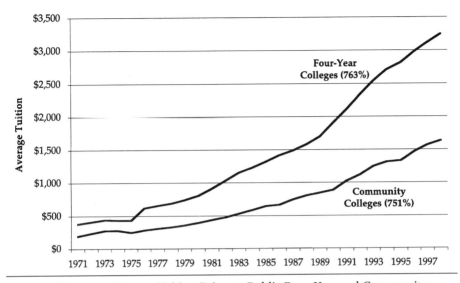

Figure 1.2. Average Tuition Prices at Public Four-Year and Community Colleges, 1971–1998.

Prices are in current (non-inflation-adjusted) dollars. Tuition amounts are for resident undergraduate students and are enrollment-weighted—they represent the price paid by the average student in each sector nationally. The increases from 1971 to 1998 are shown in parentheses. Data from the College Board (1999a), Table 5.

greater, increasing by 70 percent, from 6.0 million in 1971 to a peak of 10.2 million in 1992.

The enrollment increases were driven by two factors: (1) an increase of 156 percent in the number of "nontraditional" college attendees, students outside the cohort of 18- to 24-year-olds who had historically represented the bulk of college-going youth; and (2) an increase of 32 percent in the enrollment of 18- to 24-year-old students, despite the demographic declines of the 1980s (National Center for Education Statistics, 1999, Table 174).[2]

Examined in the light of data on recent college prices, these trends seem contradictory. Even though college and university tuition prices have risen at rates far in excess of inflation over the last two decades (as amply reported by the media) and the college-age cohort has been declining, college enrollments have continued to grow. Clearly, increasing recognition of the importance of a college education (as found in the two polls described earlier) has been offsetting concerns about the rising price. Figure 1.2 shows the average public four-year and community college tuition prices since 1971. Between

1971 and 1998, the Consumer Price Index increased 297 percent while tuition prices in both sectors increased more than 750 percent.

In the following sections I analyze the affordability of undergraduate education from a number of perspectives and attempt to explain the apparent contradiction of rising prices and enrollments. After examining alternative ways of measuring college affordability and explaining the methodology used in this chapter, I examine in detail how college affordability has changed over the last two decades. I then relate these changes to the history of increasing enrollments and offer some concluding thoughts.

Measures of College Affordability
The Price of College

The affordability of college can be measured in a number of ways. Perhaps the simplest is to look at the price.[3] For college, however, *price* has a number of meanings. The first issue to consider is what needs to be included in the price. For example, almost all students pay some form of tuition, though in many institutions this is referred to as "fees." Whatever the name, these charges are generally levied to cover the cost of courses and related services.

Some students, particularly those who live in university-provided residences, also pay for housing and meals provided by the institution. Many researchers exclude these "room and board" expenses in the calculation of college prices, assuming that these subsistence costs would be borne by the individual even if not attending college.[4] Nevertheless, these charges are real to the students (and their families) who have to pay them, and they often contribute to the "sticker shock" felt by those thinking of attending college.[5]

In addition to tuition, room, and board, many institutions charge additional fees to cover a variety of goods or services. For example, a college may require all students to pay an athletic fee to help defray the cost of interscholastic and intramural athletic programs. Technology fees to help cover the cost of computer and network infrastructures have become more popular in recent years. In a recent study conducted by the Campus Computing Project (1998), 46 percent of the colleges and universities surveyed imposed some form of technology fee, up from 28 percent three years earlier. Students in science courses may pay laboratory fees for the use of equipment and supplies. Besides these charges levied by the institutions, most college students must purchase other goods or services; textbooks, for example, can add hundreds of dollars to the price of college. Students attending an institution far from home may face significant transportation costs.

A second issue when examining the price of college is the role of financial aid, an important part of the college financing model in the United States. A college education, like many other goods or services, is often discounted below the "sticker price" given in college catalogs, admissions materials, and bursar bills. This discount is provided in the form of financial aid, which generally consists of (1) grants or scholarships, which are a straight reduction from the sticker price; (2) loans, which help defray the initial price of college but must be repaid at some later date; and (3) work study, in which the student agrees to provide some services to the college in return for hourly wages. Financial aid can come from a variety of sources: the federal government, state governments, private sources, commercial financial institutions, and the colleges and universities themselves.

Financial aid has grown in importance in recent years. In 1971, the total aid available from federal, state, and institutional sources was $5.3 billion; by 1998 this had grown to $43.6 billion, an increase of 723 percent (College Board, 1999b) during a period in which total college enrollment (as shown in Figure 1.1) grew 60 percent. Interestingly, the growth in financial aid mirrors the tuition price increases noted in Figure 1.2.[6]

Not only is more money available for aid, but a larger proportion of students are receiving aid. The National Center for Education Statistics (1998) has conducted large-scale surveys on the financing of college over the last decade. The National Postsecondary Student Aid Survey, conducted every three years from 1986 to 1995, is a nationally representative survey of postsecondary students in the United States. Its data, derived from institutional financial aid records at more than six hundred colleges and universities around the country, can be used to examine how the awarding of financial aid has changed over the years.

Table 1.1 shows the percentage of students in four-year institutions (public and private together, and public alone) receiving any type of financial aid and the percentage receiving grants during the 1989–90 and 1995–96 academic years. For every type of student and for both categories of aid recipients, the percentage receiving aid increased by at least six percentage points over this period. Among all students in both public and private four-year institutions, the proportion receiving any aid increased from just under half in 1989 to more than 60 percent six years later. In public institutions, the percentage of all students receiving any type of aid increased from 42 to 56 percent in the same period. These data demonstrate the increasing importance of taking financial aid into account when discussing the prices paid by college students.

Although financial aid is important, a good deal of evidence indicates that students' lack of knowledge about the availability of aid may dampen its

Table 1.1. Students in Four-Year Institutions Receiving Financial Aid,
1989–1990 and 1995–1996 (Percentage)

Category	Any Financial Aid		Grants	
	1989–90	1995–96	1989–90	1995–96
All institutions				
All students	49%	61%	41%	47%
Full-time students	55	70	47	55
Dependent students	49	62	40	48
Full-time, dependent students	52	67	43	52
Public institutions only				
All students	42	56	34	41
Full-time students	49	65	39	48
Dependent students	41	57	32	40
Full-time, dependent students	45	62	34	44

Source: Author's calculations from National Center for Education Statistics (1998).

effect on their enrollment decisions. Michael Mumper (1996) has summarized the dilemma of policymakers seeking to use financial aid to lower the
cost of higher education for needy students. "A plan which may look good in
an economics class may prove counterproductive in the real world of college
finance. In this view, lower-income students are likely to become discouraged
by rapid increases in the 'sticker price' of higher education. This occurs because information about tuition levels is much more widely known and
available than is information about financial aid programs" (p. 45). Reviews
of the literature on the economics of student demand for higher education
have found different student responses to sticker prices and financial aid
(Heller, 1997b; Jackson & Weathersby, 1975; Leslie & Brinkman, 1987). Although the enrollment of some types of students responds more to the
posted sticker price, other students seem better able to take the availability of
financial aid into account.

Ability to Pay

The price of a good or service tells only part of the story of its affordability. The demand for the good or service is determined by a number of
factors, including price, quality, availability and price of competing goods,
availability and price of substitute goods, consumer perception, and consumer income. As for other goods, incomes play an important role in determining the demand for and affordability of higher education. All other

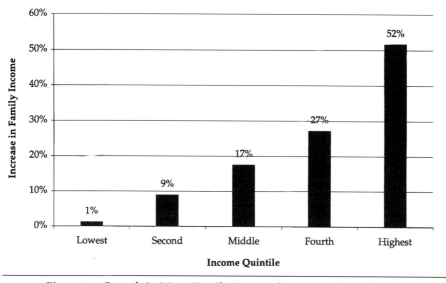

Figure 1.3. Growth in Mean Family Income, by Income Quintile, 1971–1997.
Income growth is in constant (inflation-adjusted, 1997) dollars.

things being equal, an individual from a higher-income family is more able to afford the price of a particular college than is someone from a lower-income family.

To examine the role of income in college affordability and how that role changes over time, we can examine how families in different sectors of the national income distribution have fared.[7] A common method is to rank all families from lowest to highest income and then divide them into five groups, or quintiles, with 20 percent of all families in each. For example in 1997, the average family in the lowest (first) income quintile (the poorest 20% of all families) had an income of $12,057 (U.S. Bureau of the Census, 1999a), whereas the mean income of families in the highest (fifth) income quintile was $134,285.

Figure 1.3 shows the growth in mean income of each quintile between 1971 and 1997, in constant (inflation-adjusted) dollars. Faster growth occurred among the higher income quintiles. While families in the lowest group saw an income increase of only 1 percent in real terms over these twenty-six years, families in the highest income quintile saw an increase of more than 50 percent. It is important to note that although individual families may move from one quintile to another as their incomes grow or shrink, the data in Figure 1.3 provide a sense of how similar groupings of families fared during this period and how the distribution shifted over time. And as the data show, throughout this era, the rich got relatively richer and the poor got relatively poorer.[8]

Bringing Together Price and Ability to Pay

Two key factors—the price charged by colleges and universities and the resources available to students to pay for college—can be examined in tandem to provide a key measure of college affordability. By expressing the price of college—either tuition alone or fully loaded (including the other costs discussed above), and either excluding or including financial aid—in relation to students' ability to pay, we get a more telling measure of college affordability.

The methodology used in the next section of this chapter is based on a fairly simple calculation of affordability, the ratio of price to income: P_{it}/Y_{jt}, where P_{it} is the price of college i in year t, and Y_{jt} is the income of group j in year t. As described earlier, the price can be (1) tuition (and other required fees) alone; (2) tuition plus optional expenses, such as room and board; or (3) either (1) or (2), taking into account financial aid. In addition, we can examine the price of all public institutions or only certain types (such as four-year versus community colleges). Income can also be any number of measures, such as (1) median income; (2) measures of low or high income, such as quintile groupings; or (3) income of population subgroups, such as different racial groups or regions within the country.

The affordability analyses in the next section use a number of measures of price and income, but all are based on this same ratio.[9]

Changes in Affordability of Public Colleges and Universities

As described earlier, for almost three decades public tuition prices have increased at a rate more than twice that of general inflation. This sustained increase has caused major changes in the proportion of family income required to send a student to college. In 1971, a family with the median income used 3.7 percent of its income to pay tuition for a single student attending a public four-year institution.[10] By 1997 this proportion had almost doubled, to 7.0 percent.

Figure 1.4 shows these same proportions for the mean-income family in each of the income quintiles. For families in the two poorest groupings, the proportion of income required to pay for one year's tuition at a public four-year institution more than doubled over the twenty-six years. For students

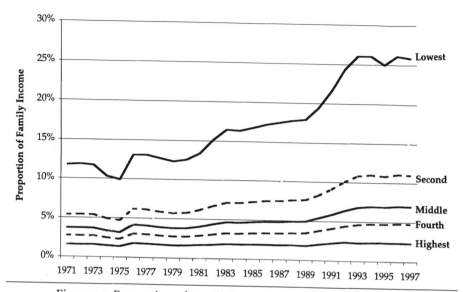

Figure 1.4. Proportion of Family Income Required to Pay Public Four-Year Tuition, by Income Quintile, 1971–1997.

Author's calculations from the College Board (1999a), Table 5; and U.S. Bureau of the Census (1999a).

from families in the fourth quintile (the 80th percentile), the proportion increased approximately three-quarters (from 2.7% to 4.8%), and for the highest quintile the proportion increased 44 percent (from 1.6% to 2.3%). The more affluent families were more insulated from the rapid growth in tuition increases by the growth in their incomes.

Adding room, board, and other required institutional charges to tuition, we see a similar picture (Figure 1.5). Between 1971 and 1997, the proportion of income required to pay total costs at four-year colleges and universities increased twenty percentage points for families in the lowest income quintile; for families in the highest quintile, the proportion dropped slightly.

In the United States, race plays an important role in separating families by income. Figure 1.6 shows median family income by race (in constant dollars) from 1972 to 1997. As a comparison, the Consumer Price Index increased 278 percent during this period. The incomes of white families were significantly higher than those of African American and Hispanic families throughout this period, with the gap greater in 1997 than twenty-five years earlier.[11] Figure 1.7 shows for each racial group the proportion of income required to pay the average four-year public tuition.[12] Because of the income differ-

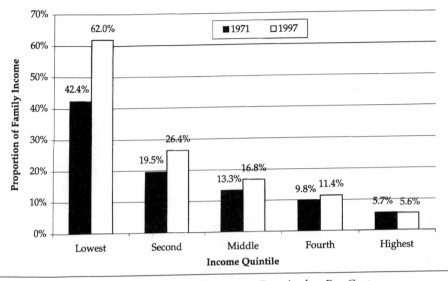

Figure 1.5. Proportion of Family Income Required to Pay Cost
of Attending Public Four-Year Institutions, by Income Quintile,
1971 and 1997.
Author's calculations from the College Board (1999a), Table 8; and U.S. Bureau
of the Census (1999a).

entials, African American and Hispanic families have had to pay a much
higher proportion of their income for students' tuition than have white and
Asian American families.

Affordability When Financial Aid Is Included

We have few reliable time-series data on tuition and other charges paid
by individual students after financial aid is included in the equation. For a
number of years the College Board (1999b) has published an annual report
summarizing the total federal, state, and institutional spending on financial
aid, with data collected from a variety of sources. Although useful in understanding the overall trends in financial aid spending, the data provide no information about the actual net tuition price paid by individual students in
public institutions. This limitation has several causes:

1. The amounts in the report represent total spending on financial aid
   (grants, loans, and work study), but do not include any per-student averages.
2. No distinction is made between awards to undergraduates and awards

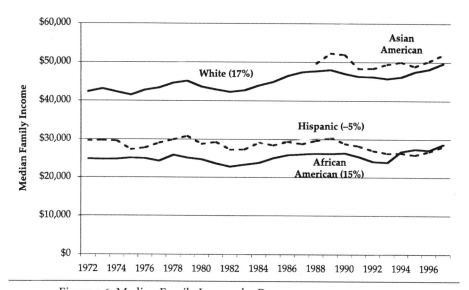

Figure 1.6. Median Family Income by Race, 1972–1997.

Income is in constant (inflation-adjusted, 1997) dollars. The increases from 1971 to 1997 are shown in parentheses (except for Asian Americans; the Census Bureau started publishing median-income data for these families in 1988). Data from U.S. Bureau of the Census (1999b).

to graduate students (with the exception of programs, such as Pell Grants, that are restricted to one group or the other).

3.   Data on financial aid are not broken down into awards for public versus private institutions.

Although the College Board figures provide few data with which to calculate the effect of financial aid on the discounting of tuition sticker prices for all students, they do permit some estimates. Included in the report is a listing of the maximum award under the Pell Grant program each year. Since Pell Grants are awarded only to needy undergraduates, these amounts can be used to calculate the effect of awarding a Pell Grant on the tuition and other charges paid by a typical low-income student. Figure 1.8 shows the maximum Pell Grant awarded each year as a percentage of the cost of attendance for students at public four-year institutions. When the Pell Grant program was first fully funded in 1975, the maximum grant provided almost 85 percent of the cost of attendance. This percentage then steadily declined and by 1996 covered little more than one-third of the cost. This drop in the "purchasing power" of Pell Grants for students attending public colleges and universities occurred during a period when the public institutions were capturing an in-

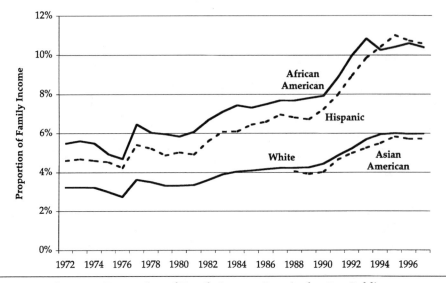

Figure 1.7. Proportion of Family Income Required to Pay Public
Four-Year Tuition, by Race, 1972–1997.

Author's calculations from the College Board (1999a), Table 5; and U.S. Bureau
of the Census (1999b).

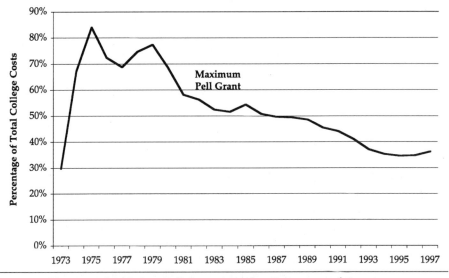

Figure 1.8. Maximum Pell Grant Award as Percentage of Cost
of Attending a Public Four-Year Institution, 1973–1997.

Data from the College Board (1999b), Tables 3 and 7.

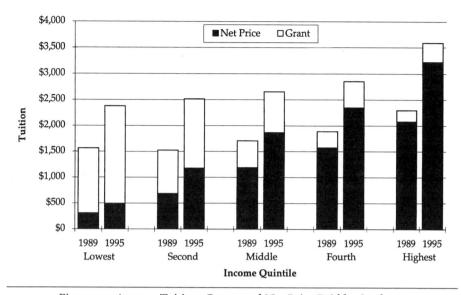

Figure 1.9. Average Tuition, Grant, and Net Price Paid by Students in Public Four-Year Institutions, by Income Quintile, 1989 and 1995.

Tuition is net price plus grant. Author's calculations from National Center for Education Statistics (1998) and U.S. Bureau of the Census (1999a).

creasing portion of the Pell Grant dollars provided by the federal government.[13]

Reliable data on average financial aid awards are not available for every year, but the National Postsecondary Student Aid Surveys (NPSAS) allow researchers to calculate national estimates of different types of financial aid awards for the years the surveys were conducted. Information included in the surveys can be used to estimate the average tuition paid and grant received for students in different income groups.

Figure 1.9 uses income quintiles and NPSAS data to calculate the average grant received and net price paid (tuition minus grants) by students in public four-year institutions. Two patterns are apparent: (1) students from wealthier families attend higher-priced institutions, and (2) students from lower-income families have a larger percentage of their tuition paid through grants. The latter finding is not surprising given that most financial aid awards are based on financial need.[14] Even though students from poorer families receive larger grants, the percentage change in the net price they paid from 1989 to 1995 was greater than for higher-income students. Students in the first (lowest) and second income quintiles saw an average increase in net

Table 1.2. Components of Average Tuition Price Paid and Proportion of Average Family Income, by Income Quintile, 1989–1990 and 1995–1996

	Income Quintiles				
	Lowest	Second	Middle	Fourth	Highest
1989–90					
Tuition	$1,563	$1,523	$1,703	$1,887	$2,296
Grants	1,258	842	516	314	221
Net price	305	681	1,187	1,573	2,075
Net price as % of average income	3.4%	3.3%	3.7%	3.4%	2.4%
1995–96					
Tuition	$2,378	$2,514	$2,652	$2,853	$3,589
Grants	1,886	1,339	789	506	371
Net price	492	1,175	1,863	2,347	3,218
Net price as % of average income	4.7%	4.8%	4.8%	4.1%	2.8%
Increase in net price as % of average income, 1989–90 to 1995–96	38%	45%	30%	20%	14%

Source: Author's calculations from National Center for Education Statistics (1998) and U.S. Bureau of the Census (1999a).

price of 61 and 73 percent, respectively, whereas students in the fourth and highest income quintiles saw an increase of 49 and 55 percent.

In the years from 1989 to 1995, poorer students saw the largest increases not just in the net price but also in the proportion of family income required to pay to attend these institutions. Table 1.2 shows the components of the average tuition paid by students in each of the income quintiles, along with the proportion of family income required to pay the net price. For students in the lowest and second income quintiles, the proportion of income required to pay the net price increased 38 and 45 percent, respectively; for students in the highest two income quintiles, the increases were only 20 and 14 percent. Although financial aid does somewhat insulate poorer students from tuition increases, these students lost ground during this period.

Similar information for students from different racial groups is given in Figure 1.10. African American and Hispanic students receive larger grants (on

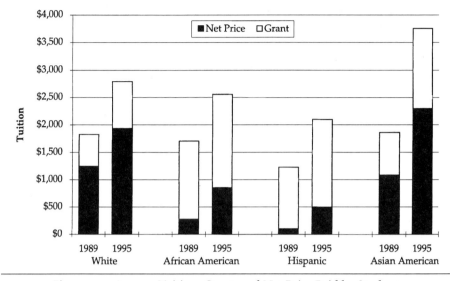

Figure 1.10. Average Tuition, Grant, and Net Price Paid by Students
in Public Four-Year Institutions, by Race, 1989 and 1995.

Tuition is net price plus grant. Author's calculations from National Center
or Education Statistics (1998) and U.S. Bureau of the Census (1999a).

average) than do white and Asian American students. Again, this is largely
because of their greater financial need (as demonstrated by the income
differentials shown in Figure 1.6). However, African American and Hispanic
students saw a much larger increase in the average net price to attend these
institutions (208% and 414%, respectively) than did white and Asian American students (56% and 113%).

The effects of these price changes on the proportion of income required
to attend college are shown in Table 1.3. In both academic years, African
American and Hispanic students used less of their family incomes (on average) to pay the net price after grants, but for both groups the increase in that
proportion between 1989 and 1995 was larger than for white and Asian American families.

The data presented here clearly demonstrate the impact of rising tuition
on students and their families. Paying for college is taking a greater share of
families' financial resources, and this increasing burden has been felt disproportionately by lower-income, African American, and Hispanic students—
all groups that historically have been underrepresented in higher educa-

Table 1.3. Components of Average Tuition Price Paid
and Proportion of Average Family Income, by Race, 1989–1990
and 1995–1996

	White	African American	Hispanic	Asian American
1989–90				
Tuition	$1,826	$1,704	$1,224	$1,860
Grants	586	1,429	1,127	783
Net price	1,240	275	97	1,077
Net price as % of average income	3.5%	1.4%	0.4%	2.9%
1995–96				
Tuition	$2,789	$2,555	$2,099	$3,756
Grants	853	1,707	1,600	1,461
Net price	1,936	848	499	2,295
Net price as % of average income	4.6%	3.4%	2.1%	5.0%
Increase in net price as % of average income, 1989–90 to 1995–96	29%	141%	361%	69%

Source: Author's calculations from National Center for Education Statistics (1998)
and U.S. Bureau of the Census (1999b).

tion.[15] Although financial aid has helped cushion the impact of rising prices,
it has not been sufficient to offset the positions of these students relative to
those from more advantaged families.

Reconciling Rising Prices and College Enrollments

Given the information provided above, how can we reconcile increasing
college enrollments (and participation rates) with the rapid increases in
price? The evidence seems to refute the downward sloping demand curve,
which, according to economists, applies as much to higher education as to
other goods and services. All other things being equal, we would expect
higher prices (especially relative to other goods or to people's ability to pay)
to result in lower college enrollments, but enrollments have continued to
climb over the last two decades.

In fact, other things are not equal; over time, the U.S. economy and society have undergone important structural changes. Chief among these is the
increasing value placed on higher education by labor markets. Some form of
higher education is seen as the ticket to jobs that provide a "livable wage"—
one that provides a salary and benefits to support a family in (at least) a mid-

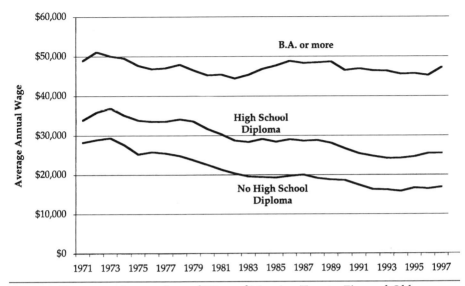

Figure 1.11. Average Annual Wage of Men Age Twenty-Five and Older, by Educational Attainment, 1971 and 1997.

Wage amounts are in constant (1997) dollars. Data from U.S. Bureau of the Census (1998a), Table C-8.

dle-class lifestyle. Economists have posited a number of explanations for why higher education has become more highly valued in recent years, including declining unionism, the need for more technical skills than are developed in high schools, and the movement of blue-collar manufacturing jobs overseas (Levy & Murnane, 1992; Murnane, Willett, & Levy, 1995; Murphy & Welch, 1992, 1993). Regardless of the favored explanation, the data are immutable: the wage premium for a college education is increasing.

Figure 1.11 shows the average wages for men aged twenty-five and older by their level of educational attainment, from 1971 to 1997. The data are in constant (1997) dollars in order to demonstrate changes in real wages since 1971. The gap between the wages of college graduates and those with less education widened during the twenty-six years, not because of growing wages for the graduates but because of the declining real wages of workers with less than a college education. The wages of college graduates declined 4 percent during this period, but workers with less education saw their average wages drop even more precipitously—25 percent for high school graduates and 40 percent for those who dropped out of high school.

The net effect of these changes was an increase over time in the earnings

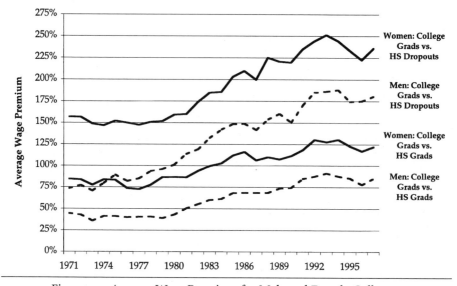

Figure 1.12. Average Wage Premium for Male and Female College Graduates Age Twenty-Five and Older, 1971–1997.

The premiums are measured versus high school (HS) graduates (with diploma) and high school dropouts (no diploma). Author's calculations from U.S. Bureau of the Census (1998a), Table C-8.

premium for college graduates. As Figure 1.12 shows, the average college graduate earned much more than the nongraduate. For example, male college graduates in 1971 earned (on average) 44 percent more than men with only a high school diploma and 73 percent more than those who had dropped out of high school. Twenty-six years later, these premiums increased to 85 and 180 percent, respectively. Women saw similar gains in wage premiums for graduates.[16]

The increasing value of a college degree in the labor markets is not the only reason for increased enrollments. Affirmative action, begun in the 1960s during the Civil Rights era, helped open the doors of college to students from minority groups.[17] Table 1.4 shows the college enrollment rates of high school graduates by race, as well as each group's share of undergraduate enrollments, in 1976 and 1996. All groups increased their undergraduate enrollment rates, but white students' overall share decreased during this period. Minority students, particularly Asian Americans and Hispanics, gained in their overall representation among undergraduates.

Table 1.4 also demonstrates the gains made by women during this pe-

Table 1.4. College Enrollment Rates and Shares of Undergraduate
Enrollment, 1976 and 1996 (Percentage)

	Enrollment Rate[a]		Share of Undergraduate Enrollments		Change in Share
	1976	1996	1976	1996	
White	48.9%	67.5%	82.2%	71.2%	(13.4%)
African American	41.9	59.6	10.0	11.0	10.0
Hispanic	52.0[b]	56.7[b]	3.7	8.7	135.1
Asian American[c]	—	—	1.8	5.8	222.2
Native American[c]	—	—	0.7	1.0	42.9
Nonresident aliens	—	—	1.5	2.2	46.7
Men	47.2	60.1	52.0	44.1	(15.2)
Women	50.3	69.7	48.0	55.9	16.5

Source: National Center for Education Statistics (1999), Tables 183, 184, and 207.
[a]Percentage of high school graduates who enrolled in college within 12 months of graduation.
[b]Owing to small sample sizes, rolling averages are used.
[c]The Census Bureau, which calculates these figures from the Current Population Survey, does not publish enrollment rates for Asian Americans or Native Americans because the sample sizes are too small.

riod. Although both men and women increased their college-going rates, the faster growth among women changed the gender balance among undergraduates. In 1976, 52 percent of all undergraduates were men; by 1996, women's share had grown to 56 percent. The growth in women's enrollment may be due in part to affirmative action efforts, but women's increasing participation in the labor force also helped drive their demand for higher education. In 1980, the labor force participation rate of women aged sixteen and older was 47.7 percent; by 1997 this had increased to 56.8 percent. Men's labor force participation rates during this period declined slightly, from 72.0 percent in 1980 to 71.3 percent in 1997 (U.S. Bureau of the Census, 1998b, Table 646).[18]

A last factor that should be noted is the role of parental education levels on college-going behavior. Almost all studies on the effect of family background characteristics on the decision to attend college have found that a key predictor is whether the student's parents attended college (Blakemore & Low, 1983; Hossler, Schmit, & Vesper, 1999; Kodde & Ritzen, 1988; Manski & Wise, 1983; Savoca, 1990). Having parents who attended college is strongly and positively correlated with a person's decision to enroll in college: "Parents' education has a strong effect on the college aspirations of high school

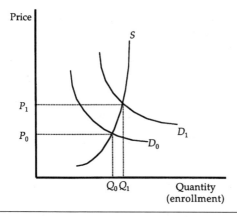

Figure 1.13. Shift in the Demand Curve for Higher Education.

The D and S curves represent the demand for and supply of higher education, respectively; P and Q, price and level of college enrollment; subscripts o and 1, points before and after various influences on college enrollment. With these influences, the equilibrium point for market supply and demand shifted from $P_0 Q_0$ to $P_1 Q_1$, as described in the text.

students and an even stronger effect on the actualization of their plans" (Hossler et al., 1999, p. 105). Thus, in a snowball effect, as more people attend college, their children will be more likely to enroll, notwithstanding the other factors influencing college enrollment.

All these influences on college enrollment—the growing wage premium for college graduates, affirmative action, and increased labor force participation by women and minorities—caused what economists describe as an outward shift in the demand curve for higher education (Figure 1.13). The curve D_0 represents the demand for higher education before these changes occurred; S, the supply of higher education; P_0 and Q_0, the average price and total enrollment, respectively, in the United States, or the *equilibrium point* given the market supply and demand before any changes. Curve D_1 is the demand for higher education as influenced by the forces described above; the new equilibrium point is at the higher price P_1 and the increased enrollment Q_1.[19] In the absence of such a demand shift, higher education institutions would not have been able to sustain the price increases of the last two decades *and* increase enrollments as they did.

The coexistence of rising prices and rising enrollments is no contradiction at all. Changing economic and societal conditions helped increase the demand for higher education, thus creating an era in which more students attended college in the face of rapid price increases.

What will the future hold for college prices and enrollments in the public sector? There are some signs that tuition price increases may be abating. Annual tuition increases in four-year institutions averaged 10 percent annually in the first half of the 1990s, but since 1995 they have averaged less than 5 percent annually (College Board, 1999a). Some states, including Massachusetts, California, Virginia, and New York, have instituted or proposed tuition freezes or cuts, and many states have developed or are considering new financial aid programs (Hebel, 1999a, 1999b; Ma, 1999). These moves in recognition of the magnitude of the price increases in recent years have been made possible by the strong fiscal conditions in most states and the willingness of legislators and governors to increase state appropriations to make up for lost tuition revenue.

But these generous fiscal conditions are not likely to continue indefinitely. As one report on recent trends in state spending on higher education warns, "Given past state budget patterns of coping with fiscal deficits and avoiding tax increases . . . projected shortfalls [in state revenues] will lead to increased scrutiny of higher education in almost all states, and to curtailed spending for public higher education in many states. The bad news is that if economic growth is slower than 'normal,' if taxes are reduced, *or* if state spending increases for areas outside of higher education, then the outlook for support of public higher education will be even *less* favorable" (Hovey, 1999, p. vi). Given the experiences of the late 1980s and early 1990s, when states faced fiscal declines and appropriations to higher education suffered, increased pressure on state budgets in the future will most likely result in constricted or even declining allocations to higher education. This in turn will press state coordinating boards and institutional governing boards to make up for lost state revenues by increasing tuitions. (See Chapter 3 for an analysis of the link between state appropriations and tuition-setting policy.)

On the demographic side, the demand for higher education is unlikely to lessen. After bottoming out at 2.5 million in the early 1990s, the number of U.S. high school graduates is expected to grow almost 30 percent, to a peak of 3.2 million in 2008 (Western Interstate Commission, 1998). The growth in the number of high school graduates is projected to be greatest among Asian American, Hispanic, and Native American students, followed by lower growth rates for African American and white students. Even though Hispanics and African Americans have lower college-going rates than the other groups, these rates have been increasing in recent years (Heller, 1999). We can expect these future high school graduates to attend college at rates at least equal to those of current cohorts; labor market demands continue to point to the importance of a higher education, with no identifiable factors to mitigate this pressure. We do not yet know whether the challenges to affirmative action outlined in Chapters 5 and 6 will mitigate the growth in college attendance among minority students or whether institutions and states will find other means to encourage college attendance by these traditionally underrepresented groups.

Some may argue that we have reached, or soon will reach, the practical limit of what people can afford to pay for a college education. College has become much less affordable over the last two decades for all but the wealthiest students. Yet one way or another, the students keep coming. Policymakers have the responsibility to monitor these trends and to ensure that a public college education is, if not *affordable,* at least *attainable* for all Americans.

Notes

1. The "$1,000-a-week price tag" was the cover story of a *Newsweek* article (Morganthau & Nayyar, 1996; see also Larson, 1997). Books on the topic of college affordability include those by Fossey and Bateman (1998), King (1999), McPherson and Schapiro (1991), and Mumper (1996). The government panel reports can be found in National Commission on Responsibilities for Financing Postsecondary Education (1993) and National Commission on the Cost of Higher Education (1998).

2. These enrollment increases are for all higher education students (public and private, undergraduate and graduate). The National Center for Education Statistics does not publish time-series data on enrollments by age, level of study, and institutional control.

3. *Price* is used here to describe the amount paid by the student to attend college, as distinct from college *costs,* a term generally used to describe the amounts spent by the college to provide that education. The economic analogy is that of consumer (student) and producer or supplier (college). The consumer pays a price for a good or service produced by the supplier at a particular cost, the sum of the labor, capital, and materials required in production and any profit or surplus earned by the supplier. For more on the distinction between prices and costs, see National Commission on the Cost of Higher Education (1998).

4. See Heller (1997a) for a discussion of this issue.

5. Room and board charges have increased much more slowly than tuition charges (College Board, 1999a).

6. Some believe this relationship between financial aid growth and tuition price increases is more than coincidental. Former Secretary of Education William Bennett (1987), in a view shared by others, stated, "If anything, increases in financial aid in recent years have enabled colleges and universities blithely to raise their tuitions, confident that Federal loan subsidies would help cushion the increase . . . Federal student aid policies do not cause college price inflation, but there is little doubt that they help make it possible" (p. A31).

7. The Census Bureau tracks incomes for households and individuals as well as

for families. Measures of family income are used in this analysis because of the role of families in helping to pay for the postsecondary education of many students.

8. Many authors have written about changing income distributions and the rise in income inequality in the United States. For econometric analyses, see, e.g., Bradbury (1996), Levy (1988), and Levy and Murnane (1992); for more general descriptive analyses, see Cassidy (1995) and Phillips (1990).

9. This analysis focuses on the relative affordability of college over time. It leaves open the question of absolute affordability of college: is college affordable enough? This is a difficult question to answer, but the affordability of college can at least be compared with that of other goods and services in the economy. As shown in Figure 1.2, tuition prices at public four-year institutions and community colleges increased more than 750 percent from 1971 to 1998. During this same period, the Consumer Price Index increased 297 percent, the increases in its major categories ranging from a low of 107 percent (for telephone service) to a high of 550 percent (for medical care) (U.S. Bureau of the Census, 1998b).

10. All tuition and other prices are from the College Board (1999a) and all income figures are from the U.S. Bureau of the Census (1999a, 1999b).

11. The Census Bureau began publishing the median income of Asian American families in this series in 1988. It does not publish national estimates of the income of Native American families because of small sample sizes.

12. Note that this is not the income proportion of the average price actually paid by each group, but the average income of each group divided by the average price paid by all students (of all races) in the country.

13. From 1982 to 1995 (the latest year for which figures are available), the percentage of total Pell Grant spending reported by public colleges and universities increased from 52 to 66 percent (author's calculations from National Center for Education Statistics, 1997, 1999, various years).

14. For more on the use of need-based aid versus merit aid, see Heller and Nelson Laird (1999), McPherson and Schapiro (1994, 1998), and Wick (1997). Note that most grants are awarded based on the total price paid by the student (including room, board, and miscellaneous expenses), not just the tuition price.

15. For information on historical college participation rates by race and income group, see College Board (1999a), Heller (1999), Mortenson (1995), and National Center for Education Statistics (1999).

16. Careful observation of Figure 1.12 will show that women earned higher wage premiums for a college education than did men, in part because women who graduated from college were more likely to be working full-time (and thus enjoying the wages of full-time work) than were women without a college degree. Men, both with and without a college degree, were more likely to be working full-time than were their female counterparts. In 1971, 80 percent of men and 45 percent of women were working full-time; in 1997, 90 percent of men and 61 percent of women worked full-time (author's calculations from U.S. Bureau of the Census, 1998a, Tables C-7 and C-8).

17. Many researchers have examined the role of affirmative action in extending access to higher education for minority students. See, e.g., Bowen and Bok (1998), Jackson (1990), Kane (1990, 1998), Nettles, Perna, and Edelin (1998), Orfield (1992, 1998), and Orfield and Ashkinaze (1991).

18. The effect of graduating from college on labor force participation appears to be greater for women than for men. In 1997, 71.4 percent of 25- to 64-year-old women with only a high school diploma held jobs; for college-educated women of the same age, 83.2 percent were employed, a difference of 11.8 percentage points. For the same age group of men, 86.4 percent of high school graduates and 93.5 percent of college graduates held jobs, a difference of 7.1 percentage points (U.S. Bureau of the Census, 1998b, Table 648).

African Americans and Hispanics, who benefited from affirmative action in higher education, also made gains in labor force participation. For African Americans aged sixteen and older (males and females together), participation grew from 52.2 percent in 1980 to 58.2 percent in 1997. Hispanic participation grew from 57.8 to 62.6 percent in the same period (U.S. Bureau of the Census, 1998b, Table 646).

19. This explanation assumes that the supply curve (S) for higher education stayed essentially the same over this period, an assumption generally made in student demand studies conducted by economists (Heller, 1997a; McPherson & Schapiro, 1993). A strong argument can be made for this supposition, as there were few new suppliers in the higher education market during the 1980s and 1990s. Almost all the increased undergraduate enrollment (from 10.5 million in 1980 to 12.3 million in 1997) occurred in existing institutions. Although this enrollment growth may have led to some outward shift in the supply curve, one would not necessarily expect the same effect on the equilibrium price as would occur with new suppliers in the market who chose to compete on price. If the increasing prices had pulled new suppliers into the market, thus shifting the supply curve outward, one would expect this to have helped hold down the price increases. But the increase in average tuition price at public four-year and two-year institutions (about 300%) during this period was far greater than the enrollment increase (17%).

This supposition of a constant supply curve may be tested in the near future, however, with the explosion onto the scene of virtual universities and distance education programs in the late 1990s. Whether these new suppliers of postsecondary education will compete primarily on price, quality, convenience, or some other basis remains to be seen. See the Conclusion to this volume for more on this topic.

References

Bennett, W. (1987, February 18). Our greedy colleges. *New York Times,* p. A31.

Blakemore, A. E., & Low, S. A. (1983, October). Scholarship policy and race-sex differences in the demand for higher education. *Economic Inquiry, 21,* 504–519.

Bowen, W. G., & Bok, D. (1998). *The shape of the river: The long-term consequences of considering race in college and university admissions.* Princeton: Princeton University Press.

Bradbury, K. L. (1996, July–August). The growing inequality of family incomes: Changing families and changing wages. *New England Economic Review,* pp. 55–82.

Campus Computing Project. (1998). *The 1998 national survey of information technology in higher education: Colleges struggle with IT planning.* Claremont, CA: Author.

Cassidy, J. (1995, October 16). Who killed the middle class? *New Yorker,* pp. 113–124.

College Board. (1999a). *Trends in college pricing.* Washington, DC: Author.

College Board. (1999b). *Trends in student aid.* Washington, DC: Author.

Fossey, R., & Bateman, M. (1998). *Condemning students to debt: College loans and public policy.* New York: Teachers College Press.

Freeman, R. (1976). *The overeducated American.* New York: Academic Press.

Hebel, S. (1999a, February 12). Many governors are making college issues prominent in 1999 legislative sessions. *Chronicle of Higher Education,* p. A38.

Hebel, S. (1999b, March 12). Virginia lawmakers approve a 20 percent cut in public-college tuition. *Chronicle of Higher Education,* p. A30.

Heller, D. E. (1997a). *Access to public higher education, 1976 to 1994: New evidence from an analysis of the states.* Unpublished doctoral dissertation, Harvard University, Cambridge.

Heller, D. E. (1997b). Student price response in higher education: An update to Leslie and Brinkman. *Journal of Higher Education, 68*(6), 624–659.

Heller, D. E. (1999). Racial equity in college participation: African American students in the United States. *Review of African American Education, 1*(1), 5–29.

Heller, D. E., & Nelson Laird, T. F. (1999). Institutional need-based and non-need grants: Trends and differences among college and university sectors. *Journal of Student Financial Aid, 29*(3), 7–24.

Hossler, D., Schmit, J., & Vesper, N. (1999). *Going to college: How social, economic, and educational factors influence the decisions students make.* Baltimore: Johns Hopkins University Press.

Hovey, H. (1999). *State spending for higher education in the next decade: The battle to sustain current support.* San Jose, CA: National Center for Public Policy and Higher Education.

Ikenberry, S. O., & Hartle, T. W. (1998). *Too little knowledge is a dangerous thing: What the public thinks and knows about paying for college.* Washington, DC: American Council on Education.

Immerwahr, J. (1998). *The price of admission: The growing importance of higher education.* San Jose, CA: National Center for Public Policy and Higher Education.

Jackson, G. A. (1990). Financial aid, college entry, and affirmative action. *American Journal of Education, 98*(4), 523–550.

Jackson, G. A., & Weathersby, G. B. (1975). Individual demand for higher education. *Journal of Higher Education, 46*(6), 623–652.

Kane, T. J. (1990). *Black educational progress since 1970: Policy lessons* (Working Paper H-90−8). Cambridge: Harvard University, Kennedy School of Government.

Kane, T. J. (1998). Racial and ethnic preferences in college admissions. In C. Jencks & M. Phillips (Eds.), *The black-white test score gap*. Washington, DC: Brookings Institution.

King, J. E. (1999). *Financing a college education: How it works, how it's changing*. Phoenix, AZ: Oryx Press

Kodde, D. A., & Ritzen, J. M. M. (1988). Direct and indirect effects of parental education level on the demand for higher education. *Journal of Human Resources, 23*(3), 356−371.

Larson, E. (1997, March 17). Why colleges cost too much. *Time*, pp. 46−50.

Leslie, L. L., & Brinkman, P. T. (1987). Student price response in higher education. *Journal of Higher Education, 58*(2), 181−204.

Levy, F. (1988). *Dollars and dreams*. New York: W. W. Norton.

Levy, F., & Murnane, R. J. (1992). U.S. earnings levels and earnings inequality: A review of recent trends and proposed explanations. *Journal of Economic Literature, 30*, 1333−1381.

Ma, K. (1999, February 19). Governor opposes plan by U. of Massachusetts to increase tuition and fees. *Chronicle of Higher Education*, p. A43.

Manski, C. F., & Wise, D. A. (1983). *College choice in America*. Cambridge: Harvard University Press.

McPherson, M. S., & Schapiro, M. O. (1991). *Keeping college affordable: Government and educational opportunity*. Washington, DC: Brookings Institution.

McPherson, M. S., & Schapiro, M. O. (1993). *Paying the piper: Productivity, incentives, and financing of U.S. higher education*. Ann Arbor: University of Michigan Press.

McPherson, M. S., & Schapiro, M. O. (1994). *Merit aid: Students, institutions, and society*. Williamstown, MA: Williams Project on the Economics of Higher Education.

McPherson, M. S., & Schapiro, M. O. (1998). *The student aid game: Meeting need and rewarding talent in American higher education*. Princeton: Princeton University Press.

Morganthau, T., & Nayyar, S. (1996, April 29). Those scary college costs. *Newsweek*, pp. 52−56.

Mortenson, T. (1995). Educational attainment by family income 1970 to 1994. *Postsecondary Education Opportunity, 41*, 1−8.

Mumper, M. (1996). *Removing college price barriers: What government has done and why it hasn't worked*. Albany: State University of New York Press.

Murnane, R. J., Willett, J. B., & Levy, F. (1995). The growing importance of cognitive skills in wage determination. *Review of Economics and Statistics, 77*(2), 251−266.

Murphy, K. M., & Welch, F. (1992). The structure of wages. *Quarterly Journal of Economics, 107*(1), 285−326.

Murphy, K. M., & Welch, F. (1993). Occupational change and the demand for skill, 1940–1990. *American Economic Review, 83*(2), 122–136.

National Center for Education Statistics. (1997). *Digest of education statistics, 1997.* Washington, DC: U.S. Department of Education.

National Center for Education Statistics. (1998). *National postsecondary student aid survey, restricted-use files, 1989–90 and 1995–96* [Computer data files]. Washington, DC: U.S. Department of Education [Producer and Distributor].

National Center for Education Statistics. (1999). *Digest of education statistics, 1998.* Washington, DC: U.S. Department of Education.

National Center for Education Statistics. (various years). *Integrated postsecondary education data system, finances survey* [Computer data files]. Washington, DC: U.S. Department of Education.

National Commission on the Cost of Higher Education. (1998). *Straight talk about college costs and prices.* Phoenix, AZ: Oryx Press.

National Commission on Responsibilities for Financing Postsecondary Education. (1993). *Making college affordable again: Final report.* Washington, DC: Author.

Nettles, M. T., Perna, L. W., & Edelin, K. C. (1998). *The role of affirmative action in expanding student access at selective colleges and universities.* Fairfax, VA: Frederick D. Patterson Research Institute, College Fund/UNCF.

Orfield, G. (1992). Money, equity, and college access. *Harvard Educational Review, 62*(3), 337–372.

Orfield, G. (1998). *Chilling admissions: The affirmative action crisis and the search for alternatives.* Cambridge: Harvard Education Publishing, Harvard Graduate School of Education.

Orfield, G., and Ashkinaze, C. (1991). *The closing door: Conservative policy and black opportunity.* Chicago: University of Chicago Press.

Phillips, K. (1990). *The politics of rich and poor.* New York: Harper Perennial.

Savoca, E. (1990). Another look at the demand for higher education: Measuring the price sensitivity of the decision to apply to college. *Economics of Education Review, 9*(2), 123–134.

U.S. Bureau of the Census. (1998a). *Measuring 50 years of economic change using the March Current Population Survey.* Washington, DC: U.S. Department of Commerce.

U.S. Bureau of the Census. (1998b). *Statistical abstract of the United States: 1998.* Washington, DC: U.S. Department of Commerce.

U.S. Bureau of the Census. (1999a). *Mean income received by each fifth and top 5 percent of families (all races): 1966 to 1997* [On-line]. Washington, DC: U.S. Department of Commerce [Producer and Distributor]. Available: http://www.census.gov/hhes/income/histinc/f03.html

U.S. Bureau of the Census. (1999b). *Race and Hispanic origin of householder—Families by median and mean income: 1947 to 1997* [On-line]. Washington, DC: U.S. Department of Commerce [Producer and Distributor]. Available: http://www.census.gov/hhes/income/histinc/f05.html

Western Interstate Commission on Higher Education. (1998). *Knocking at the college door: Projections of high school graduates by state and race/ethnicity 1996–2012.* Boulder, CO: Author.

Wick, P. G. (1997). *No-need/merit scholarships: Practices and trends.* New York: College Board.

2 The Paradox of College Prices: Five Stories with No Clear Lesson

MICHAEL MUMPER

Public college prices have increased steadily, often remarkably, since the early 1980s. Nationally, the average tuition for an in-state student at a public four-year college in 1998–99 was more than $3,000 per year. This represents an increase of 20 percent in the last five years and 80 percent in the last ten years. In New Jersey, Pennsylvania, Massachusetts, Vermont, and Connecticut, the price tag was more than $4,000 per year. These developments have spurred broad public concern about college affordability. A recent poll by the American Council on Education (ACE, 1998) revealed that American parents are more concerned about the rising price of college than about the quality of public K–12 schools, health care for their children, and even the possibility of their children being the victims of crime. Moreover, in order to pay these rising prices, student borrowing has mushroomed. A survey by the USA Group found that students who left four-year colleges in 1997 had an average Stafford (federally guaranteed) loan debt of more than $9,000 (Scherschel, 1998, p. 16).

But this widespread agreement on the rapid rise of public college prices has not led to any coherent or coordinated efforts to address the problem. This is certainly not for a lack of attention. More than two dozen states have put together commissions, taskforces, or working groups to study the problems associated with rising college prices. Even the federal government has become involved. In 1997, Congress appointed a national commission to study the issue and make public policy recommendations. Still, no consensus has been achieved on what government can or should do about tuition inflation. The causes of tuition inflation may vary substantially from state to state and from sector to sector, of course, and may differ today from those of the 1980s. But even among policymakers and analysts in the same state, after examining the same data for the same time periods, heated differences often have emerged over what to do about rising prices. Some states have instituted tuition caps; some have mandated increased teaching loads at public colleges; some have centralized governance structures and others have decentralized those structures; some have experimented with performance budgeting and others have moved heavily to supplement traditional institutions with distance learning, and virtual programs.[1] This wide range of policy responses reflects an underlying disagreement over the causes of tuition inflation.

This chapter attempts to sort out the competing explanations of why public college prices have increased so rapidly and explain why this seemingly straightforward question has proven so difficult to answer. I begin by reviewing research on the causes of tuition inflation at public colleges, a review that reveals the substantial problems facing researchers in this area. I then explore the different ways in which state policymakers understand the causes of tuition inflation and how these different views shape the policies they see as appropriate and effective. The focus of this chapter is limited to tuition increases at public colleges and universities since the mid-1980s. It does not address the issue of tuition inflation at private universities, where the revenue and expenditure patterns are quite different.

Research on the Causes of Tuition Inflation

The reasons for the differences in public college tuition from state to state have not been the subject of a great deal of research. Those studies that have been conducted have produced some interesting insights, but they have not resolved the debate about the causes of tuition inflation. One approach to answering this question attempts to sort out the relationship between tuition levels and a number of economic, social, and political variables. To facilitate such research, Kent Halstead (1998) and Edward Hines (1996) have developed extensive data sets on trends in tuition, state spending levels, tax rates, and economic development levels. In one of the most comprehensive studies of this type, James Hearn, Carolyn Griswold, and Ginger Marine (1996), using 1980 data, disaggregate the impact of several independent variables on public college tuition and student aid levels in the states. Their study makes several important findings. First, region of the country is the variable most closely associated with tuition rates. States in the Northeast and Midwest have high tuition and high aid levels; states in the Southwest and West have low levels of tuition and student aid. Second, they find that economically developed states are more likely to have low-priced entry points into the higher education system: the higher the personal income in a state, the lower the tuition at two-year colleges. Finally, states with planning agencies and strong coordinating boards have higher tuition levels at four-year colleges. These findings point to important underlying factors that may drive changes in college prices. But, at least in the short term, such findings provide limited guidance for policymakers. A state's region is fixed. Its level of economic development is largely fixed in the short term. Even the governance structure of the state's colleges may be quite difficult to adjust.

Perhaps the most highly publicized study of the causes of tuition inflation was conducted by the National Commission on the Cost of Higher Education (1998), appointed by Congress in 1997. The commission was in operation for less than a year, but its final report, *Straight Talk about College Costs and Prices*, is the most comprehensive work on the subject to date. It brought together a wide range of opinions and made use of extensive quantitative analysis and expert testimony. Yet, in the end, the commission members were unable to reach agreement on the causes of college price increases. They did agree on five "convictions," including such noncontroversial positions as "The concern about rising college prices is real" and "The public and its leaders are concerned about where higher education places its priorities" (p. 13).

One of the most interesting sections of the National Commission's 1998 report is a series of appendixes intended to answer specific questions about the link between rising prices and several alleged causes. Yet, after providing pages of statistical and testimonial data on each potential cause, the commission hedges its conclusions. Its answer to the question "Have increases in college and university administrative costs affected tuition increases?" is a definitive "Possibly" (p. 248). In response to the question "Have costs to construct and renovate campus facilities affected tuition increases?" the answer is "Probably" (p. 266). And its answer to "Have technology costs driven tuition up?" is "Possibly" (p. 266). Such answers, of course, are less than satisfying, but the fault does not lie with the commission or its staff. These tentative conclusions reflect the substantial and heated disagreement among the experts on these issues. Indeed, the best answer to the question "Why have college prices increased?" remains the one presented by Arthur Hauptman (1990) in a report for the College Board and the ACE. "What is the bottom line reason for the college price spiral? This report identifies a number of hypotheses, each of which is found by the subsequent analysis to have something to contribute to the argument. But the bottom line is that there is *no* overarching explanation" (p. vii).

The Paradox of College Tuition

Where does this leave us? Given such tentative research findings, how can state and campus leaders formulate policy to confront and control rising college prices? The answer is that each participant in the tuition-setting process must construct for him- or herself an operational understanding of

the contested dynamics that drive college costs and prices. It is from this often very personal understanding that policymakers approach the problem.
Since many different constructions are possible, the resulting policies can
proceed in quite different directions.

The study of tuition inflation and the creation of policy to remedy it are
so difficult because the dynamic driving them can be constructed in so many
different ways. In this light, a recent study by the Institute for Higher Education Policy (IHEP, 1999) describes tuition as a "puzzle." It can also be seen as
a paradox. In *Policy Paradox: The Art of Political Decision Making,* Deborah
Stone (1997) begins by noting that "paradoxes are nothing but trouble. They
violate the most elementary principle of logic: Something cannot be two
different things at once. Two contradictory interpretations cannot both be
true. A paradox is just such an impossible situation, and political life is full
of them" (p. 1). The problem of public college tuition inflation is such a paradox. The ambiguity over the causes of rising college prices has its roots in two
conditions. First, the processes by which public college tuition is set are complex and negotiated. Second, there is an ongoing confusion over the definition and use of the terms of the debate. In combination, these factors create
a situation in which participants in a conversation about tuition are often
talking about different things at the same time. Everyone is using the same
words, but each participant attaches a different meaning to those words.

Almost every state has established a clear process that public college
leaders and state officials follow as they set tuition rates. Most states have also
enacted a tuition policy to guide them through the process. But under pressure from structural shifts in campus and state budgets, these processes and
guidelines are often set aside. The IHEP's 1999 report described it this way:
"The authority to set tuition is generally shared among the legislature, governor, governing boards, and sometimes the campuses in multi-campus systems. As such, decisions about tuition changes occur where there is a broad-
based shared responsibility between government and higher education,
rather than the authority to act unilaterally, which is clearly held by one side
or the other. This means that tuition decisions are political, and that a number of interest groups try to influence the process" (p. 24). It also means that
accountability and responsibility for those decisions are blurred. No one is
clearly to blame, or able to take credit, as tuition changes. The IHEP report
went on to worry that "because tuition increases are a political hot potato
and because responsibility for approving them is shared between the academy and state government, the result is a form of tuition 'chicken' where each
waits for the other to take the initiative" (p. 25). Given that tuition levels in

each state are negotiated among many institutions through a process in which guidelines are regularly ignored, the perspectives of the individual participants inevitably shape the outcome. Yet, those participants may enter the negotiation with different assumptions and understandings of the dynamics that drive tuition rates.

To add to the confusion, there is substantial disagreement about the definitions of the fundamental terms used in the negotiation. The National Commission on the Cost of Higher Education (1998) describes the relationship between the terms as "opaque" (p. 12) and goes on to complain that "the terms of analysis used by different parties are not always consistently defined; institutional costs and student costs are two different things, prices and costs are not the same, and prices charged and prices paid often bear very little relationship to each other. The persistent blurring of terms (both within and beyond higher education) contributes to system-wide difficulties in clarifying the relationship between cost and quality; defining the difference between price and cost; distinguishing between what institutions charge and what students pay; and ultimately to systemic difficulties in controlling costs and prices" (pp. 14–15).

Looked at one way, tuition inflation may simply reflect the rising prices of the goods and services purchased by campus leaders. But looked at another way, such increased campus expenditures are not really a cause at all. College leaders' choice to increase their spending does not mean that those increases were necessary or justified. Thomas Sowell (1992) makes the point that when "a college expends its range of resources first, and then calls it 'increased costs' later, this tends to . . . erode the very concept of living within one's means" (p. 24). He continues, "When parents are being asked to draw on the equity in their home to pay rising tuition, it is not simply to cover the increased costs of educating their children, but also to underwrite the many new boondoggles thought up by faculty and administration, operating with little sense of financial constraints" (p. 24). But how do policymakers decide which campus expenditures constitute legitimate costs and which unnecessarily drive prices up?

In the absence of a shared understanding, participants must define terms for themselves and must create a model, or metaphor, to guide their decision making. How each policymaker assesses the dynamics of the problem, in turn, shapes the policy options he or she sees as appropriate to dealing with that problem. The solutions policymakers are drawn to if they see the price spiral as driven by inadequate state support, for example, will be quite different from those they support if they see the problem as driven by wasteful spending by campus leaders. Thus, in order to understand the problem of tuition inflation and the policies required to remedy it, we must begin by examining how policymakers understand the causes of the problem.

Data and Method of This Study

As explained by Stone (1997), causal narratives provide the logic on which policy is built. A causal narrative is simply the story that interested persons tell about how and why a problem has developed. Analysis of these narratives provides insight into how policymakers understand the issue and why they make particular decisions. The data for this analysis are drawn from extensive interviews with state and campus policymakers, in which they were asked to relate their own explanations for tuition inflation in their states. I use the resulting narratives to examine the different ways in which policymakers construct the causes of college price increases (Foss, 1989; Kirkwood, 1985; Mumby, 1987).

Between 1995 and 1999 I visited eleven states (Colorado, Connecticut, Iowa, Louisiana, New Mexico, New York, North Carolina, Ohio, Texas, Vermont, and Virginia). These states were chosen because they represent a wide range of tuition levels, economic conditions, and regions. In each state I interviewed a cross section of the state's higher education policymakers.[2] I began each interview by asking the policymaker to tell me what she or he saw as the cause or causes of rising public college prices in that state and whether these prices presented a serious problem to residents. This gave the participants the opportunity to explain how they saw the causal links. In analyzing the interview transcripts, I categorized the resulting narratives into five "stories" based on shared assumptions or common characteristics.

The Five Stories of Tuition Inflation

When policymakers were asked to explain the increases in public college tuition in their states, no single causal narrative emerged. All participants were willing to give me their views on those causes, but the stories they told varied remarkably. The variation was evident across states, across professional responsibilities, and sometimes between policymakers in adjacent offices. I was able to sort the vast majority of these stories into five, reasonably distinct causal narratives of college tuition inflation. Each of the five stories was full of detail and supported by tables, handouts, or written reports. Some stories had villains, others had innocent victims, and a few had both. Each was evident, to one degree or another, in every state. These five ideal-type narratives form the unspoken understanding on which many of the decisions about tuition levels are based. In some states, one or another of the narratives had achieved a kind of dominant position, with many people describing the events and dynamics in the same way. In most states I visited, however, there was an ongoing competition among policymakers over which narrative would become dominant.

I recount here each of the five narratives. The first two focus on changing trends in campus and state revenues. In different ways, they link rising college prices to insufficient revenues. The second two focus on increases in campus expenditures, linking higher prices to changes in campus spending patterns. The fifth focuses on the counterintuitive link between rising prices and enrollments (a relationship explored in Chapter 1). In each case I lay out the narrative in composite form, using the words of the participants whenever possible. For each meta-narrative, or composite story, I explore the assumptions, numbers, symbols, and metaphors used in its construction, then present some of the evidence proponents use to support that story. Based on these interview data and the written material I gathered while conducting the interviews, I do my best to tell each of the five stories fairly.

Narrative 1: The States Made Prices Rise

In the first narrative, rising college prices are explained as the inevitable result of the decline in state support for higher education. During the last few years, the state appropriation to higher education has been reduced (or at least not increased fast enough) and colleges have been forced to find other sources of funds. The only way they could respond to these reductions was to raise tuition. A legislative staff member in New York State described the state's tuition increases as "inevitable." He went on, "Under the circumstances, there was really nothing else that we could do." A vice president at the University of Vermont described the situation this way: "In the early 1990s we experienced tremendous increases in tuition, especially in-state tuition. And this isn't a bitch or a gripe, but that was the result of the inability of the state to appropriately fund higher education. At that point, the only option available to the then-president was to increase tuition."

In this view, state legislators, governors, and campus leaders are not decision makers who chose to increase prices; they are just responding to overwhelming budgetary pressures. According to the financial aid director at a public college in Virginia, "It was all because of the economy that the state was unable to fund higher education. That is what caused tuition to increase faster than normal." If you accept that colleges have only two major revenue sources, tuition and state appropriations, and that institutional expenditures are fixed, tuition becomes a variable in a simple algebraic problem. If appropriations go down or increase more slowly than expenditures, tuition must go up to keep the equation in balance.

The popularity of this narrative among campus leaders is easy to understand. It presents campuses as innocent victims of forces beyond their control. The responsibility for rising college prices rests with those off-campus. Sometimes the villain of this narrative was cyclical change in the state's economy. Sometimes the state legislature or the governor was the villain for cutting the appropriation to higher education. A legislative staff member in Louisiana was emphatic about this point. "Why has college tuition gone up? The answer comes right back to the point that the legislature hasn't put up its share so the colleges have gone somewhere else to get it. They [legislators] don't like to hear this because the finger keeps pointing back at them. It is because they haven't put up the money that these numbers are so skewed and where there has been this tremendous increase in tuition."

Here, the states are viewed as victims of economic problems beyond their control. As the economic difficulties of the early 1990s reduced the revenues available to states, they had no choice but to pass the cuts along to colleges in the form of reduced appropriations. Public colleges, in turn, simply passed them along to parents and students in the form of higher tuition. A member of the Virginia House of Delegates explained tuition inflation in such a way. "During the recession of the early 1990s, Virginia was one of only two states that did not raise tuition. We haven't raised the corporate income tax since 1971. We have the lowest tax rates in the country—lower than our neighbors in [North] Carolina or anywhere. So as we went through the recession we had to start cutting spending. And that is when we made the cuts in [higher education] that led to the tuition increases."

A look at the changing composition of campus revenues illustrates the point. In 1980, public colleges received about 44 percent of their revenues from state and local governments. In 1997–98, these sources accounted for less than 36 percent of revenues (Mortenson, 1999). To compensate for these declining state and local dollars, colleges are relying more on tuition revenue. In 1980, tuition accounted for only about 13 percent of public college revenues; by 1997–98 this had increased to more than 20 percent.

This pattern of substituting tuition revenue for state support is evident in Figure 2.1. Since 1985, state support has become an ever smaller part of public colleges' revenue. The share of total revenue they received from state government declined by 18.2 percent between 1985–86 and 1995–96. During the same time, the portion of their total revenue derived from tuition and

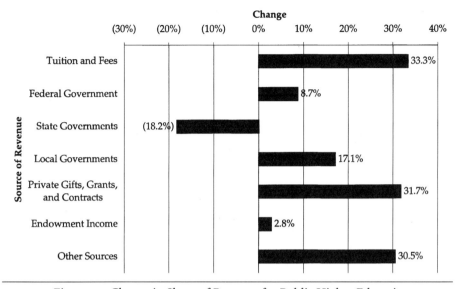

Figure 2.1. Change in Share of Revenue for Public Higher Education (Excluding Sales and Services), 1985–86 to 1995–96.
Data from National Association of State Budget Officers (1997).

fees increased by 33.3 percent. The decline in state support was particularly large in a few states. In Virginia, for example, state support for higher education was reduced by $500 million (27%) between 1990 and 1995 (Hsu, 1995). Figure 2.1 also shows that public colleges have sought to increase their revenue from other sources to compensate for declining state support. The share of total revenues from private gifts, grants, and contracts, as well as federal support and endowment income, all increased during the decade.

When the causes of tuition inflation are seen in this way, none of the participants have to accept responsibility for the outcome. Thus, they feel little reason to change their behavior to control the problem in the future—there is little they can do. Campus leaders may seek to lobby their state government more aggressively for increased appropriations. But until the external conditions that "caused" the price increase are reversed, little can be expected to change. Indeed, from this viewpoint, it is easy to conclude that tuition increases are here to stay. One policymaker described this as a "new age" in which "costs are likely to continue to rise." Another explained with resignation, "At least in this state, the days of low tuition are over."

Narrative 2: Medicaid and Prisons Made Prices Rise

Of course, the level of state appropriation to higher education need not be seen as fixed, nor tuition as mechanically set. Both can, of course, be seen as the result of conscious decisions. A second narrative explaining the causes of tuition inflation focuses the blame on other items that are demanding increased state appropriations and crowding out college funding. In this view, rising college prices were not an inevitable outcome of changes in the financial situation of state governments but the result of choices made by legislators and governors, and even the public. Thomas Mortenson (1997) describes the trends this way: "Clearly, the funding priorities of state and local governments have shifted and continue to do so. Presumably, these priorities reflect the will of the voters, and the changing priorities of the voters over the last forty-five years. Between the mid-1950s and 1982, voters appear to have supported increased expenditure shares for higher education in state and local government budgeting. Since 1982, however, that has reversed with resources shifted from higher education to new budget priorities of medical care and corrections—and tax cuts."

A staff member of the Louisiana House of Representatives described a similar situation. "Any responsible finance person, and most members of the state legislature, will tell you our problem with the budget is that everything is dedicated. They [legislators] have no discretion. When a crunch comes, higher education, health and hospitals, and welfare are the only areas where there is not a commitment either through a federal court order [mandating state spending] on corrections management, debt pay off, or whatever. The portion of the budgetary pie that they can actually play with is relatively small."

For many policymakers, especially state legislators and their staff, the decision to shift funding away from higher education or to stabilize the rate of growth in the higher education appropriation was portrayed as a very difficult choice. But with insufficient revenue to cover all the legitimate demands, cuts had to be made somewhere. According to the vice president of a public university in Connecticut, many members of the legislature concluded that they "just could not continue to fund higher education at ever higher levels—no matter how good it is." He went on, "I have never been critical of the legislature in our state, because I can understand the dilemma facing the appropriations committee. Higher education comes in talking about what a great value they are to the state and how they are an investment for the future. But then corrections comes in and says 'we've got people living three to a cell. All our gyms are full. We can't provide appropriate medical care.' And then the social service people come in and they bring families with infant children and no money and say 'we can't even provide them with milk and food.' With a limited budget and with so many needs, it is understandable."

A legislative staff member in Virginia told a similar story. "I think solely one factor caused the tuition increases. We had a general fund crisis that started in 1989 and got progressively worse. When the recession eased, we got a new governor who wanted to spend more on corrections. I think the public also wanted more money spent that way. But [the department of] corrections is now really driving the state budget. Medicaid was the problem a few years ago, now it is corrections."

In the context of growing pressure on state budgets, the higher education appropriation stood out as the logical place to cut—often not because of dissatisfaction with the performance of the colleges. Many policymakers were well aware that the cuts would be painful to campus budgets and would require them to raise tuition. But public colleges had a mechanism to raise new revenue to replace the funds lost in state cuts. In the words of a member of the Ohio House of Representatives, "It was easier to cut something that could be replaced. When we made the budget cuts, we really felt that we were not hurting higher education." Thus, from the perspective of a state, higher education could be cut without being forced to close campuses, eliminate programs, or even reduce staff. Indeed, cutting appropriations to public colleges and universities was seen as quite different from cuts to corrections, transportation, or other agencies that had no way to secure replacement revenues. A legislative staff member in New York explained the difference this way: public colleges and universities "are unique among state agencies because . . . they have a source of revenue that other agencies don't. The Department of Corrections can't charge tuition and room and board. The Department of Transportation can't charge people to drive on Delaware Avenue out into Delmar."

This view of the causes of tuition inflation appears to be popular with state legislators and their staff. Indeed, in a survey of chairpersons of state education committees, a strong majority (68%) believed "the ability of colleges to raise their own money through tuition, research grants, and gifts" was a significant factor in determining how much money the legislature would appropriate to higher education (Ruppert, 1996, p.9).

Those who approach the problem of rising college prices from this perspective can provide compelling numerical evidence to support their view. Figure 2.2 illustrates the changes in state spending patterns from 1986 to 1996. The only areas increasing their share of state budgets were Medicaid and corrections. The biggest losers in that reallocation were higher education, transportation, and cash assistance programs such as welfare and unemployment insurance.

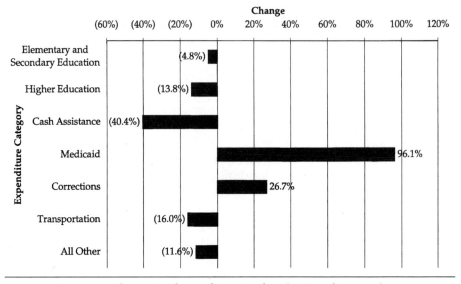

Figure 2.2. Change in Share of State Budget (National Average), 1986–1987 to 1996–1997.
Data from National Association of State Budget Officers (1997).

Figure 2.3 illustrates the relative share of state spending allocated to higher education and Medicaid between 1987 and 1997. As recently as 1989, higher education accounted for the second largest share of state budgets, following elementary and secondary education. Medicaid stood in fourth place, behind transportation spending. But beginning in the late 1980s and accelerating into the 1990s, Medicaid spending grew dramatically. By 1990 it had surpassed both higher education and transportation to become the second largest share of state budgets.

The growth of Medicaid spending has slowed considerably since 1994, but it continues to command a significant portion of state spending. A recent report by the National Association of State Budget Officers (1997) speculated that "the easing of spending pressure from Medicaid has allowed states to focus on other priorities" (p. 2). Those who see declining state support as the primary cause of tuition inflation view this as a very hopeful sign. Higher education must still compete with demands from elementary and secondary education, transportation, and other program areas that also feel neglected by years of declining state support. But from this view, the answer to the question "Why did college prices increase?" is clear: Medicaid and the pris-

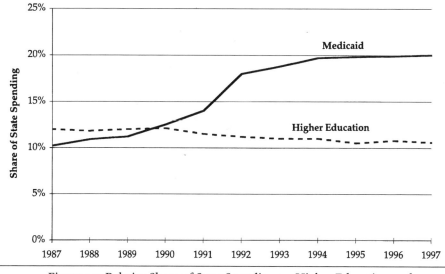

Figure 2.3. Relative Share of State Spending on Higher Education and Medicaid (National Average), 1987–1997.
Data from National Association of State Budget Officers (1997).

ons did it. And, if spending in these other areas slows, higher education will be the beneficiary.

Narrative 3: Quality Programs Cost Money

Not everyone sees tuition inflation as driven primarily by changes in campus revenue patterns. A third narrative traces the causes to changes in the spending patterns of public college campuses. Seen this way, the problem of rising college costs is a straightforward matter. Certain expenditures are required to provide a high-quality higher education, and public colleges and universities were faced with a simple choice: either spend the money needed to keep up or fall behind. A member of the New York General Assembly put this narrative in its most blunt form: "Look, we had a choice to make. We could let tuition increase or we could cut back on quality." A vice president at a public institution in Iowa explained that "people just don't understand how expensive it has become to run a university these days. Our health insurance costs have gone through the roof. Our heating costs have gone up because we have so many old buildings. And we have done more in the past few years to get faculty salaries in line with our peer institutions. These changes have really increased our costs."

This story often made use of the metaphor of the "fork in the road." When policymakers reached the fork, they could take the route that led to higher quality but higher prices or the one that led to lower quality accompanied by lower prices. The implicit conclusion was that, given the choice, the road to higher prices was the right one. Indeed, the heroes of this story are those who have fought to maintain quality in the face of pressure to cut programs. A staff member at the State University of New York system said, "We have a lot of bean-counters in the legislature this term. They don't seem to be interested in anything but cutting spending. Sure we can be more efficient, but you don't get there in one year. We don't want to compromise the quality of our programs in the long term."

Policymakers often began this narrative with a review of items in the public college budget that have grown rapidly in recent years. A number of general spending needs and specific expenditures were mentioned, including rising health care costs, federal and state regulations and mandates, the higher salaries necessary to retain "star" faculty, and the perceived demand by students for increased recreational and support services. But the two areas of increased spending mentioned in almost every narrative of this type were technology and deferred maintenance. Spending in these areas was presented as absolutely essential to the continued health of the higher education system. These narratives were peppered with reminders that public colleges and universities had actually underspent in these critical areas and that more, not less, spending would be necessary in the future.

Colleges are indeed spending more on technology, and at least some of these costs are passed on to students in the form of higher tuition. According to the National Commission on the Cost of Higher Education (1998), "Institutions must provide equipment for faculty and students as well as the infrastructure to accommodate it. Given the age of many campus buildings, and the state of the infrastructure to support this equipment, this expense is substantial" (p. 11). The commission goes on to conclude that "increasing costs for technology almost certainly translate into higher prices charged to students" (p. 11). This view was echoed by a staff member of the State University of New York system, who observed that "technology has been a major expenditure issue for us for several years now. We really haven't tracked it closely, but anecdotally, it is clear that a huge amount of money has gone into technology." A staff member of the Colorado Council on Higher Education explained, "We have invested heavily in technology in the past few years, both for regular instructional use as well as for distance learning. These infrastructure expenditures have been expensive, but they were essential. Given the increases in enrollments that are projected for our system, we could not afford to wait too long. We needed to spend that money now. And frankly, I am worried that we have not spent enough."

The decaying physical plant of the nation's public colleges—no doubt exacerbated by years of deferred maintenance and repairs—has presented colleges with an increasing cost simply to keep their programs operating. A National Science Foundation (1996) survey of scientific and engineering research facilities estimated the deferred maintenance costs to replace or repair these facilities at $9.3 billion. Another recent report placed the total cost of deferred maintenance at the nation's colleges at $26 billion (Kaiser, 1996). In addition to these ongoing repairs and renovations, institutions face the extra costs of improving the quality of the infrastructure. As the National Commission (1998) put it, "Thus, not only are many college and university buildings and laboratories old and outdated in terms of computer wiring and other infrastructure needs, but they are also struggling to maintain quality information access within the walls of these buildings on our nation's campuses" (p. 265).

The view that rising college costs are driven primarily by the high costs of providing a high-quality education was clearly laid out in an op-ed article in the *New York Times* by Charles Kiesler (1993), chancellor of the University of Missouri at Columbia. He argued that policies to control college prices are based on a misunderstanding of the problem of college costs. "Most law makers and policymakers are misled by standards of measure that betray an inadequate grasp of the financial challenges we face, especially at major research universities." This misunderstanding has arisen because the Consumer Price Index and the Higher Education Price Index, the most common measures of the costs facing colleges, present a distorted picture. In Kiesler's view, both measures "dramatically underestimate the institutions' true cost of doing business—costs over which the institutions often have no control." Seen this way, the causes of the problem are simple, even if often misunderstood. The increasing costs of a quality higher education caused college prices to rise. As operating expenditures for colleges increased, tuition was increased as higher costs were passed along to students. The quality of higher education has been maintained, but unfortunately, that important outcome could be achieved only at the expense of higher college prices.

Narrative 4: Those Unaccountable Public Colleges Made Prices Rise

The fourth causal narrative places the blame for rising college prices squarely on the shoulders of the colleges themselves. This story is built on the assumption that one job of campus leaders is to make choices about where to spend their limited funds. In this view, as the goods and services that colleges must purchase increased in price, the institutions should have been more responsible; they should have reexamined their spending priorities rather than simply continuing past purchasing patterns. Colleges' proper response to rising prices was not simply to pay but to reexamine their expenditures. Like all public agencies, colleges should find a way to live within their budgets by changing priorities, improving efficiency, or increasing productivity.

All too often, however, campus leaders proved unwilling to take such unpopular yet necessary steps. A legislator in New York explained that instead of setting priorities, the public colleges tried "to be all things to all people unfortunately, there is just not enough money to continue doing things that way." A former senior member of the Ohio governor's staff put it this way: "Colleges need to learn to control their spending. During the 1980s, we increased their appropriations every year and they continued to increase tuition at double-digit rates. There was just no accountability." In Colorado, a state representative told me that, after years of trying to get control of spending, "eventually the legislature said to higher education 'look you *have* to change.' You have to do business differently." The vice president for finance at Ohio State University put it more delicately. "The assumption used to be that higher education was a good investment—now they [these institutions] are being asked to prove that they are not inefficient" (Mathesian, 1995, p. 21).

In this view, the villain in the story of college prices is the unaccountable and unresponsive campus leader. The heroes are legislators and governors fighting to ensure that public monies are spent in the most efficient and effective ways. At the heart of this portrayal is a disagreement over the proper priorities of public higher education. Campus leaders, and especially university faculty, are presented as primarily interested in research, whereas state officials and the public see undergraduate education as the priority. Seen this way, the story of college prices is a struggle between those who want to ensure efficient and productive public spending and those—unaccountable campus leaders—who refuse to spend the money on undergraduate instruction.

Figure 2.4 presents evidence to support this view. Between 1985 and 1995, public colleges and universities increased their spending on research by more than 12 percent, but spending on instruction actually decreased by nearly 7 percent. Indeed, spending per full-time equivalent (FTE) student on administration, student services, and scholarships increased as spending on instruction was declining. Colleges were clearly directing a larger share of their spending toward other priorities at the expense of instruction.

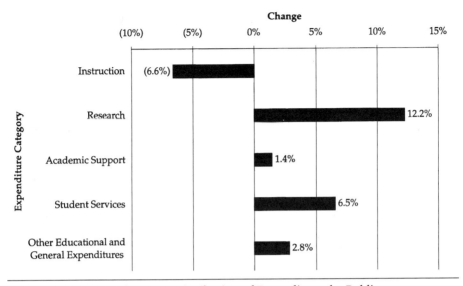

Figure 2.4. Change in Distribution of Expenditures by Public
Institutions of Higher Education, 1985–1986 to 1995–1996.
Data from National Center for Education Statistics (1999).

The numbers in Figure 2.4 should be interpreted with caution. Increased
research spending, for example, is often the product of rising levels of external grants and sponsored projects, restricted funds that can be spent only in
ways designated by the funding agency. Campus administrators have very little discretion over how these funds are spent. Thus, increased research spending, especially when originating from external sources, is not necessarily an
indication of an explicit decision to shift funds from instruction to research.

Nevertheless, the view that colleges do not spend their money in appropriate ways appears to be widely shared by state policymakers. A recent survey of legislators conducted by the Education Commission of the States
(1998) revealed that "many believe that higher education does not spend its
money wisely, and that tuition increases could be avoided if colleges re-
aligned their spending with those areas the public most cares about, especially undergraduate education and job preparation" (p. 13). Similarly, a survey by the National Education Association found that 68 percent of the
chairpersons of education committees in state legislatures "feel strongly that
colleges and universities should focus more of their attention on undergraduate education as the core of their enterprise" (Ruppert, 1996, p. 14). A
committee chairperson quoted in this report summed up this view: "In times

of decreased financial support, we should put the money where it serves the greatest number of people, and that is basic core education" (p. 14).

Many state policymakers believe this is precisely what public college campuses have *not* done. A legislative staff member in New York told me a story about how Governor Pataki, in response to a rally by public college faculty to oppose proposed budget cuts, issued a statement saying that "rather than trying to stir people up, the faculty should be working on increasing their productivity. He ticked off several requirements. He said that if every faculty member would spend an additional hour a week in the classroom, it would save something like $17 million. If they taught an additional class it would save $20 million. If sabbaticals were canceled, for a year it would save $15 million." This position neatly expresses the type of policy that makes sense if policymakers see tuition increases as driven by the irresponsible, or at least unaccountable, spending by public colleges. Limiting price increases must begin by controlling and changing those spending patterns.

Many legislators explained to me, in a frustrated and even angry tone, that they had increased the higher education appropriation several times in past years and had still seen large tuition increases at public institutions. Campuses were not spending their money in the way state leaders wanted them to. A member of the Iowa General Assembly noted, "Frankly, I have a hard time figuring out where all the money goes. Many of us deeply want to improve higher education. But the more money we give them, the more they want. They never seem to recognize that we have other needs in the state." She went on to complain that "they don't even want to give us the kind of information we need to make good decisions. Everyone in state government is looking for ways to improve productivity, but higher education doesn't even want us to measure their productivity. Their view is 'give us the money' and leave us alone." According to an Ohio state representative, "those in the ivory tower need to come down, get a little dirty, and explain the whole process of what they do" (Mathesian, 1995, p. 22).

Evidence supporting this view of tuition inflation was largely anecdotal. Legislators, their staff, and members of the governor's office all seemed to have a favorite story to illustrate the problem. Sometimes it was a story about a faculty member who seemed to be paid a large salary yet did almost no teaching. Sometimes it was about a university administrator who was earning more than the governor. More often, the story was based on a personal experience. As a legislative staff member in Iowa explained, "When I went to the University of Iowa, I rarely had a class over thirty-five or forty students. The professors seemed to genuinely care about our education. But my niece goes there today, and all her classes are in huge auditoriums or taught by T.A.s [teaching assistants]. It really makes me wonder if she is getting her money's worth." A member of the Colorado General Assembly explained, "We have a problem here known as 'mission creep.' Every institution aspires to be like the ones that have more status. All the community colleges want to be four years. All the four years want to be research universities. They are all expanding their range of classes and increasing their research capacity. Nobody is happy just being what they are. And it all ends up costing a lot of money."

Perhaps the most analytical expression of this narrative was presented by William Massey in his testimony to the National Commission on College Costs. He argued that colleges and universities make spending decisions in accordance with a theory first offered by Howard Bowen in his classic treatise *The Costs of Higher Education* (1980), paraphrasing Bowen by stating, "Universities will raise all the money they can and spend all the money they raise" (Massey, 1998, p. 86). Seen this way, institutional spending decisions are constrained only by the funds they can raise. Massey went on to observe that "there is no mystery about how institutions can contain or even cut costs: the job is painful, but it can be done" (p. 86). In this view, public colleges chose not to cut costs because they did not have to cut costs. They could simply increase tuition to generate the revenue to cover their costs. According to Massey, with little incentive to control spending, institutions have fallen victim to a number of "cost drivers," one of which is institutionally funded research. In his view, this research serves as an "academic ratchet" that constantly forces up expenditures, because intrinsic and extrinsic incentives drive faculty toward research and away from teaching. The faculty marketplace rewards research, not teaching. Promotion, salaries, and prestige favor research. Moreover, PhDs are socialized for research, not teaching. This dynamic, Massey argues, is an important element of the tuition spiral as pressure to increase research causes institutions to reduce teaching-load norms and increase the demand for support services. In the end, this dynamic may produce more research, but that increase comes "at the expense of educational quality" (p. 86).

The relationship between tuition inflation and increased spending on research, especially sponsored research, remains sharply contested. Many find Massey's position overly simplistic. They counter that if research is the cause of rising prices, tuition should rise more rapidly at institutions that conduct lots of research and more slowly at institutions that conduct less. There is no empirical evidence of this pattern.

If policymakers begin with this view of the causes of public college tuition increases, they will design policies starkly different from those proposed by policymakers who accept any of the first three stories. More state money is not the answer. More campus autonomy would be counterproductive. Public colleges need to be made more accountable through either direct top-down control or altered incentives such as performance-based budgeting. One example of the policy emerging from this approach is the position taken by Ohio's Managing for the Future Taskforce in 1992. The final report of the taskforce argued that undergraduate teaching had been shortchanged in favor of research and recommended that the state mandate a 10 percent increase in teaching loads for all faculty across the state (Tucker & Voelker, 1995).

Narrative 5: It Only *Looks* Like a Problem

The final story about what underlies tuition inflation is not really about a cause at all. Instead, this perspective challenges the premise of the question. By asking "Why has tuition increased in your state?" I was implicitly saying that these increases are important and need to be addressed. But some policymakers thought this assumption was misguided. When asked whether the rapid tuition increases of the early 1990s presented a barrier to college in the state, a staff member at the Iowa Board of Regents replied, "Many legislators in our state are aware that enrollments in our public colleges and universities increased even as record tuition charges were being imposed. This caused them to conclude that we didn't have an affordability problem. If students can still afford to go to college, why should the legislature, which is facing lots of other demands, worry about it?"

A staff member of the House Education Committee of the Virginia House of Delegates told the same story. "You know, it [tuition inflation] really wasn't a problem. My chairman will tell you that he got more complaints about his constituent's children not getting into the school of their choice. He just didn't hear about it. I think it's just a function of the wheel not being squeaky enough." And I heard the same view from a staff member at the Colorado Commission on Higher Education. "I would say that the General Assembly is not concerned about rising tuition because the most rapid increase occurred during a time of enrollment growth. Most of our institutions did pretty well—despite the higher tuition. Fortunately, enrollment growth fit nicely with the fiscal crisis."

When seen in this way, college price increases should become a concern only when they begin to stop students from entering public colleges. To be sure, most of those who view the problem this way are aware that rising prices could depress participation rates in ways not evident simply by looking at total enrollments. Students who might otherwise attend the flagship university may elect to attend a community college. Students who might have gone

Table 2.1. Changes in Tuition and Enrollments at Four-Year Public
Colleges in Selected States, 1986–1987 to 1996–1997

	Public College Tuition (1996 dollars)			Public College Full-Time Equivalent Enrollment		
	1986–87	1996–97	Change	Fall 1986	Fall 1996	Change
California	$1,476	$2,720	84.3%	402,115	434,560	8.1%
Texas	1,267	2,028	60.1	290,961	336,716	15.7
North Carolina	1,171	1,841	57.2	112,418	132,690	18.0
Illinois	2,445	3,522	44.0	160,812	159,822	20.6
Virginia	2,963	3,968	33.9	122,272	140,484	14.9
U.S. Total	2,024	2,987	47.6	4,295,494	4,737,248	11.0

Source: Snyder, Hoffman, & Geddes (1998).

away to college may attend a school where they can live at home. But faced
with tight budgets and fierce competition for state dollars, these were
tradeoffs that some policymakers were willing to make.

As with the first four narratives, there is numerical evidence to support
the view that despite higher prices, students are indeed finding their way to
college in record numbers (an outcome described in Chapter 1). The study
by IHEP (1999) makes this point. "Access to college, as measured by the proportion of people going to college, is being maintained despite the higher
prices . . . When the higher prices are compared to the economic costs of not
going to college, clearly the costs of not going outweigh the price of attendance, even at the higher tuition levels" (p. 5).

Table 2.1 provides some evidence to support this view. Between 1986–87
and 1996–97, tuition at four-year public colleges increased, in constant dollar terms, by nearly 50 percent nationally. Yet, during that same time, FTE enrollment at four-year public colleges increased by 11 percent. Moreover, in
states where the percentage increase in tuition was especially large (such as
Texas), FTE enrollment increased even more. Certainly some states were
starting from a very low tuition level. But even in Virginia, which had one of
the most expensive state college systems during the decade, FTE enrollment
increased by nearly 15 percent.

This trend toward larger enrollments at public colleges is even more remarkable given the decline in the number of high school graduates during
the same period. Between 1986 and 1997, the number of high school graduates dropped 6.2 percent nationally. In the Northeast and Midwest the declines were even sharper. Yet, despite fewer high school graduates and higher

tuition, public college enrollment continued to increase. It is easy to see how policymakers with limited resources may not see the rise in tuition as an urgent problem. Indeed, to many, enrollment increases may have made efforts to reduce state support for higher education in order to fund other state priorities especially appealing.

Conclusion

As public college prices continue to rise, many policymakers believe they need to take action to limit those increases. But what actions should they take? Countless proposals have been suggested, almost all of which can be supported with a plausible rationale. As policymakers struggle to sort out the merits of these plans, the conclusions they reach will be shaped, perhaps even determined, by how they understand the dynamics of college prices. A proposed solution will make sense to policymakers only if it conforms to their view of the causes of price increases. Thus, to understand why policymakers form the policies they do, we must understand how they construct the problem they are trying to solve.

This chapter has identified four relatively distinct understandings of the causes of public college tuition inflation and another that denies this is a problem at all. Each position is supported by numbers, stories, and other evidence. These narratives compete with one another to win the support of the policymaking community. The one that achieves the dominant position will shape the policy that eventually emerges. If the cause is seen as insufficient state support, the appropriate policy response is to ensure that states have sufficient nontuition resources to keep prices low. If the problem is seen as unaccountable college spending, policies should seek to force colleges to live within their means. If rising public college prices are not seen as a problem, no policy response is needed.

Seen in this way, public college tuition and the problem of tuition inflation are inherently political. Advocates of competing viewpoints struggle to manipulate numbers, metaphors, and symbols in order to persuade others of the validity of their interpretation. However, at least in the states examined here, no dominant interpretation has emerged. The competition among the conflicting interpretations continues.

Assessing the validity of these competing narratives is a difficult, perhaps impossible, task. They are five stories without a clear lesson. Each seems to be based on a reasonable set of assumptions and can be constructed into a plausible description of the causes of the problem. Moreover, each story is convincingly argued by a number of well-informed policymakers. But rising public college prices remain a paradox. In this complex and ambiguous context, state and campus policymakers struggle to sort out the merits of particular solutions. Does performance-based funding improve performance? Will state mandates, which cap tuition or require improved productivity, harm the quality of instruction? The answers to these questions will be determined by the way in which policymakers have constructed the dynamics of college tuition. In the absence of clear thinking about these underlying dynamics, policy debates will inevitably lead to confusion and frustration. Indeed, such debates can never be resolved by examinations that focus on the particular remedy itself: those who construct the causes differently will evaluate the remedies differently. But by understanding the different constructions on which policy remedies are based, policymakers can more accurately assess the impact of plans to control college costs. This, in turn, might lead to more coherent state policies.

Notes

This research was supported by a grant from the Ohio University Research Committee. It benefited from the careful research assistance of Robert Welch.

1. For a review of the variety of state responses to rising public college prices, see Mumper (1998).

2. In each state I interviewed members of the state legislature (from the education or appropriations committees), staff in the governor's office, legislative staff, staff at the state board of higher education, and the director of the state's Student Aid Commission. In each state I also visited two four-year colleges. At both campuses I interviewed the director of financial aid and the vice president for finance. I also interviewed as many other people as were suggested by the original set of interviews.

References

American Council on Education. (1998). *Research on public perceptions of college costs and student aid.* Washington, DC: Author.

Bowen, H. R. (1980). *The costs of higher education: How much do colleges and universities spend per student and how much should they spend?* San Francisco: Jossey-Bass.

Education Commission of the States. (1998). *Survey of perceptions of state leaders.* Denver, CO: Author.

Foss, S. (1989). Narrative criticism. In *Rhetorical criticism: Exploration and practice* (pp. 229–288). Prospect Hills, IL: Waveland Press.

Halstead, K. (1998). *State profiles: Financing public higher education 1985–1995.* Washington, DC: Research Associates of Washington.

Hauptman, A. (1990). *The college tuition spiral.* Washington, DC: College Board and American Council on Education.

Hearn, J., Griswold, C., & Marine, G. (1996). Region, resources, and reason: A contextual analysis of state tuition and student aid policies. *Research in Higher Education, 37,* 241–278.

Hines, E. (1996). *State higher education appropriations 1995–1996.* Denver, CO: State Higher Education Executive Officers.

Hsu, S. (1995, January 23). Virginia failing in funding, colleges say: Business leaders warn of cuts' effect. *Washington Post,* p. A1.

Institute for Higher Education Policy. (1999). *The tuition puzzle.* Washington, DC: Author.

Kaiser, H. (1996). *A foundation to uphold: A study of facilities conditions at U.S. colleges and universities.* Alexandria, VA: Association of Higher Education Facilities Officers.

Kiesler, C. (1993, July 28). Why college costs rise and rise and rise. *New York Times,* p. A19.

Kirkwood, W. (1985). Parables as metaphors and examples. *Quarterly Journal of Speech, 71,* 422–440.

Massey, W. (1998). Remarks on restructuring higher education. In National Commission on the Cost of Higher Education, *Straight talk about college costs and prices.* Phoenix, AZ: Oryx Press.

Mathesian, C. (1995, March). Higher ed.: The no longer sacred cow. *Governing,* pp. 20–24.

Mortenson, T. (1997). FY 1997 state budget actions. *Postsecondary Education OPPORTUNITY, 55,* 10.

Mortenson, T. (1999). Refinancing higher education 1952 to 1997. *Postsecondary Education OPPORTUNITY, 79,* 10–20.

Mumby, D. (1987). The political function of narratives in organizations. *Communications Monographs, 54,* 113–127.

Mumper, M. (1998). State efforts to keep public colleges affordable in the face of fiscal stress. In J. Smart (Ed.), *Higher education: Handbook of theory and research.* New York: Agathon Press.

National Association of State Budget Officers. (1997). *Executive summary, 1997 state expenditure report* [On-line]. Washington, DC: Author. Available: http://www.nasbo.org/pubs/exprpt/serxec.htm

National Center for Education Statistics. (1999). *Digest of education statistics, 1998.* Washington, DC: U.S. Department of Education.

National Commission on the Cost of Higher Education. (1998). *Straight talk about college costs and prices.* Phoenix, AZ: Oryx Press.

National Science Foundation. (1996). *Scientific and engineering research facilities at colleges and universities.* Washington, DC: Author.

Ruppert, S. (1996). *The politics of remedy: State legislative views of higher education.* Washington, DC: National Education Association.

Scherschel, P. (1998). *Student indebtedness: Are borrowers pushing the limits?* (New Agenda Series Vol. 1, No. 2). Indianapolis, IN: USA Group Foundation.

Snyder, T., Hoffman, C., & Geddes, C. (1998). *State comparisons of education statis-*

tics: 1969–70 to 1996–97. Washington, DC: U.S. Department of Education, National Center for Education Statistics.

Sowell, T. (1992). The scandal of college tuition. *Commentary, 95,* 24.

Stone, D. (1997). *Policy paradox: The art of political decision making.* New York: Norton.

Tucker, J., & Voelker, J. (1995). Public higher education in Ohio. In C. Lieberman (Ed.), *Government, politics, and public policy in Ohio* (pp. 213–231). Akron, OH: Midwest Press.

3 · Reforming the Ways in Which States Finance Higher Education

ARTHUR M. HAUPTMAN

States vary considerably in how they finance higher education. Despite these differences, policymakers in every state have at their disposal three basic financing mechanisms: (1) the allocation of taxpayer resources to publicly supported state institutions; (2) the setting of tuition prices at public institutions, either directly by the state or indirectly through the state's review of decisions by institutional officials; and (3) the funding levels and rules for determining eligibility and award size for state-funded student aid programs.

Over the last half-century, the ways in which states use each of these financing mechanisms have undergone significant evolution. For most of U.S. history, virtually all state funds for higher education were allocated to public institutions for the purpose of maintaining low or no tuitions for students. But policies over the last quarter-century have incorporated more of a mix in the three elements of state financing. As a result, the naturally intense politics of state support for higher education have been tempered by greater reliance on the principles of policy and systems analysis.

Despite this progress, the system of financing in most states is insufficient to ensure the future accessibility and affordability of higher education for a broad range of Americans. This includes many minority and disadvantaged students, who will constitute an increasing proportion of the population demanding higher education.

In this chapter I examine how state policies can promote accessibility and accountability. I first review the evolution of the three key state financing policies—resource allocation, tuition setting, and student aid—and compare this evolution to changes in the federal role in providing student aid. I then assess why the current policies in most states are not sufficient to meet the challenges ahead and suggest some improvements. I make two basic recommendations for increasing the effectiveness of state financing in meeting the goals of greater accessibility and affordability. First, states need to achieve greater coordination among the three financing policies. The lack of coordination, evident in most states, results in policies that work against each other. For example, funding policies may serve to limit access while stu-

64

dent aid programs are designed to increase access. The net result is that none of the policies achieve their desired objectives. Second, state financing policies should be more student-oriented and less focused on meeting institutional financing needs alone.

Evolution of State Financing Mechanisms

State funding remains one of the largest sources of revenues in American higher education. By the late 1990s, the fifty states collectively provided $50 billion annually in support of higher education. We can place this $50 billion in perspective in a number of ways:

- State funding for higher education is one of the largest categories of state spending, representing more than 10 percent of all state budgets.
- States spend roughly twice as much as the federal government to support higher education, including student aid, campus-based research, and other categorical aid.
- State funds represent about one-quarter of total revenues for all institutions of higher education (public and private combined). Tuition revenues now constitute roughly one-third of the total revenues for all institutions, but just one-fifth for public institutions.

The importance of state funding is most critical at public institutions; despite some decline over the last several decades, it continues to represent one-third of all their revenues. Although tuitions and fees at public institutions have been increasing at twice the rate of inflation for the last several decades, they still are only half the size of state appropriations. State student aid programs make up a small proportion of total state funding, representing (on average) about 5 percent of what states collectively spend on higher education.

I describe here the evolution of policies governing trends in the use of the three components of states' higher education financing: allocations to public institutions, tuitions at public institutions, and state student aid programs. Figure 3.1 outlines these developments.

State Allocations to Public Institutions

More than 90 percent of state funding for higher education is in the form of support to public institutions. These allocations of taxpayer dollars have historically been political decisions, as institutions seek to maximize the funds they are eligible to receive. But in the late 1950s, state governments concluded that this large taxpayer support could not be distributed simply on the basis of political strength. This coincided with the impending demo-

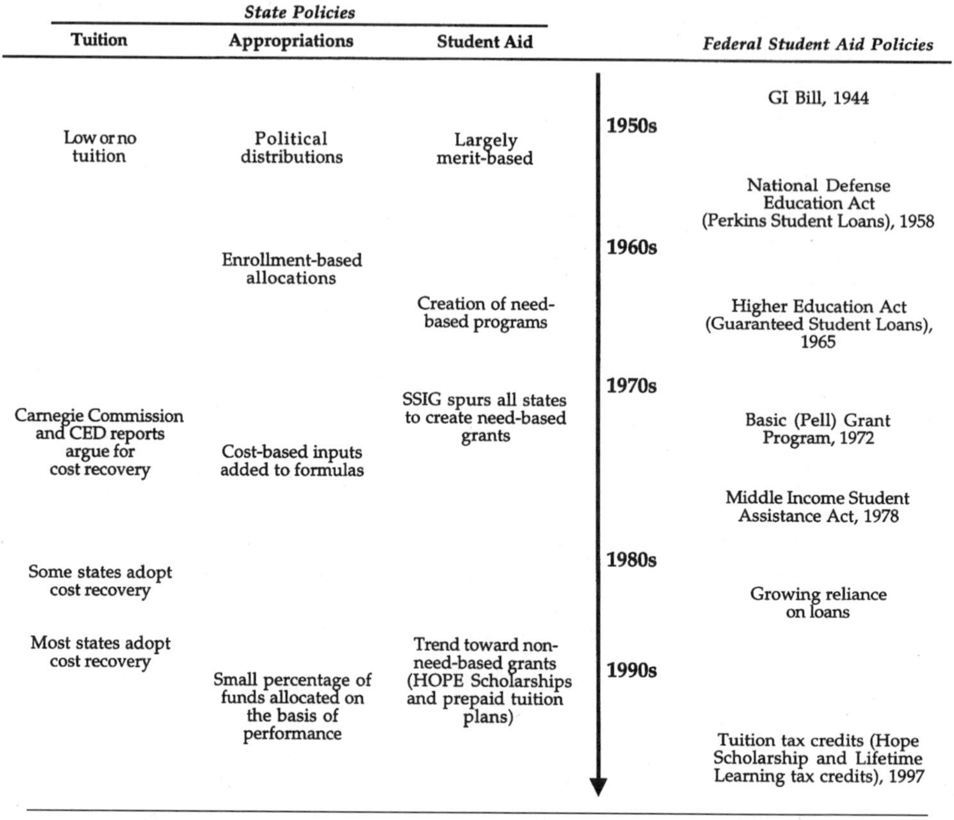

State Policies				Federal Student Aid Policies
Tuition	**Appropriations**	**Student Aid**		*Federal Student Aid Policies*
				GI Bill, 1944
Low or no tuition	Political distributions	Largely merit-based	**1950s**	
				National Defense Education Act (Perkins Student Loans), 1958
	Enrollment-based allocations		**1960s**	
		Creation of need-based programs		Higher Education Act (Guaranteed Student Loans), 1965
Carnegie Commission and CED reports argue for cost recovery	Cost-based inputs added to formulas	SSIG spurs all states to create need-based grants	**1970s**	Basic (Pell) Grant Program, 1972
				Middle Income Student Assistance Act, 1978
Some states adopt cost recovery			**1980s**	Growing reliance on loans
Most states adopt cost recovery	Small percentage of funds allocated on the basis of performance	Trend toward non-need-based grants (HOPE Scholarships and prepaid tuition plans)	**1990s**	
				Tuition tax credits (Hope Scholarship and Lifetime Learning tax credits), 1997

Figure 3.1. Evolution of State and Federal Policies for Financing Higher Education.

CED, Committee for Economic Development; SSIG, State Student Incentive Grant program.

graphic change: demand for higher education was about to grow tremendously as baby boomers reached college age and the underlying college participation rate increased. Enrollments in public higher education doubled between 1955 and 1965, then doubled again from 1965 to 1975 (National Center for Education Statistics, 1997, Table 172).

State support of public institutions was one of the two primary policy vehicles for funding the expansion of higher education over the last half-century. The GI Bill provided greater access to higher education for veterans returning from World War II and the Korean War in the late 1940s and the

1950s, and state support was just as critical in the expansion from the 1950s through the mid-1970s.

Most states dealt with the projected growth in the number of college students in the 1960s by using debt to fund the capital expenses required for building new public campuses or expanding existing ones. This decision to expand access by borrowing to build was accompanied in a number of states by a shift from politically based distributions of funds to allocations for re-current expenses based on the number of enrollments. By the end of the rapid expansion of higher education in the mid-1970s, enrollment-driven formulas had replaced strictly political distributions as the primary approach for allocating state funds to public institutions to support recurrent expenses.

In the 1970s, for distributing state dollars to public colleges and universities, a number of states began to shift from formulas based only on enrollments to those also taking into account the use of resources, inputs in the form of costs per student. This occurred principally because formulas based solely on enrollments failed to recognize the varied structures and histories of the institutions.

Beginning in the late 1980s, a further shift occurred as some states began to allocate some of their funding on the basis of performance measures. States adopting these performance-based approaches typically set aside a small portion of funds—typically less than 5 percent of their higher education budgets—to be allocated on the basis of such performance measures as graduation rates and an institution's demonstrated ability to reduce costs per student. Tennessee took the lead in this, followed by several other states; South Carolina was the most aggressive in adopting a performance-based system of allocating funds in the 1990s. But as the 1990s came to a close, the experience with performance-based funding was disappointing to those who believed that outcomes, not inputs, should determine state funding priorities. Fewer than a dozen states have adopted performance-based systems, setting aside a small share of total higher education funding into special funds allocated according to performance measures. Few states have built performance into their basic funding formula. (See Chapters 7 and 9 for more on performance funding.)

In the 1990s, the pattern of state policies for allocating funds to institutions was mixed. A handful of additional states adopted funding formulas based on enrollments, costs, or some combination of the two. But perhaps an equal number moved in the opposite direction, rejecting the use of formulas and adopting policies largely based on historical allocations, with adjustments for inflation and enrollment shifts. Virginia is a good example of the latter group; for most of the 1990s, the amount of state funding to public institutions was principally a function of how much they received the year before.

Tuitions at Public Institutions

States vary widely in how tuitions are set at their public institutions. In some states, legislatures play a major role in setting tuitions by stipulating what those tuitions should be. In a smaller number of states, governors and their staffs have a direct role in the tuition-setting process. In most states, however, public institutions now have the principal responsibility for setting tuitions, and governors and legislators ensure that these increases do not exceed some politically determined maximum.[1]

States also vary in the handling of tuition revenue. In a number of states, tuition revenues from public institutions are retained in the state treasury then reallocated back to the institutions. In other states the funds are retained by the institutions for use as they see fit. In Massachusetts, for example, tuition revenue is retained by the state but fees (nontuition charges to students, set by each campus board) are not, with the result that fees have increased much faster than tuition rates.

Regardless of the role of state and institutional officials in setting tuition and fees or the retention of these funds by institutions, in virtually all states there is a direct relationship among the level of public sector tuition and fees, the amount of state funding, and the cost of providing the education. The more the state provides, the lower is the tuition for any given level of costs per student. Put another way, state and local taxpayer support allows public institutions to charge tuitions and fees far below the actual cost to educate students.

Maintaining low or no tuition has been the principal public policy mechanism for providing access to higher education for most of U.S. history. This tradition helps explain why states spend as much as they do for higher education: paying all, or almost all, of the cost of this education is very expensive. And this traditional policy of maintaining low or no tuition was predominant throughout the expansion of higher education in the 1960s and into the 1970s.

But in the early 1970s, two national reports presaged a movement away from traditional state policy. One of these reports was issued by the Carnegie Commission on Higher Education (1973); the other was the product of the Committee for Economic Development (CED, 1973) an influential national group of business and community leaders. Both reports contained a re-markably similar recommendation: states should move away from a policy of low tuition to one based more on the notion of cost sharing between the states and the students and their families, such that tuitions should even-tually reflect one-third of the education costs. The notion behind this de-parture from traditional low-tuition policies was that students (and their families) should pay for the private economic benefits of a public higher ed-ucation, namely, the higher incomes that accrue to people who attend and graduate from college.

When these reports were first published in the early 1970s, neither the Carnegie Commission nor the CED generated much support for their prin-cipal recommendation of cost sharing. Most state policymakers remained re-luctant to move away from the traditional low-tuition approach. There were some exceptions, perhaps most importantly the decision at the City Univer-sity of New York to charge tuition, for the first time, for 1975–76, a result of New York City's fiscal crisis. But as the data in Table 3.1 indicate, the average tuition at public institutions across the country remained low and actually declined in real terms in the first half of the 1970s as high inflation eroded the value of public tuitions. The increase in public tuition rates (71%) in the second half of the 1970s was not much greater than inflation as measured by the Consumer Price Index (56%).

Not until the recession of the early 1980s did public sector tuition begin to climb substantially in real terms. As public institutions were squeezed by the falloff in state revenues, caused by the recession and its effect on states' ability to generate tax revenues, state legislatures and public institutions be-gan to look more favorably on the idea of cost sharing, mostly as a means for maintaining institutional budgets in the face of state spending shortfalls. In the first half of the 1980s, public sector tuition rates increased by two-thirds (more than 20% in real terms). With easing of the recession and sustained economic growth throughout the rest of the 1980s, renewed growth in the state funding of public higher education slowed the growth of public sector tuition, which increased only 15 percent in real terms in the second half of the 1980s.

The recession of the early 1990s, however, cemented tuition as an im-portant and permanent component in the financing of public higher educa-tion. Most states moved toward a system of cost recovery in which tuition rates are set formally or informally as a proportion of costs per student. Tu-ition at public four-year institutions grew by more than one-third in real terms in the first half of the 1990s. As a result, tuition also became a more sig-

Table 3.1. State and Federal Higher Education Trends, 1970–1998

	1970	1975	1980	1985	1990	1995	1998
Total state funding of higher education[a]	$6.5	$12.0	$19.2	$28.6	$39.2	$42.9	$49.4
Total state funding of higher education[b]	29.0	37.8	40.4	44.1	50.4	46.5	49.8
State spending for student aid[a]	0.2	0.4	0.8	1.2	1.7	2.8	3.4
Federal spending for student aid[a]	0.7	1.5	5.5	9.0	9.9	11.7	13.0
Tuition at public four-year institutions	325	432	738	1,228	1,696	2,705	3,111
Tuition at public four-year institutions (1999 dollars)	1,450	1,361	1,551	1,895	2,180	2,935	3,139
State spending for student aid as % of:							
Total state funding for higher education	3.1%	3.3%	4.2%	4.2%	4.3%	6.5%	6.9%
Federal spending for student aid	29	27	15	13	17	24	26
Federal spending for student aid as % of state funding for higher education	11	13	29	31	25	27	26

Sources: College Board (1998a,b), Gillespie and Carlson (1983), and Hines (1998).
[a]Billions of dollars.
[b]Billions of 1999 dollars.

nificant revenue source for all public institutions, growing to almost 20 percent of all revenues—after a period in which it was 13 percent of revenues or less (National Center for Education Statistics, 1997, Table 325).

State Student Aid Programs

State-level student aid has always played a secondary role in the financing of public higher education in the United States. Table 3.1 confirms that although funding for state student aid programs grew consistently in real terms over the last three decades, these programs represent a small percentage of total state spending for higher education. Throughout the 1960s, as states poured money into the expansion of public higher education, state student aid programs were decidedly in the background. Less than half the states had a financial aid program of any kind, and only a few states had programs of any significant magnitude. At the end of the decade, student aid represented 3 percent of total state funding of higher education.

This picture changed somewhat with passage of the State Student Incentive Grant program as part of the 1972 reauthorization of the Higher Education Act (HEA). The purpose of the program was to stimulate the creation of state student aid programs to complement the expansion of federal programs proposed in the same legislation. Despite relatively modest levels of funding, the State Student Incentive Grant program succeeded in meeting this goal. By the end of the 1970s, virtually all states had at least one need-based student grant program, and a number of states had several such programs.

Although the primary focus of states' aid to students has been on need-based grants, some states have a number of other programs that award aid on a basis other than financial need. Many of these non-need-based programs are targeted at particular groups of students, such as the children of deceased veterans, police disabled in the line of duty, and other categories of public safety officials. The trend in the 1990s was toward greater use of merit-based and other non-need-based programs, as a number of states sought to address middle-class concerns about college affordability by moving eligibility for aid programs up the income scale or instituting new programs with middle-class students as the primary beneficiaries. In 1997–98, nearly one-fifth of state aid was not based on financial need.[2] The best example of the state tilt toward helping the middle class is the prepaid tuition plans now offered in more than a dozen states. Middle- and upper-income families disproportionately participate in and benefit from these prepaid plans because they have the funds to make the prepayments and receive the largest tax benefits of tax-exempt income accrual.

Trends in Federal Student Aid

To put the state developments in context, Table 3.1 also indicates trends over the last half-century in federal support for higher education.[3] The principal difference in the federal and state roles in higher education is that the federal government has focused more on helping students pay for college expenses and the states on providing operational support to public institutions, enabling them to charge low tuitions; student aid has played a much smaller role in the state programs. Thus, one could maintain that the federal role, with its focus on student aid, has been more devoted to access, whereas the states, by seeking to keep public sector tuition low, have focused more on affordability.

The federal role in supporting college students began with passage of the initial GI Bill in 1944, which provided education benefits to World War II veterans. Subsequent versions of the GI Bill for Korean and Vietnam War veterans cemented the notion of federal aid provided in exchange for service. The first major federal aid program based on financial need was contained in the National Defense Education Act of 1958, now known as the Perkins Student Loan Program, which uses new federal capital and repayments into a revolving fund to provide low-interest loans to students with financial need. It was incorporated into the campus-based programs of grants, loans, and work study as part of the HEA legislation in 1965. In these campus-based programs, the federal government provides funds to institutions, which then identify recipients of need-based aid. The HEA legislation also created the Guaranteed Student Loan program to help students from a broader range of family incomes borrow for tuition and other college expenses.

The federal commitment to providing financial aid for the neediest students deepened in 1972 with creation of the Basic Education Opportunity Grant program, now known as Pell Grants. The Pell Grant program was a sharp departure from the campus-based approach in that it was designed to act more like a voucher program in which students vote with their feet and institutions reap the benefits of federal funding. One of the sharper distinctions between the federal role in higher education and the state student aid programs is that the major federal programs—GI Bill, student loans, and Pell Grants—were designed as vouchers: they are portable across institutions and must be used for educational expenses.[4] Few of the state student aid programs could reasonably be described as vouchers.

This commitment to helping the neediest students ebbed in 1978 with passage of the Middle Income Student Assistance Act, enacted as an alternative to tuition tax credits at all educational levels. The legislation expanded eligibility for Pell Grants up the income scale and removed the income limits for receiving subsidized loans in the Guaranteed Student Loan program. Although a need-based limit on subsidized borrowing was reestablished in 1981, the principle of federal aid reaching farther up the income scale had been established. This contributed to the growing reliance on student loans in the 1980s and 1990s. The shift in the federal role toward providing affordability was reinforced in 1997 with passage of two tuition tax credits for higher education: Hope Scholarships and the Lifetime Learning Tax Credits.

Problems with the Current Structure of State Financing and Suggestions for Improvement

As the preceding discussion indicates, although states vary greatly in the specifics of their higher education financing, the evolution of financing policies in most states over the last fifty years has led to systems with the following general characteristics:

- State funding of public institutions is based primarily on the number of students enrolled and the costs per student.
- Tuitions at public institutions are set through the political process or as a matter of cost recovery, with tuitions pegged to a percentage of costs per student.
- State student aid plays a relatively modest role, averaging about 5 percent of total state funding for higher education.

This financing structure has contributed to some remarkable accomplishments over the last half-century. The number of students enrolled in public institutions grew from just over one million in the late 1940s to more than eleven million in the 1990s (National Center for Education Statistics, 1997, Table 172). Total college participation rates have more than doubled for all income groups, with most of that increase occurring at public institutions. Overall, two-thirds of each class of high school graduates now attends college; although statistics were not kept at the time, this figure was surely less than a third in 1950 (National Center for Education Statistics, 1997, Table 183).

This remarkable expansion in the number of students and college participation rates occurred while resources per student were also expanding dramatically. Expenditures per student (in constant dollars) at public institutions rose from $12,000 in 1970 to approximately $15,000 in the 1990s, an increase of 25 percent after adjusting for inflation (National Center for Education Statistics, 1997, Table 336). This growth in spending per student in the face of tremendous expansion in the number of students represents a remarkable commitment to public higher education on the part of the states.

Although these figures confirm that the states have been remarkably successful in allowing a dramatic expansion in higher education, substantial structural problems also exist. These problems have often been disguised by the sheer level of resources devoted to the effort, overwhelming the inefficiencies in the system.

The challenge for the future lies in the likelihood that states will be unwilling or unable to muster sufficient resources to deal with changing demographic and economic realities. These demographic realities include a growing demand for higher education among traditionally underrepresented low-income and minority groups. The economic reality is that given the competing demands for resources, public higher education is unlikely to receive increased public resources sufficient to keep up with the growth in demands. The longstanding structural problems in how states finance higher education must therefore be addressed if future demand for public higher education is to be satisfied. Here I outline the major problems and suggest some solutions.

Problem: The financing structure in many states results in the highest proportion of funds being distributed to the institutions with the highest cost per student.

Most states now distribute funds based on historical allocation patterns or cost-based funding formulas. Under either approach, institutions with higher costs per student tend to receive a higher proportion of taxpayer dollars. This is not a policy concern if the higher costs are a function of higher proportions of students enrolled in high-cost programs such as engineering or the sciences. But if the higher costs per student are the result of undersubscribed courses or light teaching loads without correspondingly higher research activities, then distributing funds on the basis of cost per student or historical patterns may be rewarding greater inefficiency more than higher quality.

Suggested improvement: Use the process of allocating funds to institutions to encourage greater efficiency in the use of public resources.

Cost-based allocation procedures could be modified in several ways to encourage greater efficiency in distributing public resources. One way is to use average cost per student across the system, rather than actual cost per student at each institution, as the basis for allocating funds. This averaging would blunt the incentive for individual institutions to increase their cost per student since they would not be directly rewarded for doing so. Indeed, they could be penalized for having a higher than average internal cost structure.

To minimize the danger of penalizing institutions with a high percentage of enrollments in high-cost fields of study, the average cost per student should be separately calculated for different fields.

Another technique is to move to a system of normative costs rather than actual costs. As the name implies, normative costs are calculated from a series of formulas that use student/faculty ratios, space utilization rates, and other factors based on some notion of what ought to be rather than what is. Again, normative costs should be separately calculated for different fields of study so as not to penalize institutions with high proportions of students in high-cost fields.

Problem: Tuition-setting policies based on cost-sharing principles may encourage cost escalation rather than cost moderation.

Most states now (directly or indirectly) link tuition and fees at their public colleges and universities to the institutions' cost per student. This widespread adoption of cost sharing reflects the commonsense notion that students should pay a portion of their education costs to reflect the private benefits they will receive in the form of higher incomes. But taking cost sharing into account in tuition setting has some negative characteristics: it may encourage institutions to increase their costs per student in various ways so as to receive higher tuition revenues in the future.

Suggested improvement: Consider making tuition a measure of ability to pay by setting it as a percentage of a general economic index such as gross domestic product (GDP) per capita.

An alternative to tying public tuition and fees to costs per student is to peg them to an overall index of economic activity such as state GDP per capita. Public sector tuition would then increase in line with the state's economic growth and thus with people's ability to pay for higher education. In addition, institutional officials could not influence this type of tuition-setting index as they can when tuition is linked to cost per student. Indexing tuition to the economy and people's ability to pay would make state policies more student-based than under the current, institution-based system.

Moving to such a system would not preclude the possibility of varying tuition for students at different institutions or in different fields of study. For example, the percentage of GDP per capita could be set higher at a state's best public institutions as a reflection of their higher quality, higher costs, and higher demand. Or, as in Japan, the best public institutions might charge lower tuition as a means of rewarding the best students with the lowest prices. Similarly, tuition for students in different fields of study could vary to reflect cost differentials or to carry out policy goals such as charging lower prices to encourage enrollment in fields with labor market shortages.

Problem: The financing structure in most states gives short shrift to the goal of increasing access for students from low-income families.

Although most state policymakers stipulate increased access to higher education as a critical goal, several aspects of states' financing mechanisms work against the objective of increasing the participation of students from lower-income families. The allocation formulas in most states reward public institutions equally for enrolling the well-prepared student from affluent circumstances and the inner-city student with good grades who may require substantially more resources to succeed. Students from well-to-do families tend to enroll in the best institutions in the state; they attend better K–12 schools, have better academic records, and thus are more often admitted to institutions with higher standards. Thus, students from higher-income families are concentrated in the best colleges and universities. Funding formulas that do not differentiate on the basis of students' socioeconomic circumstances may be perpetuating this pattern. And to the extent that funding formulas do not take into account the socioeconomic characteristics of the students who enroll, public institutions have little incentive to recruit and admit students from lower-income or minority families.

Suggested improvement: Use the state allocation procedures to correct past inequities by rewarding greater access for target groups of students.

Most states tend to see the process by which they allocate funds to their higher education institutions as a means to improve quality, a philosophy that contributes to the unequal distribution of resources described above. One way to correct this bias is to change the criteria for distributing state funds to public institutions.

Rather than treating all students alike for the purpose of distributing funds, states could place a higher priority on funding students from disadvantaged backgrounds. For example, states could more generously subsidize public institutions for students from low-income families or minority groups than for more mainstream students. This additional payment would recognize that students from traditionally underrepresented groups are typically less prepared for college and therefore will likely cost more to educate. By making the allocation of funds more access-based, state funding policies could be more effective in broadening college opportunities than is the more traditional approach of relying solely on student aid for promoting access.

This notion of basing the allocation of state funds on priorities can be applied to a number of other goals as well. For example, to encourage students to enter fields with labor market shortages, states could provide higher subsidies for students enrolling in those fields. Or, if degree completion rates are too low, states could appropriate funds to institutions on the basis of the number of students who graduate rather than the number enrolled. This retention feature could also be reserved for student aid recipients, to prevent creaming of the best-prepared students by the institutions.

Problem: Most states devote only a small percentage of their higher education budgets to student aid, thus shortchanging the goal of access.

Another indicator of the low priority given to access in most states is the small percentage of their higher education budgets devoted to student aid. Given that, on average, student aid represents about 5 percent of total state spending on higher education, the primary programs for improving access receive a very small share of the state's higher education funding. In most states, this small proportion of funds devoted to student aid is not a function of an explicit policy decision; more often, it is the residual of a series of decisions about the size and distribution of state funds for public institutions: whatever is left over in the budget for higher education is funneled into student aid programs.

Suggested improvement: Increase the share of higher education funding devoted to student aid.

An alternative for determining how much funding a state devotes to student aid is to make the student aid programs an integral part of the budget-making process. In many countries this practice is referred to as "top-slicing," a process by which a share of the higher education budget is set aside for student aid or other purposes before distributing funds for the operational support of public institutions. Most institutional officials in the United States and around the world oppose top-slicing because it typically results in fewer funds for operational support. They are also concerned that if aid is available for students attending private or out-of-state institutions or for off-campus living expenses, public institutions will receive less funding from the state through operational support.

These institutional concerns confirm the term *institution-based* to describe state policies that devote a small share of higher education funding to student aid. In some states, such as New York, which historically has devoted 20 percent of its higher education budget to student aid, the policies might be described as more *student-centered.* Clearly, policymakers in many states would decide to spend a much smaller share of their higher education budget on student aid than does New York, even if the decision were more explicitly made. But at least that would be a proactive policy judgment rather than the more typical decision by default.

Problem: Public sector tuition increases the most when students and their families can least afford to pay.

The pattern of public sector tuition increases in the United States over the last several decades is clear. In the last three recessions, in the mid-1970s, the early 1980s, and the early 1990s, percentage increases in public sector tuition were in double digits. Once each recession ended, the percentage increases slowed down, but rarely fell to the levels of inflation. Over good times and bad, public sector tuition rates have grown, on average, at twice the rate of inflation over the last two decades, as have tuition rates in private institutions. These public and private sector tuition patterns differ in two ways, however. First, tuition rates are much higher in private than in public institutions. Second, private tuition rates tend to increase more during economic expansions, whereas public sector prices increase faster during recessions.

The reason for the more rapid increase in public sector tuition rates during recessions is clear. Tuition represents the major difference between what states provide and what institutions need in their budgets. During good economic times, state revenues grow faster and states have more money to spend on higher education and other functions, and thus less is needed from tuition revenues to meet budget needs. During recessions, state revenues fall and tuition rates increase more rapidly to allow public institutions to maintain their budgets. This pattern of public sector tuition prices going up the most when people can least afford them is perhaps the most objectionable aspect of higher education financing in most states. (See Chapter 1 for more on this relationship between tuition and the ability of students and their families to pay.)

Suggested improvement: Set aside reserves during economic booms to reduce the volatility of public sector tuition increases.

Tying public sector tuition prices to an economic index such as GDP per capita would correct the problem of tuition increasing the most during recessions. But it would exacerbate the situation of most public institutions, which would face a "double whammy" during recessions: their state funding would fall and so would tuition revenues. Without a correcting feature, recessions would wreak havoc on institutional budgets under this scheme.

Rather than using public sector tuitions as the flywheel, a better way for states to cope with the ups and downs of the economic cycle would be to set aside reserves during a strong economy. These reserves could then be used to stem the effects of the inevitable shortfall in funding during economic downturns. In a similar vein, states could borrow during a recession and then reserve funds during subsequent economic expansions to retire the debt. In either case, creating reserves is critical to making any state financing scheme less susceptible to the economic cycle.

A chief argument against the creation of reserves is that institutional officials lack the discipline to not spend them during the good times. The way to address this legitimate concern is to maintain the reserves at the state level and to provide clear and objective criteria that determine when in the economic cycle they can be used. The important point is for states and institutions to achieve more prudent budgeting practices by stabilizing the system, filling in some of the funding troughs that occur during recessions and lowering the peaks that can occur during expansions.

Concluding Note: A Framework for Improving Accessibility and Affordability

In this chapter I have identified a number of problems with states' systems of financing higher education and have suggested some ways in which state policies could be more effective in making public higher education more accessible and more affordable. These suggested improvements fall into two categories.

First, for state financing policies to be more effective, greater coordination in the policy development and implementation of the three types of financing mechanisms is critical. To achieve greater accessibility, for example, states should not rely solely on student aid programs. Funding formulas should improve access by factoring in the characteristics of students. Policymakers should explicitly consider how much of the higher education budget to devote to student aid, rather than letting these decisions be made by default.

Second, state financing policies should become oriented more toward meeting the needs of students and their families than toward helping institutions finance themselves. Setting public sector tuition rates as a percentage of state GDP per capita, rather than as a percentage of costs per student, is one example of a more student-based approach. Other student-based policies include recognizing the differing characteristics of students and establishing reserves so that public sector tuition prices would no longer increase most rapidly during recessions.

These two themes—coordinating state financing policies and making them more student-oriented—can serve as a framework for assessing the capacity of state policies to make higher education more accessible and afford-able. States will have to adjust their policies in these two directions if they wish to meet the demographic and economic challenges in the decades ahead.

Notes

1. For an overview of the states' policies in setting public college and university tuition rates, see Lenth (1993).

2. The annual survey of the National Association of State Student Grant and Aid Programs is the best source of information on trends in state student aid programs (New York State Higher Education Services Corporation, 1999).

3. For a fuller review of the fifty-year history of federal support for higher education students, see Gladieux and Hauptman (1995).

4. For a fuller discussion of the use of vouchers in higher education, see Hauptman (2000).

References

Carnegie Commission on Higher Education. (1973). *Higher education: Who pays? Who benefits? Who should pay?* New York: McGraw-Hill.

College Board. (1998a). *Trends in college pricing.* Washington, DC: Author.

College Board. (1998b). *Trends in student aid.* Washington, DC: Author.

Committee for Economic Development. (1973). *The management and financing of colleges.* Washington, DC: Author.

Gillespie, D. A., & Carlson, N. (1983). *Trends in student aid, 1963 to 1983.* Washington, DC: College Board.

Gladieux, L., & Hauptman, A. (1995). *The college aid quandary.* Washington, DC: Brookings Institution.

Hauptman, A. (2000). Vouchers and American higher education. In C. E. Steuerle, V. D. Ooms, G. Peterson, & R. D. Reischauer (Eds.), *Vouchers and the provision of public services.* Washington, DC: Brookings Institution and Urban Institute.

Hines, E. R. (1998). *State higher education appropriations 1997–98.* Denver, CO: State Higher Education Executive Officers.

Lenth, C. (1993). *The tuition dilemma.* Denver, CO: State Higher Education Executive Officers.

National Center for Education Statistics. (1997). *Digest of education statistics, 1997.* Washington, DC: U.S. Department of Education.

New York State Higher Education Services Corporation. (1999). *NASSGAP annual survey report.* Albany: Author.

II ACCESS

4 Reframing Access and Opportunity: Problematic State and Federal Higher Education Policy in the 1990s

PATRICK M. CALLAN

The new century has arrived, and during its first decades we will most likely be debating our traditional concepts of access and opportunity in higher education. Significant changes in the societal context of U.S. colleges and universities—demographic, economic, and technological—are already beginning to force us to reconsider traditional policies and practices. This reconsideration and reframing will become even more urgent, and in this chapter I propose several elements or dimensions of opportunity that should be a part of the discussion. The focus is on technical and academic education beyond high school, on undergraduate collegiate work, and on inclusive criteria for determining who should benefit from opportunity. Opportunity in higher education has expanded throughout American history, and until recently our concept of opportunity has been derived largely from experience with the phenomenal growth of enrollment and participation since World War II. This chapter provides support for the belief that recent trends indicate a narrowing of opportunity. I outline six dimensions of opportunity that we need to consider (among many others) as we reframe traditional concepts.

Expansion of Opportunity after World War II

The expansion of access and participation in higher education has been a major theme of American social and economic history in the post–World War II era. Accessibility broadened dramatically in the half-century following passage of the GI Bill, the policy that brought educational opportunities to World War II veterans. Stimulated primarily by public policies instituted by the nation and the states, colleges and universities successfully accommodated first the veterans and then the baby boomers. Responding in part to the Civil Rights movement, public policies stimulated colleges and universities to expand educational opportunity once again, this time for "nontraditional" students—that is, minority students who traditionally had been underrepresented in American colleges and universities, as well as adults beyond the traditional college age who usually attended college part-time.

Financial aid to students, enlargement of existing educational facilities, and, in the public sector, an unprecedented construction of new campuses were the major policy tools used by government during these last five decades of expansion.

In the process of broadening opportunity, the very definition of higher education changed. This had happened before. The Morrill Act of 1862 and establishment of Land Grant colleges extended college education to new populations and expanded the curriculum to include practical and applied areas. Similarly, the creation of community colleges altered the definition of higher education to encompass a broader array of vocational and academic opportunities for a larger number of people. These historical changes were attributable less to evolutionary forces *within* higher education than to *external* social and economic pressures. As throughout much of American history, the expansion of educational opportunity was driven primarily by utilitarian considerations. Government policies supported higher education as a *means* to a wide range of larger national *public purposes:* avoiding large-scale unemployment; competing for scientific and technological superiority during the Cold War; responding to the moral imperatives of the Civil Rights movement; encouraging national, state, and regional economic growth; and promoting opportunity and social mobility.

The GI Bill, the development of student financial assistance, and the growth of public higher education were all political and governmental responses to significant public needs. The responses differed as the perceived needs differed, but they shared a common theme that cuts across the large array of public policies and programs. This common theme was individual opportunity, a growing national belief that every American who was motivated and could benefit from education and training beyond high school should have that opportunity, regardless of personal or family financial resources and race or ethnicity.

By the late 1990s, education and training beyond high school was no longer just one of several options that individuals might pursue to better themselves economically and socially. In the years following World War II, the expansion of opportunity had taken two roads. One road was the expansion of the U.S. industrial base, leading to growth of the middle class, to suburban life, and to expectations that one's children would have an even better life. The other was the expansion of education, which led to increasing numbers of students and higher education institutions and ultimately to the present information-based, global economy. These roads were equally important for several decades, but the one based on the old industrial economy has narrowed substantially in recent years. Domestically, technological advances have increased productivity and fewer unskilled workers are required. In contrast, education is now the only road to opportunity for most people. Education beyond high school is now a virtual necessity for those aspiring to maintain or achieve employment that provides a middle-class standard of living. It has become a necessary, though not sufficient, condition for the employment to which most people aspire, employment that provides economic sufficiency and the conditions correlated with civic, community, and cultural life. If opportunity is broadly defined as the chance to participate fully in society, higher education has become the only road to opportunity for most Americans.

Narrowing of Opportunity in the 1990s

The ideal of opportunity for all Americans to participate fully in society, and to have access to higher education as a means to that end, must now be reframed. Recent state and federal policies require us to reexamine this issue. By 2008, some two million additional students will seek entry into our colleges and universities (National Center for Education Statistics, 1998), but projected state support will not be commensurate with that growth. Costly construction of new facilities, the past solution to growth, is unlikely, given the political limits to raising taxes and shifting funds from other public services, such as public K–12 schools, health care, or welfare, all of which have legitimate claims on public funds (Hovey, 1999; see also Chapters 2 and 7 for more on the competition for state appropriations).

As we approach this new era of constrained resources for higher education, recent trends show disproportionate increases in subsidies for middle-income students and families and decreased public concern for those with lower incomes. These trends can be traced, in large part, to the national economic recession of the early 1990s and the responses of state governments. Although this recession may now be just a blip on the charts of those concerned with the nation's economy, it was of great and immediate consequence for higher education in many states. And, more critically, it foreshadowed the important long-term implications of constrained resources. In state budgets during that recession, higher education was the biggest loser with respect to share (Gold, 1995). For the country as a whole, the share of higher education in state budgeting dropped from 14 percent in 1990 to 12.5 percent in 1994, a 10.7 percent reduction in overall spending for higher education. Even more significantly, between 1992 and 1994, for the first time in forty years, there was an absolute decline in state dollars spent on higher education (Callan, Finney, Bracco, & Doyle, 1997). The response of states, colleges, and universities to the deep cuts in state budgets was to increase tuition. In 1993–94, tuition increases surpassed state appropriations as the largest revenue source for higher education (National Center for Education Statistics, 1997, p. 343).

Ironically, the recession of the early 1990s came at a time of increasing recognition of the need for education or training beyond high school. The economic imperative was—and remains—powerful; simply stated, a college graduate earns more than someone with only a high school diploma. As shown in Figure 1.11 in Chapter 1, in 1971 a male with a baccalaureate degree earned about 50 percent more than a worker with only a high school diploma; by the late 1980s that differential was 60 percent, and by 1997 it was 70 percent.

The differential was largely accounted for by the deteriorating economic prospects of those with a high school diploma or less education, whose real income decreased by 25 and 41 percent, respectively, between 1970 and 1997. Academic or vocational education beyond high school does not guarantee a middle-class life, but the penalty for not pursuing it is even greater now than twenty-five years ago. Almost all those who held their own or improved their income over the last quarter-century had some college education or either a baccalaureate or advanced degree.

The need for education or training beyond high school is not a secret confined to statisticians. The economic volatility of the 1980s and 1990s made that need clear to most Americans. In a recent national public opinion survey, one question asked whether a high school graduate should go on to college or take any decent job offer; 86 percent of those polled recommended college (Immerwahr, 1998, p. 4). In the same survey, some 75 percent of the respondents believed that a college education was more important in 1998 than ten years earlier; only 5 percent thought it less important. One need not discount the intangible social and intellectual benefits of education to understand the enormous economic pressure on the young to enroll in college, as well as the growing pressure on many older individuals to enroll in or return to college to raise their educational and skill levels.

Just as the gap in economic opportunity between college-educated and non-college-educated Americans widened in the latter years of the twentieth century, the gap between the rich and poor also widened, despite a major economic expansion in the middle and late 1990s. The participation of all income groups in higher education has risen in recent years—from just over 50 percent in 1977 to more than 65 percent in 1997 (Institute for Higher Education Policy, 1999, p. 21). But the gap in the extent of participation, like the income gap between rich and poor, has widened. High school students from families in the highest income quartile (with an annual income above

$72,000 in 1996) have an 80 percent chance of entering college by age twenty-four. Students from families in the lowest income quartile (less than $24,500 in 1996) have a 35 percent chance of entering college by the same age (Mortensen, 1998, p. 5). Today, a major challenge for our society, and for higher education's role in it, is to address the gap in wealth and income that is paralleled by a disturbing gap in educational opportunity.

State and federal policies in the 1980s and 1990s did little to address the educational opportunity gaps as they emerged and widened. From the early 1980s to the mid-1990s, states shifted responsibility for higher education away from taxpayers and toward students and their families, as tuition rates for public higher education increased by about a third (in real terms) without commensurate increases in need-based student financial assistance. Between 1980–81 and 1994–95, the percentage of college and university revenues derived from tuition increased by 32.9 percent, while that derived from state government declined by 21.6 percent (National Center for Education Statistics, 1998, p. 343). During roughly the same period (1976–77 to 1996–97), tuition and fees at public institutions increased by 375 percent, although the Consumer Price Index increased by slightly more than 150 percent (Institute for Higher Education Policy, 1999, p. 12). The incomes of some segments of the population may have matched these increases in tuition, but the increases had a decidedly disproportionate and adverse impact on low-income families (see Figure 1.4, Chapter 1)

In 1971, tuition for one student at a public four-year institution required 12 percent of the income of a low-income family; in 1997 it required more than 25 percent. For many students and families, all this added up to increases in tuition at a time of high unemployment, economic stagnation, and decline in personal incomes. In New York State, for instance, between 1990 and 1995, tuition increased from 4.2 to 7.7 percent of median household income; in California, the increase was from 1.7 to 3.1 percent (Halstead, 1998, pp. 11, 67). In California, the combination of tuition increases and reduced state appropriations drove down higher education enrollments (particularly in the state university and community college systems) by two hundred thousand at a time when the rate of unemployment was approaching 10 percent (Usdan & Callan, 1998, p. 29). The public perceived the tuition increases as excessive and the consequence has been a political backlash against even modest increases, a backlash that continues into the new century with tuition reductions.

Public opinion surveys during this time of economic volatility and significant hardship showed that the middle class in particular feared that higher education, just when it seemed more essential than ever, was becoming less accessible. As middle-class families weighed in on this issue, political leaders, first at the state and then at the federal level, began searching for ways to relieve the anxiety about access to higher education. By the mid-1990s, of the five states that had raised tuition by the highest percentage from 1990 to 1995 (California, Massachusetts, New York, Oregon, and Virginia), four had either frozen tuition or slowed the rate of growth significantly. In California and New York, Governors Pete Wilson and George Pataki advocated or supported steep tuition increases in the early and mid-1990s. Facing adverse public opinion and with reelection campaigns ahead, both governors backed away from their earlier positions. In Governor Wilson's case, this meant the reversal of a negotiated agreement with public college and university leaders that called for future tuition increases of 10 percent a year. Prior to Wilson's reversal, Gray Davis—the prospective gubernatorial candidate who became governor of California in 1999—proposed a (failed) amendment to the state constitution that would have frozen tuition and restricted future increases.

In many states, the growth of programs providing financial support to academically successful students regardless of need outstripped the growth of need-based financial aid. Basically, non-need-based programs give subsidies to students who are already college bound. The best known of these, the Georgia HOPE Scholarship, was structured to exclude the participation of low-income students who received federal Pell Grants, a kind of reverse means testing. This program influenced the trend toward publicly supported grants that do not consider financial need. Because of this program, in "1995–96, non-need-based dollars for undergraduates . . . *increased* by almost 11 percent from the previous year . . . whereas need-based grants had *decreased* by 2 percent" (Education Resources Institute & Institute for Higher Education Policy, 1998, p. 10). Georgia's HOPE program not only influenced other states but gave its name to new—and costly—federal tax credits.

At the federal level, at least two developments have, in the opinion of many, helped jeopardize opportunity. First, over the last two decades the federal financial aid system has been transformed—without major policy debate—from one characterized predominantly by need-based grants to a national aid system in which loans are the predominant form of financial aid. As Figure 4.1 illustrates, from 1987 to 1997, loans from all sources increased 106 percent in constant dollars, from about $17 billion to $36 billion. Grants from all sources increased only 57 percent, from $15 billion to $24 billion. During this same period, federal support of need-based Pell Grants grew only 19 percent, from $5 billion to $6 billion.

The rich as well as the poor can borrow money to attend college. The poor, however, are more likely to have a cumulative debt exceeding $20,000

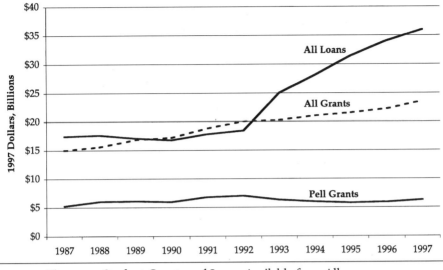

Figure 4.1. Student Grants and Loans Available from All Sources, and Pell Grant Spending, 1987–1997.
Data from the College Board (1998).

(Baum & Saunders, 1998). And borrowing is a much greater burden on poor families. In 1996, for example, total undergraduate student loans amounted to 26 percent of family income for the lowest income quintile, 6 percent for the middle quintile, and only 1 percent for the highest (National Center for Education Statistics, 1996; loan amount by income quintile). Equal availability of federal loans to all income groups does not result in equal opportunities for affordable college participation.

The second development at the federal level was middle-class relief from college costs in the form of tuition tax credits. Tested in polls and focus groups in the 1996 elections, the tax credit idea linked tax relief—promised by presidential candidates of both parties and many congressional candidates as well—with the equally popular concept of assisting the middle class in meeting college costs. The result, the Taxpayer Relief Act of 1997, is expected to cost some $40 billion in foregone revenues from 1998 to 2002—the largest infusion of federal aid for college since the GI Bill. Two nonrefundable tax credit programs are at the heart of the federal law: the Hope Tax Credit, for the first two years of college tuition expense, and the Lifelong Learning Tax Credit, for tuition expense after the first two years. As Table 4.1 shows, these programs ease the burden of college costs for the middle class—maximum benefits are

Table 4.1. Estimated Benefits of Federal Student Aid and the Hope Tax Credit, by Taxable Family Income

Taxable Income	Pell Grant	Loan Subsidy	Hope Tax Credit	Total Federal Aid
Two-year public colleges and universities[a]				
$10,000	$3,000	$200	$0	$3,200
20,000	3,000	200	0	3,200
30,000	2,450	200	0	2,650
40,000	950	200	550	1,700
50,000	0	0	1,250	1,250
60,000	0	0	1,250	1,250
70,000	0	0	1,250	1,250
80,000	0	0	1,250	1,250
90,000	0	0	625	625
100,000	0	0	0	0
Four-year public colleges and universities[b]				
$10,000	$3,000	$875	$0	$3,875
20,000	3,000	875	0	3,875
30,000	2,450	875	550	3,875
40,000	950	875	1,500	3,325
50,000	0	875	1,500	2,375
60,000	0	0	1,500	1,500
70,000	0	0	1,500	1,500
80,000	0	0	1,500	1,500
90,000	0	0	750	750
100,000	0	0	0	0
Four-year private colleges and universities[c]				
$10,000	$3,000	$875	$0	$3,875
20,000	3,000	875	0	3,875
30,000	2,450	875	1,500	4,825
40,000	950	875	1,500	3,325
50,000	0	875	1,500	2,375
60,000	0	875	1,500	2,375
70,000	0	875	1,500	2,375
80,000	0	875	1,500	2,375
90,000	0	875	750	1,625
100,000	0	875	0	875

Source: Hauptman and Rice (1997).
Note: Calculations are for full-time freshman students. Income is defined as adjusted gross income for taxpayers filing jointly with two dependents. Pell Grants are for families of four with one child in college. Loan subsidy is based on the maximum subsidized loan for freshman students, $2,625. Eligibility for tax credit is determined by tuition minus all grants, scholarships, and other tax-free educational assistance. Tax credit is $0 if family income is less than $30,000 or net tuition is negative. Maximum allowable tax credit is $1,250 for two-year colleges and $1,500 for four-year colleges.
[a]Average tuition = $1,500; average cost of attendance = $4,500.
[b]Average tuition = $3,000; average cost of attendance = $10,000.
[c]Average tuition = $13,000; average cost of attendance = $20,000.

received by students and families in the $40,000 to $80,000 income bracket—and exclude the lowest-income students and families.[1]

About $9 billion in foregone revenue for these tax credits was incurred in 1998, the first year in which the act was implemented. In contrast to this $9 billion spent for middle-income taxpayers, Congress appropriated $650 million in 1998 to increase the maximum Pell Grant awards and to broaden eligibility for these grants. The Pell Grant program serves the lowest-income students.

Even those who do not believe, as I do, that the tax credit provisions of the 1997 Taxpayer Relief Act are lacking in distributive equity must recognize the law's significant policy implications. The new tax credits can be viewed as a clear step toward federal reframing of generally accepted concepts about the financing of opportunity in the United States. Clayton Spencer (1999), for example, finds two indications that the federal reframing threatens traditional financial aid policy. The first is that tax benefits—essentially automatic entitlements—enjoy a "mechanical" budgetary advantage over traditional, discretionary student aid programs because the latter require annual appropriations from available funds. At both the federal and state levels, political leaders will find it easier to enact tax credits than to appropriate general fund support for direct student aid, particularly in an economic downturn or when other entitlements limit available funds.

The second indication is perhaps even more alarming: the tax credit provisions may be evidence of an erosion of the coalition that has supported traditional student financial aid for the last thirty years. This coalition consisted of those with a direct interest in an individual student—the student, his or her family, the financial aid officer who evaluated need and packaged aid, and the college or university that received the dollars. The interests of these participants and the award itself intersected at a specific time and place—the time a student enrolled at a particular college or university. But under the new law, this coalition has little part in the tax credit programs. Students enroll in September, but the benefits are not received until April of the following year—and then the money may or may not be used for educational purposes. Instead of individual need evaluated by the financial aid officer, eligibility for a tax credit is calculated by an accountant. Colleges and universities are no longer partners in determining and conferring an educational benefit. If the traditional coalition will no longer be a viable advocate for opportunity, who will?

In the face of growing evidence of gaps in wealth, income, and opportunity, state and federal policy has centered on easing the burdens of those who are already college bound, not on closing the country's opportunity gap.

Moreover, some aspects of the new federal tax credit legislation may actually undermine states' commitments to opportunity. For instance, the program is structured to the disadvantage of states in which public institutions charge low tuition; that is, eligible students and families in low-tuition states will receive lower federal tax benefits than those in states with high-tuition policies. Similarly, for many students in states with generous need-based student financial assistance, such as California, Illinois, New York, and Pennsylvania, their state grants will reduce the amount of their or their families' federal tax credits. In other words, one effect of the federal legislation is to penalize students in states that have most generously subsidized college opportunity through low tuition, large need-based financial aid programs, or both.

At the beginning of the new century, it is unclear how tax credits will ultimately play out with respect to access or affordability. Having provided a powerful economic incentive for higher education institutions and states to *increase* tuition in order to capture federal tax dollars and shift cost to the federal government, the Clinton administration and Education Secretary Richard Riley (1998) used the "bully pulpit" to advocate against tuition increases in the short term. During the present strong economy and with growing state appropriations to higher education, states and colleges are unlikely to move aggressively to raise tuition in order to capture federal dollars. However, when the economy turns down, states will face lower revenues and colleges and universities will see reduced budgetary increases, perhaps even cuts. Whether the states and the higher education institutions will continue their self-imposed restraints on large tuition increases remains to be seen.

The public policies of the 1990s emphasized reducing the financial burden on students who are in college or most likely to attend college, and their families. The same thrust of policy rewards high-achieving students through grants that are not means tested. As a consequence, public benefits have made college somewhat more affordable for students from upper- and middle-income families. Moreover, they have expanded the college choices for these students—those who currently enroll in high proportions. Michael McPherson and Morton Schapiro (1998), writing after the Clinton administration proposed the federal tax credits but before enactment by Congress, observed that "people's willingness to accept the vision of providing equal educational opportunity through need-based student aid has come increasingly into question at all levels" (p. 14). In contrast—and reflecting the political tenor of the early and mid-1990s—President Clinton (1999) appears to have already declared victory in the quest for equal opportunity in higher education. In his 1999 State of the Union Address, he asserted that the new federal tax credit programs "finally open the doors of college to all Americans" (p. 4).

I respectfully disagree. Rather than opening the doors of opportunity, these new tax credits may well epitomize recent trends that point to political, but not necessarily public, reluctance to maintain opportunity.

Six Critical Dimensions of Opportunity

Historically, public policy—state and federal—has been the engine driving opportunity in the United States. Whenever the nation has sought to expand opportunity or to create a more level playing field, colleges and universities have responded. And in the future as in the past, the defining element of educational opportunity will be access: which individuals and groups are included and which excluded. Opportunity will continue to flow from society's values and priorities as expressed in the policies of state and federal political bodies. Higher education opportunity is inextricably tied to overarching questions about the distribution of public resources and to the priorities and incentives—explicit and implicit—that affect government's support of students and institutions.

Federal and state higher education policies of the middle and late 1990s seem to reflect the broad political trends that Nicholas Lemann (1998) has called "the new American consensus," a consensus focused on the primacy of suburban middle-class interests. According to Lemann, this consensus dominates both major political parties and is based on an extremely narrow view of the purposes and role of government. This view emphasizes the responsibility of government to protect middle-class interests and eschews politically uncomfortable issues, such as the responsibilities of citizens for the common good and the growing disparities of wealth and income. Lemann describes this as a pinched view of civic obligation in a democracy and as a constricted concept of the government's responsibility to those who are not part of the new consensus—a consensus he characterizes as one of "government of, by and for the comfortable" (p. 37). Lemann's analysis of the national political environment is a useful backdrop for understanding the federal and state policy directions described above. It also suggests that neither the problems nor the solutions to the issues of opportunity are likely to be found by examining higher education in a vacuum. While not claiming to predict how the societal, political, economic, and educational scenarios will play out in the first decade of the new century, I do believe we can identify several elements that may help us reframe and revitalize opportunity and access.

Lowering Financial Barriers

Money matters, as most Americans know. Family income is highly correlated with enrollment in higher education and completion of degrees. As recent trends show, government policymakers believe that public subsidies are an effective way to encourage college attendance for middle- and upper-income families. Couldn't a powerful political and substantive case be made for the potential impact of subsidies for the less affluent? Assuredly, but the Clinton administration did not attempt to make this case in its tax credits proposal. It chose instead to propose modest and much less expensive increases in the federal Pell Grant program for low-income students. The principal problem with federal tax credits and many of the new state initiatives is not that they make higher education more affordable for those already attending college, but that they systematically exclude others from participation—potential students in the lower-income strata, those who attend college in the lowest numbers.

By their recent initiatives at the state and federal level, political leaders have responded to anxieties that financing college is a major problem for the middle class. This may be well and good, but as public opinion surveys show, Americans consistently and by large majorities hold two beliefs about higher education opportunity that are not reflected in the recent policies of their elected leaders (Ikenberry & Hartle, 1998; Immerwahr, 1997, 1998):

1.   Every American who is motivated and can benefit should have college opportunity, and no one should be denied opportunity because of lack of personal or family financial resources.
2.   College opportunity is most problematic for persons of low income (in contrast, for instance, to ethnic minorities, part-time students, and the middle class).

I offer two hypotheses for reframing public policy on opportunity and access. First, opportunity will be enhanced if public programs and subsidies that address financial aspects of access to higher education link the interests of the middle class and the less affluent rather than divide them. For example, at the state level, merit-based scholarship programs should be open to low-income students in states where they are not, such as Georgia. At the federal level, an approach similar to the federal earned income tax credits should be incorporated into the Hope and Lifelong Learning tax credits: refundable tax credits that benefit those who do not have federal tax liability because their income is too low.

A second hypothesis, based on public opinion surveys, is that the public will support government efforts to improve higher education opportunity for low-income Americans, particularly if the linkage suggested above is built into these efforts. The failure of recent government policies to address the opportunity gaps cannot be attributed to public resistance. Rather, political and governmental leaders, as in the example of the Clinton administration's tax credit initiatives, have not tried very hard—perhaps because, focused on appeasing the anxieties of articulate middle-class voters, they were satisfied with simply addressing those anxieties.

Closing the College-Preparation Gap

Lowering financial barriers to college will not suffice. The financial gap is all too often a preparation gap as well. Those from low-income backgrounds not only are less likely to enroll but, if they do, disproportionately require remedial assistance. The reframing of opportunity must address this preparation gap.

Improvement of public K–12 schools, particularly those serving communities sending the fewest students to college, will be a critical task. In the absence of a rigorous and well-taught curriculum, school and student accountability—testing and the reduction and elimination of college-level remedial courses, for example—will only document and intensify problems we already know exist. Care should be taken that reform measures making sense in the short term do not have adverse long-term implications. For example, elimination of remedial courses at colleges and universities, if implemented in isolation, may perpetuate the effects of poor schooling throughout a student's life. The most recent backlash against remediation (particularly in the City University of New York) and much of the public and media discourse on the issue appear to be flawed by a "one size fits all" approach to both the problem and the solution. This tends to lump students having specific, short-term needs with functional illiterates.

Addressing the preparation gap will entail the deliberate and active participation of colleges and universities. Higher education leaders must see such participation as a top priority. Improvement of teacher training and professional development is the unique task of the colleges, but other reform measures are also important (e.g., supporting standards-based public school reform and incorporating these standards in college admissions requirements, and moving from admissions policies based on curriculum and credit hours to admissions based on competency). Public policies, particularly at the state level, should encourage colleges and universities in these college-preparation efforts through incentives and accountability measures (Timpane & White, 1998).

Improving Graduation Rates

The concept of opportunity has often been oversimplified to mean only access or the opportunity to enroll. But opportunity encompasses more than this; once enrolled in college, students must have the opportunity to achieve their educational goals. According to the National Center for Education Statistics (1997), less than half the students who entered college in 1989 aspiring to four-year degrees had actually received them five years later (p. 67). By 1994, 46 percent had received a baccalaureate degree, 5 percent had received an associate degree, 18 percent were still enrolled, and 28 percent had not earned a degree and were no longer enrolled.

In an address to the American Association for Higher Education, James B. Hunt Jr. (1998), governor of North Carolina, characterized these low rates of student success as higher education's "learning deficit." He called upon colleges to address this issue constructively, "not by reducing our commitment to quality, but by increasing it, and finding ways to keep those students enrolled, studying, learning" (p. 8). Better precollegiate preparation can improve these success rates. As Governor Hunt suggested, however, colleges not only must work for school reform but also must look to themselves, to their own pedagogy and curricula, and to their policies and practices for transferring students from two- to four-year colleges. Without improving student learning and attainment *within* higher education, the reframing of opportunity and access *to* higher education will be a hollow gesture.

Opening Doors to Adult Students

Reframing opportunity must recognize a role for higher education in meeting the growing needs of the adult population for education and skills. Economic volatility, immigration, and the demands of continuing technological advances bring persons of all ages to higher education. Our rapidly changing, information-based economy will continue to create a large gap between the knowledge and skills of the workforce and the demands of the modern marketplace. It is in the interest of individuals, their communities, and society that this gap, which is also an opportunity gap, be closed. But for many adult students, high school is years or decades—sometimes even continents—behind them, and their initial educational needs are frequently basic. Of course, not all colleges and universities can or should serve all these students, but public policy should see that they are served—and served fairly and effectively. Punitive and exclusionary approaches will not serve the fundamental public interest in opportunity and in a competent workforce and citizenry.

Constraining College Costs

Escalating costs of higher education inevitably drive up prices; steep and precipitous increases in the price of college create "sticker shock." Shocked reaction to high tuition dampens the college aspirations of many low-income and first-generation students. Meanwhile, college, state, and federal leaders find that high tuition increases the costs of student financial aid. Constraining the growth of college costs is therefore a key element of preserving and enhancing accessibility. Higher costs per student threaten the long-term capacities of states, colleges, and universities to accommodate enrollment demand. In the absence of greater institutional effectiveness in containing increases in costs and prices, externally imposed cost or price controls could become a "solution" that both middle- and lower-income groups would support. This is not a scenario I would endorse, but it is not an unlikely one if most Americans believe college opportunity is moving beyond their financial grasp.

Increasing the Role of the States

The states have leverage to take the lead on the opportunity agenda. More than either higher education institutions or the federal government, states can assess the roles of public schools, of public and private colleges and universities, and of the growing number of corporate and other providers of education beyond high school. Federal tax credits, by supporting middle-income students and their parents, may free states to focus their financial aid resources on the needs of low-income students. The states also play a key role in efforts to reform the public K–12 schools; they have the unique capacity to stimulate and encourage needed collaboration between schools and colleges, to advance standards-based education, and to use their teacher certification function to encourage—indeed require—the reform of teacher training.

These six concepts are not a comprehensive strategy but rather elements of a new framework for opportunity and access. No single proposal is a panacea or silver bullet, nor are all collectively. But each addresses a piece of the opportunity puzzle.

Concluding Thoughts

The public policy of opportunity for all represents lasting and deeply held American values. Responding to the society around them, colleges and universities have been instrumental in reshaping that society and the U.S. economy in ways that place higher education in the role of gatekeeper of opportunity. Federal and state higher education policies of the 1990s and the "new consensus" that Lemann (1998) has so aptly described as "government of, by and for the comfortable" have, more by drift than by design, diminished the role of higher education as the enabler of opportunity. But the political and educational conditions required for reframing opportunity and access also are present; a recommitment to higher education's critical responsibility for opportunity is possible. The conditions for this recommitment are apparent in the values of the general public and in the traditions and capacities of the colleges and universities, demonstrated so well as they responded to state and federal policies over the half-century since World War II. We have seen higher education develop the talents and skills of individuals and groups once written off as uneducable—the veterans after World War II, ethnic minorities, and older students returning for a second chance.

Few would argue that the current distribution of income and college opportunity reflects the distribution of talent in American society. Yet, as the gaps in wealth and income have widened, so have the gaps in opportunity and college access. Higher education cannot unilaterally close the opportunity gap. This will require close collaboration with the public schools and political leadership. Without political leadership, colleges and universities may well be part of the problem—components of a social infrastructure that perpetuates and perhaps widens the opportunity gap. With such leadership, they can play an active and invaluable role in the reframing and renewal of opportunity in the new century.

Note

The Clinton administration has proposed an expansion of the tuition tax credits in its 2000–2001 budget. The expanded credits would provide three dollars in benefits to middle class students and their families for every one dollar in assistance to the neediest groups (Callan & Haycock, 2000).

References

Baum, S., & Saunders, D. (1998). *Life after debt: Results of the national student loan survey.* Braintree, MA: Nellie Mae.

Callan, P. M., Finney, J. E., Bracco, K. R., & Doyle, W. R. (Eds.). (1997). *Public and private financing of higher education.* Phoenix, AZ: Oryx Press.

Callan, P. M., & Haycock, K. (2000, March 20). Best intentions, going awry. Washington Post, p. A17.

Clinton, W. J. (1999, January). *State of the union address.* Washington, DC: The White House.

College Board. (1998). *Trends in student aid.* Washington, DC: Author.

Education Resources Institute & Institute for Higher Education Policy. (1998). *Do grants matter? Student grant aid and college affordability.* Boston: Authors.

Gold, S. D. (Ed.). (1995). *The fiscal crisis of the states: Lessons for the future.* Washington, DC: Georgetown University Press.

Halstead, K. (1998). *State profiles: Financing public higher education 1978 to 1996.* Washington, DC: Research Associates of Washington.

Hauptman, A. M., & Rice, L. D. (1997). *Coordinating financial aid with tuition tax benefits* (Brookings Policy Brief No. 28). Washington, DC: Brookings Institution.

Hovey, H. (1999). *State spending for higher education in the next decade: The battle to sustain current support.* San Jose, CA: National Center for Public Policy and Higher Education.

Hunt, J. B. Jr. (1998). *Organizing for learning: The view from the governor's office.* San Jose, CA: National Center for Public Policy and Higher Education.

Ikenberry, S. O., & Hartle, T. W. (1998). *Too little knowledge is a dangerous thing: What the public thinks about paying for college.* Washington, DC: American Council on Education.

Immerwahr, J. (1997). *Enduring values, changing concerns: What Californians expect from their higher education system.* San Jose, CA: National Center for Public Policy and Higher Education.

Immerwahr, J. (1998). *The price of admission: The importance of higher education.* San Jose, CA: National Center for Public Policy and Higher Education.

Institute for Higher Education Policy. (1999). *The tuition puzzle: Putting the pieces together.* Washington, DC: Author.

Lemann, N. (1998, November 1). The new American consensus. *New York Times Magazine,* pp. 37–43.

McPherson, M. S., & Schapiro, M. O. (1998). *The student aid game: Meeting need and rewarding talent in American higher education.* Princeton: Princeton University Press.

Mortensen, T. G. (1998, September). Educational opportunity by family income, 1970 to 1996. *Postsecondary Education OPPORTUNITY,* pp. 1–8.

National Center for Education Statistics. (1996). *National Postsecondary Student Aid Study, 1996 data analysis system.* Washington, DC: U.S. Department of Education [Producer and Distributor].

National Center for Education Statistics. (1997). *Digest of education statistics, 1997.* Washington, DC: U.S. Department of Education.

National Center for Education Statistics. (1998). *Projections of education statistics to 2008.* Washington, DC: U.S. Department of Education.

Riley, R. (1998). *Letter from Secretary Riley to college and university presidents, December 16, 1998.* Washington, DC: U.S. Department of Education.

Spencer, C. (1999). The new politics of higher education. In J. E. King (Ed.), *Financing a college degree: How it works, how it's changing.* Phoenix, AZ: Oryx Press.

Timpane, P. M., & White, L. S. (1998). *Higher education and school reform.* San Francisco: Jossey-Bass.

Usdan, M., and Callan, P. M. (1998). *The California Higher Education Policy Center: An assessment.* San Francisco: James Irvine Foundation.

5 Time for Retreat or Renewal?

Perspectives on the Effects of *Hopwood* on Campus

SYLVIA HURTADO AND
HEATHER WATHINGTON CADE

Several legal initiatives of the late 1990s have made it more difficult to determine whether selective, public educational institutions will be able to provide rapidly growing racial/ethnic communities in the United States with the necessary leadership and support for economic growth. Projections indicate that the same states that have eliminated race as a criterion in college admissions will become more economically dependent on the incomes of talented students from different racial/ethnic populations whom they are able to train and retain as residents. All of this depends on access and affordability and, specifically, on whether higher education admissions and scholarship criteria are broad and sensitive enough to identify student talent in racially/ethnically diverse communities. Until recently, these decisions were left to educators with experience in evaluating student potential relative to the rigors of the college and its stated mission.

In this chapter we use Texas as a case study to examine the dynamics of a legal challenge, a state legislative response, and a campus response to the elimination of race-conscious decisions in admissions, programs, and scholarships. From a campus perspective, the goals of achieving diversity on campus are central to the goals of serving an increasingly racially/ethnically diverse taxpayer base and educating students to participate in a diverse workforce. Our purpose here is to determine the effects on a particular campus of both a legal challenge (*Hopwood v. State of Texas,* 1994/1996) and a legislative response to meet these goals, as seen through the eyes of students, faculty, and staff.

A Case of Reverse Discrimination or Reversing Progress against Discrimination?

Texas has a history of segregation in its public K–12 schools and its system of higher education, and evidence of continuing segregation. The first African American law student at the University of Texas was asked to begin his studies in a basement, away from white students. The ensuing lawsuit, *Sweatt v. Painter* (1950), established that such separate facilities were inherently unequal to those available to white students. Among those who could attend college in the 1960s, Mexican Americans and African Americans were prohibited from living in or visiting the dorms of white students at the University of Texas (Lawrence & Matsuda, 1997). At the time that rejected applicant Cheryl Hopwood sued the University of Texas Law School for violation of her constitutional rights under the equal protection laws, desegregation lawsuits remained pending against forty different Texas school districts, and the Office of Civil Rights of the U.S. Department of Education had not determined whether Texas had made sufficient progress in eliminating its segregated system of public higher education (Lawrence & Matsuda, 1997). In 1994–95, approximately one-third of African American and 43 percent of Hispanic pupils in Texas attended schools that were more than 90 percent minority (Orfield, Bachmeier, James, & Eitle, 1997). Only in 1993 did Texas begin to equalize the financing of public schools so as to eliminate the great disparities in resources that had affected the quality of education of many African Americans and Hispanics.

In the case of *Hopwood*, the Federal District Court for the Western District of Texas held that the dual system of admissions under which the plaintiffs were rejected was not lawful. In the mid-1990s, the University of Texas Law School used separate pools for minority and white applicants in making admissions decisions, a change of practice from previous years. However, the court also held that the use of affirmative action was constitutional because it was necessary to remedy continuing effects of discrimination against students of color in primary, secondary, and higher education. Further, the court found that "in the context of law school's admissions process, obtaining the educational benefits that flow from a racially and ethnically diverse student body remains a sufficiently compelling interest to support the use of racial classifications" (*Hopwood v. State of Texas*, 1994, p. 571). The decision essentially mirrored that of U.S. Supreme Court Justice Powell in *Regents of the University of California v. Bakke* (1978), which struck down the admissions program of the University of California, Davis, medical school but supported the use of race as a "plus factor" in admissions considerations if it served an educational purpose.

In *Hopwood*, claims of reverse discrimination were essentially rejected by the district court on the grounds that a simplistic application of the Fourteenth Amendment would ignore a long history of discrimination that the amendment was adopted to remedy. Moreover, reviews of admissions files revealed that admission was offered to 109 nonminority applicants with lower scores than Hopwood's, and Hopwood had also provided the least amount of information on her background and qualifications compared with all other admissions applications reviewed by the district court. The plaintiffs won the case to dismantle an ill-conceived admissions program, but Judge Sparks awarded one dollar in damages and the right to reapply to the law school without paying additional fees. The decision was appealed and went before a three-judge panel of the Fifth Circuit Court that encompasses Texas, Louisiana, and Mississippi.

The Fifth Circuit judges (all conservative appointees of the Reagan and Bush administrations) reversed the district court decision and, in effect, rejected Justice Powell's position in *Bakke* allowing universities to use race as a factor in admissions decisions (Fifth Cir. 1996, 78 F.3d 932). Ignoring both the history of discrimination in Texas and the need to educate a more diverse student population for educational purposes, the Fifth Circuit stated, "We agree with the plaintiffs that any consideration of race or ethnicity by the law school for the purpose of achieving a diverse study body is not a compelling interest under the Fourteenth Amendment" (*Hopwood v. State of Texas*, 1996, p. 25). Three months later, the *Hopwood* case was at the U.S. Supreme Court to settle the constitutional issue. The Court, however, declined to hear the case on the grounds that the University of Texas Law School had already changed its admissions procedure to evaluate white and minority applicants in the same pool. Therefore, although the issue of whether race can be used in admissions is, in Justice Ginsburg's words, one of "great national importance," the Supreme Court "must await a program genuinely in controversy" (quoted in Lawrence & Matsuda, 1997).

The case was sent back to the district court for assessment of damages and legal fees. The judge awarded only one dollar in damages to the plaintiffs, and additional aspects of the *Hopwood* case are still (as of early 2000) under appeal. Several organizations are filing additional briefs on the compelling need to diversify law schools and to support the limited use of race in admissions in a revised admissions process. Meanwhile, the expansive opinion of the Fifth Circuit still stands and has obligated institutions in Texas to revise their admissions programs to eliminate the use of race. Standing federal court orders and the 1992 Supreme Court decision in *United States v. Fordice* (1992) to desegregate the public higher education systems in Louisiana and Mississippi have ensured that those states continue to improve their efforts to diversify their campuses; the courts have ruled that race-neutral policies are not sufficient to overcome the past and continuing effects of segregated systems of education in those states. (Texas was not under a federal order to desegregate its system of higher education because it had voluntarily complied by developing a statewide desegregation plan.)

The Fifth Circuit's ruling has widespread application in Texas because the former Texas attorney general, Dan Morales, interpreted the decision to apply not only to the University of Texas's new admissions policy but also to all state-supported universities, programs, and college scholarships. This restriction severely hampered the efforts made by the state's flagship universities (University of Texas at Austin and Texas A&M University) to recruit minorities. Texas institutions with open enrollment policies were affected, but not to the same extent as those that maintained selective admissions standards. Recruitment, retention, and scholarship programs for minorities were redefined (Montejano, 1997). Presumably in an effort to prevent further litigation, Attorney General Morales even specified that recruitment and retention programs targeted specifically to African American and Hispanic students would not stand up to the strict scrutiny application of the law (Finnell, 1998).

The end of state minority scholarships marked a significant setback in the effort to increase diversity at the flagship campuses. Scholarships targeted to African American and Hispanic students served as a reward to students for academic achievement, as well as a welcoming gesture from institutions with a history of excluding students of color. In addition, after *Hopwood,* many minority students were discouraged from applying to public institutions, believing that scholarships were no longer open to them (Finnell, 1998). Altogether, these activities had a chilling effect on Hispanic and African American enrollments for fall 1996, and as the decision took full effect, enrollments were in dramatic decline by fall 1997.

The Legislative Response: The Top 10 Percent Plan and Multiple Criteria in Undergraduate Admissions

In an effort to soften *Hopwood*'s impact, the Texas Higher Education Coordinating Board (THECB) worked to develop a strategy. First, it commissioned a study by sixteen demographers and professors at Texas colleges on ways to achieve racial and ethnic diversity without using race as a criterion in admission. The resulting report, *Alternative Diversity Criteria: Analyses and Recommendations* (THECB, 1997), revealed that no single criterion or set of criteria could replace race/ethnicity and result in the same level of minority participation in higher education in Texas. However, the information served as a basis for understanding the need for an admissions program that used multiple criteria.

Next, legislators and educators worked together in an unprecedented manner to draft Texas House Bill 588 (and Senate Bill 177), also known as the Top 10 Percent Plan. House Bill 588, introduced by Irma Rangel (Democrat), won bipartisan support. It was passed by the legislature and signed into law by Governor George W. Bush in May 1997. The bill developed a uniform admissions policy for all Texas public institutions and guaranteed Texas students who graduated in the top 10 percent of their high school classes (and who file a timely application) automatic admission to state-supported institutions. Any institution could also choose to admit students from the top 25 percent of any high school under the same guidelines. Approximately 40 to 50 percent of the entering freshman class of the flagship institutions could be filled by admitting the top 10 percent from each high school across the state. For this reason, the bill also prescribed that institutions could consider a rather innovative set of multiple admissions criteria that did not require unusually high dependence on admissions test scores (SAT and ACT) or formulas.

Under HB 588, institutions can use any of the items listed in Table 5.1 to determine admissions, depending on the institution's interest in meeting educational goals. The measure encourages institutions to use broad criteria that will ensure diversity (geographic and socioeconomic), give credit for students' drive to overcome adversity, and recognize students' potential for contributing to their communities. Because continuing disparities in the quality of Texas public schools lead to disparities in students' preparation for higher education, the law also requires higher education institutions to determine whether admitted students need additional college-preparatory work and to provide remedial assistance in efforts to improve the retention of students, particularly those from low socioeconomic backgrounds. (See Chapter 4 for more on the controversial role of remediation in higher education and on the pre-college preparation of students.)

While the law broadens the scope of students eligible for admission and appears to have stopped a precipitous decline in the enrollment of African Americans and Hispanics in public institutions (Chapa, 1999), we should note that a "race-neutral" system works in Texas because of the level of racial/ethnic segregation of the schools and the rapid growth of the African American and Hispanic populations. Moreover, the law has had relatively little effect on medical and law schools, which continue to place strong emphasis on test scores, and may increase the proportion of students selecting institutions with already high proportions of minorities (Chapa, 1999). Thus, whether Texas's elite institutions will make sufficient progress in diversifying, and whether graduates will be prepared to work in a diverse workforce after being educated in a predominantly white environment or, for African Americans and Hispanics, in a predominantly minority environment, remain important, unresolved questions.

Lawmakers respected the sovereignty of higher education's admissions

Table 5.1. House Bill 588 Multiple Admissions Criteria

Academic record	Personal interview
Socioeconomic status (SES)	Standardized test performance
First-generation college student	Field of study commitment
Bilingual proficiency	Involvement in community activities
Texas Education Agency rating of the high school	Standardized test performance compared with others from lower SES
Work and family responsibilities	Admission to comparable out-of-state institution
Region of residence and location	
Graduated in top 10% of class (guaranteed admission)	Other criteria in accordance with the institutional mission
	Graduated in top 25% of class

procedures before passage of HB 588, and the legislation attempts to honor an institution's right to select its students to achieve its educational goals. Although the measure is innovative enough to leave open the possibility of including race as a criterion in admissions if deemed central to an institution's educational goals,[1] it can also be interpreted as a legislative intrusion on decisions best left to educators. If the *Hopwood* decision is overturned, legislation allows for the consideration of race as an admissions criterion. Yet, under the circumstances, the measure was needed to prevent further declines in minority enrollment.

Study of a Campus Response

During the first year that public institutions in Texas were dealing with the repercussions of *Hopwood* and new admissions requirements, our research team was invited to conduct a study of the climate for diversity on one campus, which we will call Mesquite University. This large public university had recently introduced somewhat more selective admissions criteria as a result of increasing student applications. At the same time, until *Hopwood,* the campus had been making steady progress in increasing the representation of African American and Hispanic students. The data presented here were collected as part of a comprehensive assessment of the racial climate on campus, using a mixed-method approach including qualitative (interviews and focus groups) and survey data from undergraduates, graduate students, faculty, and staff. Campus site visits to collect documents and interview individuals occurred during the fall of 1997. We conducted surveys of 3,361 students, faculty, and staff respondents, with oversampling of minority students and female faculty to ensure broad representation of opinions from under-represented communities on campus. Weights were devised to correct for oversampling and nonresponse bias.

Our analyses followed conventional procedures for reducing data through factor analyses (i.e., principal axis factoring method and varimax rotation for estimation procedures). Appendix Table 5.A1 shows the results from the factor analyses. Items with a factor loading of more than 0.35 were used to develop the scales for subsequent analyses. As indicated by the internal consistencies (alpha), the factors had reliabilities ranging from 0.70 to 0.78. We conducted multiple regression analyses to identify factors likely to determine undergraduates' beliefs about whether *Hopwood* had a negative effect on campus. Students' background characteristics were entered as statistical controls in order to examine the effects of college experiences and attitudes about racial issues associated with views on the impact of *Hopwood*. All measures used in the analysis are shown in Appendix Table 5.A2.

The Impact of *Hopwood* on Campus

As Figure 5.1 shows, Mesquite University was making steady progress in increasing the enrollment of African American and Hispanic students until the *Hopwood* litigation. At the time of the Fifth Circuit decision, admissions offices were in full swing preparing for the fall 1996 entering class. Interviews with campus staff revealed that, even as previous admissions and scholarship procedures were in full swing, alternative criteria were being devised and additional staff members pulled into the review processes. Although the number of African American and Hispanic students admitted in 1996 was similar to that in 1995, the actual number electing to enroll at Mesquite dropped significantly. Many speculate that the drop in first-year minority enrollments, occurring across several Texas campuses, was due to media reports about *Hopwood*, prompting higher education professionals to call this the "Hopwood chill effect" (Finnell, 1998, p. 72).

However, the full impact of the Fifth Circuit decision became evident in fall 1997 enrollments at Mesquite, with new African American and Hispanic enrollments plummeting 35 percent compared with those of 1995. Fall 1998 enrollments reflected gains in minority enrollment under the new criteria selected by Mesquite to comply with the Top 10 Percent Plan, though enrollments have not returned to 1995 levels. As is evident from the data in Figure 5.1, however, white first-year student enrollments increased in 1996 while African American and Hispanic enrollments decreased. Although the expanded admissions criteria implemented by HB 588 helped increase minority enrollments in 1998, the enrollment of white students increased even

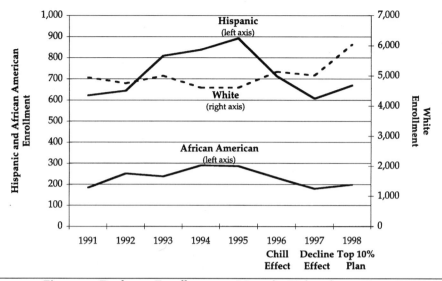

Figure 5.1. Freshman Enrollments at Mesquite University
before and after *Hopwood,* by Racial/Ethnic Group.

more rapidly that year, indicating that the expanded criteria had benefited
white students even more than minority students.

The Mesquite campus may be returning to a situation in which the vast
majority of college students have relatively little opportunity to interact with
diverse peers from Texas's racial/ethnic communities. Studies have shown
that interactions with diverse peers, on an equal basis, promote scholastic
achievement, reduction of racial prejudice, and a host of positive educational
outcomes in schools and colleges (Hurtado, 1999).

In a relatively short time, staff at Mesquite had worked hard to put in
place new review criteria in both admissions and merit scholarship awards
for fall 1997. The university used multiple criteria allowing more students to
compete for both admissions and non-need-based scholarship aid—all of
which resulted in an increased workload for staff in the review process, additional time to review files (including the need to move up deadlines), and
increased costs. Affirmative action principles had become embedded in daily
practices at Mesquite, and as noted by one staff member, "So many people
were invested in increasing the numbers [of minority students] and making
it possible to have an environment that is conducive to learning for every-
body. And then [it's as if] somebody comes and cuts off all the legs from un-
derneath" these efforts. The impact of the enrollment declines was palpable

among staff members and was manifested in a sense of frustration and despair. They believed they had been successfully recruiting a very talented group of African American and Hispanic students who would become leaders on campus and in local communities. The concern now was that the most talented, who could no longer be lured to campus with typical recruitment enticements, would go to competitive out-of-state institutions where special programs and scholarships were still available. And the numbers suggest that these students have indeed been selecting institutions they perceive as more welcoming or as providing more appealing offers.

Faculty and Staff Perspectives

Table 5.2 presents faculty and staff views on goals for diversity on campus and the impact of Hopwood. More than 90 percent of all faculty and staff agreed, in principle, that diversity is good for Mesquite and should be actively promoted. Although minority staff members were somewhat more skeptical about the centrality of diversity to the institutional mission, the majority of both faculty and staff agreed that enhancing students' overall development and ability to function in a multicultural society is part of the university's mission.[2] No significant differences were detected between minority and white faculty on these central goals and on their view that Hopwood had effectively put a stop to the institution's progress in diversifying its student population. Thus, despite the elimination of race in admissions and programs, the campus was in fairly high agreement on the importance of diversity to the educational mission and on the dilemma it now faced.

The majority of both faculty and staff also thought that the Hopwood decision had stopped Mesquite's progress toward diversifying the student population, with minority staff most likely to agree (88%) with this statement. This group may have been more aware than any other group on campus of the changing enrollment numbers. Two-thirds of minority staff thought Hopwood also had increased racial/ethnic hostility on campus, whereas only one-third of white faculty and staff members perceived the same effect. Minority faculty and staff were significantly more likely than their white counterparts to see the Hopwood decision as making discussion of diversity on campus or within classrooms more difficult. White faculty and staff were significantly more likely than minority faculty or staff to view Hopwood as making the admissions process more fair for all prospective students; some believed that the legislative response to Hopwood, the Top 10 Percent Plan, had the "potential to democratize the access to Texas' selective public institutions" (Chapa, 1999). However, whether the median incomes of selective college entrants will be substantially lower or broader in distribu-

Table 5.2. Faculty and Staff Views on Diversity and the Impact of *Hopwood* on Campus (Percentage of Responses)

	Faculty		Staff	
	White	Minority	White	Minority
The Effects of *Hopwood* have:				
Stopped Mesquite's progress to diversify the student body.	69.8%	73.6%	63.2%	87.9%***
Increased racial/ethnic hostility on campus.	34.9	44.2*	35.8	66.0***
Made the admissions process more fair for all prospective Mesquite students.	52.1	42.3**	68.0	27.5***
Made it more difficult to talk about diversity in the classroom.	21.7	34.6***		
Made it more difficult to talk about diversity on campus.			27.8	54.6***
Diversity goals				
Diversity is good for Mesquite and should be actively promoted.	93.7	91.0	92.1	93.4
Enhancing students' overall development and ability to function in a multicultural society is part of the university's mission.	84.9	82.7	81.5	69.9**

Note: Chi-square: * = $p < .05$; ** = $p < .01$; *** = $p < .001$, comparing responses of white and minority staff and faculty.

tion remains to be seen, given that merit scholarship funds have been redistributed and competition remains high for all types of non-need-based scholarships.

Staff who had been involved in making decisions about admissions and merit scholarships had been proud of their work in achieving both excellence and diversity at the institution. These staff members were now asked to implement new criteria and achieve the same level of progress toward diversity without considering race in their decisions. One staff member stated outright that their doing so made their job much more difficult. We should note that staff members were advised by legal counsel to review their practices to determine whether programs were open to all students and to redefine any services that could be interpreted as providing special benefits for minority students. The question arises, will the institution continue to assist minority students in feeling more comfortable in this predominantly white environment? Even small practices to make students feel welcome were questioned; as one administrator related, "You have some folks that are just scared to death and won't do anything [as a result of the lawsuit]. For example, we used to have a reception for our black and Hispanic graduate students . . . Well, they stopped doing that because of *Hopwood,* because that's a 'benefit'—you give blacks and Hispanics punch and cookies that you're not giving white students. [Respondent breaks his statement with levity.] We've got good punch and some very good cookies!"

In several of our visits to campus units and in conversations with administrators and staff, we were able to grasp the enormity of their effort to stay on course in terms of diversifying the campus. However, we also heard some criticism about the signal *Hopwood* sends to some on campus; as one staff member said about the decline in minority enrollments, "To me, the biggest frustration is of seeing people in this campus think, 'well, they probably really didn't belong here anyway' . . . These kids have the same drive, the same everything as their peers. We were beginning to see [progress] happening—[minority students] going to grad schools, doing all these exciting things . . . I think we played a major role in seeing that happen with the kids that we worked with." Another administrator said, "People use the *Hopwood* [decision] as a sound to retreat, it's like the bugler saying time to retreat. When you say *Hopwood,* the horn is blowing."

While some questioned the commitment to diversity on campus, others were clearly busy working toward the goals of maintaining both diversity and excellence in the student population, moving beyond retreat to a phase of renewed efforts. Another administrator indicated that the increasingly diverse voters and taxpayers in Texas would have much to do with the future of the university. "I think that if we are not a more diverse university, or at *least* a diverse university, I doubt there will be the public support in Texas to enable us to meet our goal [of becoming a premier public institution]." Thus, a decision to renew efforts to achieve diversity and excellence becomes intertwined with a campus mission to serve and remain responsive to an increasingly diverse population in the state.

Undergraduate Perspectives

We found significant differences in students' views about diversity on campus and the effect of *Hopwood* (Table 5.3). More than 81 percent of white

Table 5.3. Undergraduate Views on Diversity and the Impact of
Hopwood on Campus Undergraduates (Percentage of Responses)

	African Americans	Asian Americans	Hispanics	Native Americans	Whites
The Effects of *Hopwood* have:					
Stopped Mesquite's progress to diversify the student body.	85.0%	41.0%	59.0%	24.6%	18.6%
Increased racial/ethnic hostility on campus.	68.8	29.5	41.5	30.2	23.4
Made the admissions process more fair for all prospective Mesquite students.	22.8	72.7	62.5	78.9	86.9
Made it more difficult to talk about diversity in the classroom.	53.8	26.0	31.9	16.0	13.4
Diversity goals					
Diversity is good for Mesquite and should be actively promoted.	98.2	94.6	94.3	94.6	81.1
Enhancing students' overall development and ability to function in a multicultural society is part of the university's mission.	57.6	71.6	75.1	78.0	71.3

Note: All items are significant at $p < .001$, comparing responses across the five racial/ethnic groups.

students agreed that diversity is good for Mesquite and should be actively promoted, and more than 94 percent of nonwhite students agreed with this statement. The majority of students in all groups agreed that the university's mission involves enhancing students' overall development and ability to function in a multicultural society, though African Americans were more skeptical about the centrality of this goal (58% agreeing) at the institution. Despite the significant differences across these groups of undergraduates, these results indicate agreement, in principle, about the importance of diversity for the campus.

Perhaps because most affected by *Hopwood,* African Americans and Hispanics were more likely to agree with the statement that *Hopwood* had stopped Mesquite's progress in diversifying the student population. African American students were also more likely than other students to believe the impact had increased racial/ethnic hostility on campus and made classroom discussions about diversity more difficult. White students were least likely to perceive these effects. With the exception of African Americans, the majority of student groups believed that the admissions process had been made fairer for prospective students. Social science studies reveal that conceptions of fairness are framed by racial attitudes and beliefs (Levin, 2000); these views depend on whether students actually perceive inequality and discrimination as still prevalent in U.S. society, a finding confirmed by our multivariate analyses.

Shown in Table 5.4 are the significant determinants of undergraduate beliefs that *Hopwood* had a negative effect on campus. Controlling for all background characteristics (in the first column), we find that African American, Hispanic, and Asian American students were most likely to believe that *Hopwood* had an adverse impact on campus. In contrast, students who grew up in predominantly white neighborhoods were not likely to believe this (although the effect depends on students' beliefs about whether discrimination is still prevalent in the United States). Students who had attended college longer were more likely to believe *Hopwood* had a negative impact, but introduction of controls for attitudes about discrimination reversed the effect (Table 5.4, second column): more recent college entrants were more likely to believe *Hopwood* adversely affected the campus. Virtually all the diversity-related college experiences and current attitudes about racial issues are associated with students' perspectives on the negative effects of *Hopwood*.

The major finding of these analyses is that students who believe inequality and discrimination are no longer prevalent in American society were least likely to believe *Hopwood* had a negative impact on campus. These perspectives coincide with the Fifth Circuit opinion, which ignored both historical and contemporary manifestations of discrimination in Texas education. In contrast, students (regardless of race/ethnicity) who had observed occasions of racist behavior in the classroom or had perceived a climate of racial tension at Mesquite University were more likely to see *Hopwood* as having an adverse effect on campus. In addition, students who had some experience with diverse peers or some knowledge about diverse groups in society were also more likely to believe *Hopwood* had a negative impact. This included students reporting high levels of interaction with African American and Hispanic students or participation in some type of diversity awareness program during college. Taking a course on the experiences of different racial/ethnic minority groups was also associated with students' views, although this depended on students' beliefs about the prevalence of discrimination in American society. Overall, students' opinions about *Hopwood*

Table 5.4. Determinants of Undergraduate Beliefs that *Hopwood* Had a Negative Effect on Campus (N = 2205)

	Beta after Adding Controls for Background Characteristics	Beta after Adding Controls for Attitudes about Discrimination
Student background characteristics		
Years attended college	0.05**	−0.04*
Gender (female)	0.02	0.00
African American	0.52***	0.20***
Asian American	0.17***	0.04*
Native American	0.00	−0.02
Hispanic	0.29***	0.17***
Racial composition of neighborhood is mostly white	−0.09***	−0.02
Father's education	−0.01***	−0.03
Mother's education	0.00	0.00
Family member is alumnus of Mesquite	0.00	0.03*
Size of hometown	0.01	−0.02
College behaviors and attitudes		
Racial composition of friends on campus is mostly white	−0.15***	−0.03
Extent of interaction with African American and Hispanic students	0.03	0.04*
Attended a program focused on diversity issues	0.13***	0.08***
Participated in ethnic or cross-cultural activities or organizations	0.01	0.01
Enrolled in a course studying ethnic minorities	0.05*	0.00
Belief: discrimination no longer prevalent in the United States	−0.41***	−0.21***
Perception: racial/ethnic tension on campus	0.26***	0.19***
Perception: classroom racism	0.23***	0.22***
Sociohistorical complex thinking	−0.00	0.00
Experiences in the classroom have changed my opinion about different racial/ethnic background	0.03*	0.03*

Note: * = $p < .05$; ** = $p < .01$; *** = $p < .001$
R^2 (after adding controls for background characteristics) = .33
R^2 (after adding controls for attitudes about discrimination) = .55

seemed to hinge on some knowledge about the extent to which various groups face systematic barriers to educational and economic progress. As one white student said in a focus group, "I don't see [racial problems] because the minority groups are so small [on campus], I just haven't been at the right place at the right time to see things happen." If students have very little exposure to diversity or do not believe such barriers exist for certain groups, they are unlikely to see the need for affirmative action programs.

An Asian American student raised an important question about the declines in minority enrollments. "They can try to teach us diversity, but if there's not a diverse environment, how are you going to learn?" Students may learn about the cultural legacies that make up a pluralistic society through the college curriculum, but we found less than 15 percent of white students reporting they had taken a course on different racial/ethnic groups. Therefore, most of the learning about social differences and most experience with people from different cultures occurs through informal interactions with diverse peers on campus. As selective institutions produce new leaders, encouraging engagement and experience with diverse peers remains an important vehicle for developing skills and dispositions for a pluralistic democracy, including the ability to understand complex social problems, commitment to the betterment of society, and negotiation of differences.

Epilogue

Without question, the expansive interpretation by the Fifth Circuit Court in *Hopwood* caused widespread changes in practices as Texas colleges and universities worked toward making progress in educating an increasingly diverse population. The response by the higher education community and state policymakers was quick and effective. Although the long-term effects of the Top 10 Percent Plan are not yet evident, in the short term it has stopped a rapid decline in minority enrollments and allowed some recovery of progress in diversifying specific institutions of higher education. As is evident from this study, however, at least one institution is experiencing a declining proportion of racial/ethnic minority students relative to white students, even as it regains progress in increasing African American and Hispanic enrollment numbers. Nevertheless, lawmakers and educators are dissatisfied with these modest gains. Texas legislators plan to increase financial aid substantially in the belief that more need-based scholarships will fuel increased minority enrollments. One proposal would provide $500 million to 250,000 needy students, regardless of grades or test scores. Another would appropriate funding for older, nontraditional students. And conversations are in progress about whether a "brain drain" initiative might help to provide additional aid to talented minority students who are electing to leave the state for their education. Finding ways to train and retain the talent in the state will be a focus of both policymakers and public higher education.

On the judicial front, renewed consideration of *Hopwood* (or another legal challenge in Michigan) will eventually settle the issue of using race as a factor in admissions decisions.[3] For more than twenty years, institutions have followed the guidelines laid down by the Supreme Court in *Bakke,* and many institutions are successfully achieving both excellence and diversity as a result. Recent research in connection with the legal challenges has confirmed the substantial benefits of a diverse student population, both for campus learning environments and in the contributions of minority graduates to society (Bowen & Bok, 1998; Gurin, 1999; Hurtado, Milem, Clayton-Pederson, & Allen, 1999). At least one of these challenges will most likely result in an action before the Supreme Court.

As the Texas case shows, retaining access and affordability for a racially/ethnically diverse population will hinge on policymakers' and educators' ability to employ a broad definition of merit in admissions and in the distribution of non-need-based financial aid. Employing multiple criteria that recognize the factors affecting test scores, students' drive to achieve in the face of adversity, their determination to succeed, and their potential civic contribution to racially, geographically, and economically diverse communities is an essential starting point. As we found in our study at Mesquite, from an institutional perspective, sufficient numbers of African American and Hispanic high school students qualifying under the new criteria could be found, but this required staff expertise and created an intensive workload. However, fewer of these students could receive scholarships as an added inducement to matriculate at Mesquite. A relatively new generation of middle-class African American and Hispanic families, who do not qualify for much need-based aid, may be reluctant to take on large loans and may look for ways to offset college costs. *Hopwood* served to fuel rumors that no more state scholarship money was available for targeted groups, when, in fact, the same scholarship monies were available under redefined categories of distribution. Maintaining affordability at selective colleges and universities will be the prime determinant of whether institutions can continue to diversify their student populations.

Without additional enticements of special programs or scholarships, an institution's image looms large in students' evaluations of whether they will receive the necessary support for their educational goals. According to the survey data, minority students and staff were more likely to report negative effects of *Hopwood* on campus. The decision has done little to overcome a history of discrimination, to improve the climate for diversity, or to improve on the institutional image of exclusion at predominantly white campuses in Texas. Institutions must engage in concerted efforts to create a climate that supports diversity and achievement. A Hispanic student offered this perspective: "A lot of schools in Texas now are so afraid to praise any kind of achievement when it comes to minorities." Addressing such issues will be essential for attracting underrepresented groups, serving an increasingly diverse state population, and preparing students for participation in a diverse workforce. To maximize learning, institutions must consciously employ new strategies to engage students with diversity, to enable them to acquire the skills and dispositions necessary for leadership in a state with complex social problems, and for participation in a diverse democracy.

Appendix

Table 5.A1. Factors Used in the Analyses

Factors and Survey Items	Factor Loadings	Internal Consistency (Alpha)
Belief: *Hopwood* has had a negative effect on campus.[a]		.78
The effects of Hopwood have:		
Made the admissions process more fair for all prospective Mesquite students (reversed for analyses).	−.73	
Stopped Mesquite's progress to diversify the study body.	.71	
Increased racial/ethnic hostility on campus.	.60	
Made it more difficult to talk about diversity in the classroom.	.54	
Belief: Discrimination is no longer prevalent in the United States[a]		.77
Most people of color are no longer discriminated against in the United States.	.72	
In the generation since the Civil Rights movement, our society has done enough to promote the welfare of people of color.	.69	
The system prevents people of color from getting their fair share of the good things in life, such as better jobs and more money.	−.62	

Factors and Survey Items	Factor Loadings	Internal Consistency (Alpha)
Many whites/anglos show a real lack of understanding of the problems that people of color face.	−.59	
A person's racial background in this society does not interfere with achieving everything he or she wants to achieve.	.55	
Perception: Racial/ethnic tension on campus[a]		.77
There is a lot of campus racial conflict here.	.74	
Many minority students feel they do not "fit in" on this campus.	.71	
There is little trust between minority student groups and campus administrators.	.59	
Students from diverse racial groups communicate well at Mesquite (reversed for analyses).	.55	
Most students at this institution believe that minorities were special admits.	.55	
Perception: Classroom racism[a]		.70
I often hear students express stereotypes about different racial/ethnic groups in class.	.61	
Mesquite offers ample opportunities for students to learn about different racial/ethnic groups in a nonthreatening way (reversed for analyses).	−.58	
Faculty are not prepared to deal with conflict in the classroom.	.58	
I would like more opportunities to engage in a discussion of racial/ethnic issues in class.	.56	
I often hear faculty express stereotypes about racial/ethnic groups in class.	.47	
There are few students of color in my classes.	.46	
Sociohistorical complex thinking[b]		.74
I think a lot about the influence that society has on other people.	.80	
I really enjoy analyzing the reasons or causes for people's behavior.	.65	
I think a lot about the influence that society has on my behavior and personality.	.59	
When I analyze a person's behavior, I often find that causes are linked to a chain of events that go back in time.	.55	

[a]Responses on a four-point scale from "Disagree strongly" = 1 to "Agree strongly" = 4.
[b]Responses on a five-point scale from "Not at all like me" = 5 to "Very much like me" = 1.

Table 5.A2. Measures and Scales for Regression Model

Variable	Scale
Dependent measure	
Beliefs that *Hopwood* had a negative effect on campus	Scale items in Table 5.A1
Student background characteristics	
Size of hometown	1 = very small town (fewer than 2,500) to 7 = major urban center (1,000,001 or more)
Mother's education	0 = not applicable to 6 = JD/MD/PhD/DVM
Father's education	0 = not applicable to 6 = JD/MD/PhD/DVM
African American	Dichotomous: 1 = no; 2 = yes
Hispanic	Dichotomous: 1 = no; 2 = yes
Native American	Dichotomous: 1 = no; 2 = yes
Asian American	Dichotomous: 1 = no; 2 = yes
White (referent category)	Dichotomous: 1 = no; 2 = yes
Gender (female)	Dichotomous: 1 = male; 2 = female
Racial composition of neighborhood is mostly white	1 = all nonwhite to 5 = all or nearly all white
College experience characteristics	
Years attended college	1 = less than one year to 6 = five or more years
Family member is alumnus of Mesquite	Dichotomous: 1 = no; 2 = yes
Racial composition of friends on campus is mostly white	1 = all nonwhite to 5 = all or nearly all white
Extent of interaction with African American and Hispanic students	1 = no interaction with either group to 8 = the most interaction with both groups
Enrolled in a course studying ethnic minorities	Dichotomous: 1 = no; 2 = yes
Participated in ethnic or cross-cultural activities or organizations	1 = never; 2 = occasionally; 3 = frequently
Attended a program focused on diversity issues	1 = never; 2 = occasionally; 3 = frequently
Perception: racial/ethnic tension on campus	Scale items in Table 5.A1
Belief: discrimination no longer prevalent in the United States	Scale items in Table 5.A1
Perception: classroom racism	Scale items in Table 5.A1
Sociohistorical complex thinking	Scale items in Table 5.A1
Experiences in the classroom have changed my opinion about different racial/ethnic backgrounds	1 = agree strongly to 4 = disagree strongly

Notes

We give special thanks to the members of the research team and institutional liaison who worked on the project, including Leon Hill, Karen Kurotsuchi Inkelas, Ricardo Maestas, Michael McClendon, Ellen Meader, and Felicia Scott.

1. Institutions would still need to satisfy the federal courts that such a decision would not be in conflict with *Hopwood*.

2. Survey respondents (faculty and staff, as well as students) were asked to self-identify their race. The five categories (African American, Asian American, Hispanic, Native American, and white) are mutually exclusive

3. The University of Michigan is currently facing federal suits challenging its undergraduate and law school admissions processes. A similar suit was also filed against the University of Washington, before passage of Initiative 200 in that state in November 1998; this ballot measure outlawed the use of race and gender in admissions.

References

Bowen, W. G., & Bok, D. (1998). *The shape of the river: The long-term consequences of considering race in college and university admissions.* Princeton: Princeton University Press.

Chapa, J. (1999, January). *Hopwood effects and responses: The search for race-blind means of improving minority access to higher education.* Presented at a research conference sponsored by the American Council on Education, Washington, DC.

Finnell, S. (1998). The Hopwood chill: How the court derailed diversity efforts at Texas A&M. In G. Orfield (Ed.), *Chilling admissions: The affirmative action crisis and the search for alternatives.* Cambridge: Harvard Education Publishing.

Gurin, P. (1999). Expert report of Patricia Gurin (presented in *Gratz et al. v. Bollinger et al.* and *Grutter et al. v. Bollinger et al.*). In *The compelling need for diversity in higher education.* Washington, DC: Wilmer, Cutler, and Pickering.

Hopwood v. State of Texas, 861 F. Supp. 551 (W.D. Tex. 1994), *rev'd 78 F.3d 932 and rehearing denied en banc 84 F.3d 720 (5th Cir. 1996), cert. denied 518 U.S. 1033, 116 S. Ct. 2581, 135 L. Ed. 2d 1095 (1996).*

Hurtado, S. (1999, spring). Reaffirming educators' judgment: Educational value of diversity. *Journal of Liberal Education*, pp. 24–31.

Hurtado, S., Milem, J. F., Clayton-Pederson, A., & Allen, W. A. (1999). *Enacting diverse learning environments: Improving the climate for racial/ethnic diversity on campus* (ASHE-ERIC Report Series Vol. 26, No. 8). Washington, DC: George Washington University.

Lawrence III, C. R., & Matsuda, M. J. (1997). *We won't go back: Making the case for affirmative action.* Boston: Houghton Mifflin.

Levin, S. (2000). Social psychological evidence on race and racism. In M. Chang, D.

Witt-Sandis, J. Jones, & K. Hakuta (Eds.), *The dynamics of race in higher education: An examination of the evidence.* Stanford: Stanford University Press.

Montejano, D. (1997). On Hopwood: The continuing challenge. In *Reflexiones: New directions in Mexican American studies.* Austin: CMAS Books, University of Texas.

Orfield, G., Bachmeier, M. D., James, D. R., & Eitle, T. (1997). Deepening segregation in American public schools: A special report from the Harvard Project on School Desegregation. *Equity & Excellence in Education, 30*(2), 5–24.

Regents of the University of California v. Bakke, 438 U.S. 265, 98 S. Ct. 2733, 57 L. Ed. 2d 750 (1978).

Sweatt v. Painter, 339 U.S. 629, 70 S. Ct. 848, 94 L. Ed. 1114, *petition for rehearing denied,* 340 U.S. 846, 71 S. Ct. 13, 95 L. Ed. 620 (1950).

Texas Higher Education Coordinating Board. (1997). *Alternative diversity criteria: Analyses and recommendations. Report of the Advisory Committee on Alternative Criteria for Diversity.* Austin: Author.

United States v. Fordice, 505 U.S. 717, 112 S. Ct. 2727, 120 L. Ed. 2d 575 (1992).

6 The Contemporary Politics of Access Policy: California after Proposition 209

BRIAN PUSSER

From the summer of 1994 through the fall elections of 1996, California higher education was buffeted by a bitter political battle over access to the state's higher education institutions. Beginning with a proposal to end affirmative action at the University of California and culminating with the passage of state ballot Proposition 209, this period found California's higher education leaders fighting not just to preserve a set of access policies but also to preserve the right to make those policies.

In November 1996, California voters passed state ballot Proposition 209 by a margin of 54 to 46 percent. Proposition 209 prohibited the granting of preferential treatment to any individual on the basis of race, sex, color, ethnicity, or national origin in the operation of public employment, public education, or public contracting. Although the full ramifications of Proposition 209 were unclear before its passage, its immediate consequences for all three of California's public higher education systems—the University of California (UC), the California State University (CSU) system, and the California community college system—were widely understood. The day after the voters passed 209, UC President Richard Atkinson (1996) issued a public statement that concluded, "One idea has tended to unite people on all sides of this extraordinarily divisive and passionate debate. It is that diversity is an asset to California and can only be achieved by extending educational opportunity to disadvantaged young people. The question facing education is clear: How do we establish new paths to diversity consistent with the law?" (p. 1).

While President Atkinson pointed to the central question posed in the wake of Proposition 209, he left unspoken a question that was in many ways just as important: who should decide which paths to take? The passage of 209, and the precursor votes on affirmative action by the UC regents, forcefully ended institutional access policies that had been decades in the making. Yet the campaign to eliminate affirmative action in California also shifted the nature of the policymaking relationship between the political branches of state government and the state's higher education institutions, a relationship developed over more than a century.

The passage of Proposition 209 was considered a significant victory for Governor Pete Wilson and the state Republican party, and an equally significant blow to the state and national Democratic parties (Chavez, 1998; Pusser, 1999). In the ensuing years, significant shifts have taken place, but not precisely as expected. Many of the political forces in California that supported 209 are reeling from unprecedented losses in the November 1998 elections. A Democratic governor (Gray Davis) was elected for the first time in sixteen years, and Democrats increased their majority in the state senate and assembly and claimed the lieutenant governorship, the attorney general's office, and the superintendent of schools post. Under Governor Davis, who opposed 209 and, as a UC regent, voted to preserve affirmative action, Democrats have placed the effort to increase access and diversity in the state's higher education systems near the top of their legislative agenda.

This chapter explores the policy consequences and the unexpected dynamics emerging from the UC regents' votes to eliminate affirmative action and the subsequent statewide adoption of Proposition 209. This analysis is a portion of a larger case study of California access and diversity policy, based on a variety of legislative and institutional data sources and comprehensive interviews with California's higher education institutional leaders, state legislators, statewide officeholders, university trustees, and state education policymakers.[1] What emerges is a portrait of a most precarious transition in California's higher education, a period of intense turmoil and political competition set against a rapidly changing demographic and economic landscape. Perhaps equally important for scholars and policymakers are the challenges to prevailing understandings of education policymaking that emerge from the data and the implications for institutional autonomy and governance.

Higher Education Policymaking and Institutional Autonomy

Research on policymaking and governance in higher education has generally relied on two theoretical frames, one generally implicit, the other more often explicit. The implicit frame is a pluralist conceptualization entailing an open and democratic process of exercising authority. Elected or appointed trustees preside over the administration of public universities and are accountable to the public for their decisions (Jones & Skolnik, 1997; Kerr & Gade, 1989; Millet, 1984). The explicit frame entails theories of organizational behavior, structural propositions derived from the sociology of organizations, and theories of decision making derived from the psychology of organizations. Governance and policymaking are contingent on professional expertise linked to strategic planning, and they are increasingly based on management and decision-making models adapted from those of the corporate sector (Gumport & Pusser, 1997; Peterson, 1996).

Over the last quarter-century, research on higher education policymaking has been dominated by an open-systems, organization-environmental perspective. In this view, policy formation begins in the institution in response to demands emerging either from within the university's internal structure or from the external environment (Baldridge, 1971; Gladieux & Wolanin, 1976; Peterson, 1996). In what Baldridge called the "interest-articulation" model, the process is essentially the same for demands originating within the university (e.g., the right to form employee unions) and those originating outside (e.g., legislative demands for higher tuition). In both cases, top-level administrators within the university mediate and negotiate demands into policy, which is voted on by a board of trustees. External negotiations are conducted primarily between the university leadership and key members of the university's "task environment," a set of organizations such as government agencies, business groups, coordinating boards, other universities, the state government, and interest groups (Baldridge, 1971; Peterson, 1996).

Considerable research within the interest-articulation framework has addressed policy adoption as a function of the negotiation between state governing agencies or coordinating boards and state higher education institutions (Berdahl, 1971; Hearn & Griswold, 1994). These studies have largely focused on institutional efforts to preserve autonomy from state intervention, and they suggest that autonomy should be seen as a dynamic social phenomenon determined mainly by negotiation between the universities and outside groups (Slaughter & Leslie, 1997; Zusman, 1986). Autonomy is seen as a key element of a university's power to determine its own goals and programs and the means by which they are enacted (Berdahl, 1971). Contemporary researchers have turned attention to autonomy as an essential element in the broader contest over the social and economic benefits generated by universities (Hardy, 1990; Pusser, 1999; Slaughter, 1993).

Until recently, educational researchers have neglected the political foundations of governance and policymaking in public higher education (Rhoades, 1992). Contemporary political scientists and economists working in an arena broadly defined as the Positive Theory of Institutions have shifted attention to the effect of interest-group competition in shaping a variety of political institutions, including universities (Moe, 1995). The central focus in that research has been on the struggle to shape the organizational agenda (Kingdon, 1984), the contest over appointments to governing boards (Hammond & Hill, 1993), prospective legislative design of institutional structures (Weingast & Marshall, 1988), and control over allocating the costs and benefits of institutional policy (Wilson, 1989). Research applying the Positive Theory of Institutions to higher education policymaking views higher education as a key commodity in its own right and the policy-formation process as an interest-group struggle for that commodity value. Higher education institutions are seen as sites of contest and as instruments in broader political struggle (Masten, 1995; Pusser, 1999).

The latter formulation is particularly useful in thinking about the struggle over access and diversity policy in California's higher education. The efforts on the UC board of regents to eliminate affirmative action were opposed by the university president, all nine campus chancellors, each of the campus academic senates, the systemwide Academic Council, the system's largest union organizations, and the major UC student organizations. Although the "institutional interest" was clearly presented, the subsequent articulation and mediation process did not conform to prevailing understandings of higher education governance and policymaking. To understand the shifts in access and diversity policy following Proposition 209, we must turn our attention to the state political arena and the broader struggle for control of higher education policy.

The Regents of the University of California
Initiatives SP-1 and SP-2

> Those engaged in politics today are much more willing to use the University of California for their own purposes than they ever were before and I think that is really the change. And that is true of the Governor, that is true of the assembly and senate, it is true of Republicans and Democrats, it is a very difficult situation. (Charles E. Young, 1998, UCLA chancellor emeritus)

Before Proposition 209, Governor Wilson and his allies on the board of regents campaigned to eliminate affirmative action at the University of California. The battle over regents' initiatives SP-1 and SP-2 was widely seen as a gambit to boost the effort to put Proposition 209 on the ballot and to assist Governor Wilson's efforts to win the Republican presidential nomination in 1996 (Chavez, 1998; Schrag, 1998). Regent William Bagley (1998), a Republican, a Wilson ally, and a former member of the California assembly, put it this way: "Had Pete [Wilson] not been involved, had the governor not been involved, we would have never passed the resolutions. The governor got involved because he was running for president. The governor used my university as a forum to run for president."

Since its founding, UC has been a site of political conflict. The board of regents has been pitted against the state legislature or the governor in a number of struggles over university policies, including academic freedom (Fitzgibbon, 1968), loyalty oaths (Gardner, 1967), and free speech (Stadtman, 1970). These conflicts have persisted in spite of UC's autonomous status under the state constitution (Douglass, 1992). The university has historically been an irresistible target for political actors seeking an extremely visible platform for contesting state and national policy.

One of the most striking aspects of the regents' deliberations on the day of their votes was the presence of state political leaders who rarely appeared in the regents' public sessions (Pusser, 1999). Among those who testified were a number of ex officio regents: Governor Pete Wilson, assembly Speaker Willie Brown, Lieutenant Governor Gray Davis, and the superintendent of public schools, Delaine Eastin. Other state and national political leaders who prepared testimony for the board included the state senate majority leader Bill Lockyer, the Reverend Jesse Jackson, U.S. Congressman Tom Campbell, and a host of California senate and assembly representatives from both parties. The regents' deliberations more closely resembled a key committee session in the state capitol than the meeting of a university board of trustees. It was also a highly partisan meeting, with virtually every Democrat supporting affirmative action and every Republican seeking to eliminate the university's existing policies.

The party political efforts also went well beyond appearances by elected representatives. The president of UC Berkeley's chapter of the College Republicans described his role. "My original assignment was to bring as many students as possible to picket against affirmative action outside the auditorium. I was one of many organizers in this effort. We were supposed to concentrate on getting people there, while the Wilson campaign was to provide the picket signs. However, it soon became clear to Republican strategists that the picketing wasn't going to work. We just weren't getting the volunteers. Conservatives tend to have a real distaste for protests. They also tend to have jobs, which makes it difficult to dedicate an entire Thursday to a demonstration" (Kamena, 1995, p. 3).

After the votes were taken, assembly member John Vasconcellos (1995) expressed the anger felt by many Democrats in the legislature. As chairman of the assembly Budget Committee, Vasconcellos wielded a great deal of influence over UC's annual appropriation. The day after the votes, he wrote in a letter to the regents, "You have committed the most destructive act in modern California history. The Board has profaned its sacred trust as trustees of what once was California's great public university. You have absolutely forfeited your right to govern what was the world's most prestigious university by engaging in a blatant political act" (p. 1). He concluded, "How dare you rush to judgment—according to no public interest timetable—to join the desperate effort of a presidential candidate to jump-start his non-start campaign? How pathetic! How dare you pervert this public board of regents of this public university by a narrow vote, a political power play? If you want to join Pete Wilson's campaign committee, have the integrity to resign the public position of trust you have violated" (p. 1).

After the votes, Democratic leaders were also quick to denounce the partisan composition of the board of regents. All eighteen appointed regents on the board at the time of the votes were Republicans. The first step in the Democrats' counterattack, coming fully into play shortly after passage of Proposition 209, was a concerted effort to shift the historical character of the appointment process for UC regents.

Confirmation Dynamics

Contemporary research on the political dynamics of nominations and confirmations for governing boards focuses on two primary forms as initial frames for understanding the appointment/confirmation process: the deference model and the agenda control model (Hammond & Hill, 1993). The deference model suggests that in cases of nominations to boards having little policy discretion, the confirming body (in the UC regents' case the state senate) generally defers to a governor and confirms nominees. In such cases, those with the power to reject or confirm also have the power to constrain the efforts of board members; consequently, deference has few political costs (McCubbins, Noll, & Weingast, 1987). The agenda control model (Poole & Rosenthal, 1987) prevails when nominees can exercise considerable independence after confirmation. In these cases the confirming body is not likely to defer at the time of nomination. The nominee's ideology and party affiliation, the existence of any particularly salient issues on the political agenda, and the dominant preferences of the confirming body are fundamental to the success or failure of the nomination.

Both UC regents and CSU trustees are nominated by the governor and must be confirmed by the state senate. Regents serve twelve-year terms; CSU trustees, eight-year terms. The confirmation procedure is straightforward. When a vacancy is created on the board, the governor consults an informal advisory committee, then nominates a regent.[2] The nominee serves one year on the board, and at the end of the year the senate Rules Committee and the full senate vote on the nominee. If either body fails to confirm, the regent is out.

As California's elite public university, UC is also one of the state's elite political resources. Seats on the board have long been awarded to the state's most wealthy and influential political donors (Pusser & Ordorika, 2000). The University of California allocates an extremely scarce public resource: access to some of the nation's most coveted public campuses. The UC system is one of the state's largest employers, and it receives annual general funding of more than $2 billion. UC policy has significant state and national visibility and symbolic and practical political value.

Research on confirmation dynamics suggests that the nominees a governor offers to key boards reflect his or her own political stance and can be relied upon to monitor the institution's budget and policy in ways consonant with the governor's own beliefs. After the nomination, senators of the other political party should organize to resist the nominee in favor of an alternative choice who can be relied upon, as much as possible, to support their policy preferences.

Given UC's constitutionally autonomous status, the length of terms of the regents, and the high cost of monitoring their actions, the confirmation dynamic for the regents' appointment process should follow the agenda control model. Although both the governor and the legislature can take such measures as cutting UC's budget if it moves in directions contrary to legislative preference, such measures risk very public exposure and challenges from university supporters (Jones & Skolnik, 1997; Trombley, 1995).

Although the composition and relative autonomy of the board of regents was a significant political issue at the founding of the university, state senate confirmation of UC regents is a fairly new procedure, established by a state constitutional amendment, Measure 5, in 1972. From 1974 through 1981 the governor was a Democrat and the state senate had a Democratic majority. From 1982 through 1998, the governor was a Republican, while Democrats retained their majority in the state senate.

Table 6.1 presents a summary of the dynamics of the confirmation of UC regents between 1967 and 1998. Contrary to the predictions of contemporary political scientists, from 1972 through 1994 California state senators deferred completely to the governor's nominations, regardless of the governor's party affiliation, approving every single gubernatorial nominee to the board. A close analysis of the senate votes on each nomination shows that between 1972 and 1992 there was only one no vote. Every other nomination was unanimously confirmed, despite the presence of three Democrats on the five-member Rules Committee (Pusser & Ordorika, 2000). If, as was alleged after the regents' 1995 votes on affirmative action, the board that made those votes had been "captured" by the governor and his Republican allies, the votes were taken without a fight (Karabel, 1996).

Table 6.1. Confirmation Dynamics for University of California Regents, 1972–1999

| Governor | Governor's Party | Senate Majority | Nominees[a] | Party of Nominees | | Confirmation Outcomes | | |
				Democrat	Republican	Yes	No	Pending
Ronald Reagan[b] (1967–74)	Republican	Democrat	2	0	2	2	0	
Jerry Brown (1975–82)	Democrat	Democrat	13	13	0	13	0	
George Deukmejian (1983–90)	Republican	Democrat	18	1	17	18	0	
Pete Wilson (1991–98)	Republican	Democrat	15	0	15	9	6	
Gray Davis (1999–)	Democrat	Democrat	3	3	0	0	0	3
Total			51	17	34	42	6	3

Source: California Senate Rules Committee (1999).
[a]Nominees include nominations and renominations.
[b]Only Reagan nominations made after passage of Measure 5 in 1972 are tabulated.

The first refusal to confirm a regent came in 1994 and was in large part a protest by senate Democrats against fee increases in the UC system. The next significant challenge, in 1997, was clearly tied to the regents' votes on affirmative action, to Proposition 209, and to an awakening of senate Democrats to the importance of the regents in broader state political contests (Chavez, 1998). The question of whether the Republican party had used the regents to help advance its own political agenda, particularly the passage of Proposition 209, was at the heart of the confirmation hearing of Regent Tirso del Junco. Governor Wilson had nominated Dr. del Junco, a former chairperson of the state Republican party, for an additional twelve-year term as regent.

No witnesses had appeared to oppose del Junco at his original confirmation hearing in 1986, but fourteen witnesses representing a variety of interest groups opposed him on the first day of the 1997 hearings. The witnesses protested the regents' votes on affirmative action, the role of regents in passing Proposition 209, the apparent abrogation of shared governance on the board, and the politicization of the regents. Dr. del Junco was called to account for all these issues. In short, what had once been deferential and relatively invisible confirmation hearings had become elaborate, contentious, and very public battles.

The position of the Republicans on the state Rules Committee was that citizen del Junco had a constitutional right to express himself away from the board of regents in any way he saw fit, while he could also be a nonpartisan figure in his role as a regent. William Lockyer (1997), the committee chairperson, summed up the Democrats' position this way:

> Dr. del Junco was a Regent when he chose to be Chair of the California Republican Party, when he chose to sign a lot of questionable attack mail pieces sent against my colleagues. Now, that wasn't somebody who had much regard for the non-political role of regents. You know, I've had colleagues say to me in the senate, "I've never met this guy. I don't know him. The only thing I know about him is when I was running for the senate mail landed in my district, attacking me personally that was inaccurate, and it was signed by him as Chair of the Republican Party." So that's all I know about him. I'm voting no for that reason. So the point is this, sir. You come to us and say, "don't be political." The politics started there, not here. That's the point. We don't need to debate it. (p. 85)

Regent del Junco had a very different view of his confirmation hearing, describing it as a "political assassination" and calling for a return to a less contentious process. "You know, theoretically you would like to have a system the way you have it now—if politics would not play a major role. By that I mean the type of politics that was brought upon me. In other words, you would allow for independent intellectual thinking. Because it's very important that the regents feel free to express sincere opinions of what they think has to be done. The preservation of that constitutional right is so, so important" (del Junco, 1998).

Dr. del Junco was not confirmed for a second term. Nor did the wrath of the Democrats extend only to regents who had voted against affirmative action. Three other Wilson nominees who had not been on the board of regents at the time of the votes on SP-1 and SP-2 were forced off the board in 1997, when the chairperson of the Rules Committee refused to schedule hearings on their nominations before the expiration of their initial appointments. This action produced a response by the chairman of the regents, John Davies (Governor Wilson's former law school roommate). "Chairman Davies expressed his confidence that Governor Davis would appoint outstanding replacements for the outgoing regents, but he also pointed out that their departure represents a genuine loss for the University. He suggested that the failure on the part of the senate to confirm appointments is a disturbing trend which should not continue, representing as it does a politicalization of appointments to the Board" (Regents of the University of California, 1999, p. 6).

Since the Democrats' capture of the California governorship in November 1998, two more Wilson nominee confirmations have failed. With five more regents' terms set to expire before 2002, Governor Davis will have the opportunity to appoint ten of the eighteen appointed members on the board. And given its solid control of the assembly and senate, the California Democratic party will be in a position to significantly reshape the board for years to come.

Regents' Involvement in the Admissions Process

Increased legislative interest in the board of regents was not limited to the confirmation of new regents. In 1996 the *Los Angeles Times* reported that a number of regents, including Proposition 209 advocate Ward Connerly, had contacted UC administrators in an effort to gain preferential consideration for children of friends, business acquaintances, and relatives. In some cases, applicants who had been rejected by UC were admitted after entreaties from regents to top campus officials. Members of the assembly and senate higher education committees expressed dismay at the practice and noted the irony in such preferences being sought by regents who had voted to eliminate race and gender as criteria less than a year before. Assemblywoman Marguerite Archie-Hudson commented, "This is really to my mind the flip side

Table 6.2. Racial/Ethnic Diversity in California's Public K–12 Schools, 1997–1998 (Percentage)

Racial/Ethnic group	Enrollment (Fall 1997)	High School Graduates (Spring 1998)
American Indian	0.9%	0.9%
Black	8.8	7.7
Hispanic	40.5	30.5
Asian	11.1	14.7
White	38.8	46.3

Source: California Department of Education (1999).

of institutional racism, where you have a group of unspoken practices, assumptions and agreements based on the notion that children of people who occupy power and privilege ought to automatically have an advantage" (quoted in Ellis & Frammolino, 1996).

Hearings were held by the senate Higher Education Select Committee to explore preferential admissions and relations between UC regents and major political donors. A bill was subsequently introduced in the legislature that would have prohibited any UC regent or CSU trustee from making donations to a gubernatorial candidate. Although the bill did not reach the governor's desk, it was part of a renewed legislative participation in the conduct of the University of California and of California higher education in general.

New Commitments to Outreach and Coordination

Relations between the governor's office and Democrats in the senate and assembly could not have been much worse in the aftermath of Proposition 209, but legislative efforts to improve outreach to California's high school graduates by the UC and CSU systems received bipartisan interest. Legislators also turned attention to improving rates of transfer from California community colleges to UC and CSU and to the rates of eligibility for entrance into UC and CSU among young women and students from underrepresented racial/ethnic groups.[3] As soon became apparent, increasing diversity in higher education admissions without considering race and gender would require major policy shifts.

California's student population is richly diverse, as indicated by the data in Table 6.2. Within the K–12 cohort of nearly six million students, no racial/ethnic group constitutes more than 50 percent of total enrollment. The California Department of Education data show that Hispanic and white stu-

Table 6.3. Graduation Rates for California's Public High Schools,
by Race/Ethnicity, 1997 (Percentage)

Racial/Ethnic Group	1993 Enrollees Graduating in 1997
American Indian	62.1%
Black	55.4
Hispanic	54.3
Asian	86.7
White	73.8

Source: California Department of Education (1999).

dents comprise approximately 40 percent each, with Asians at 11 percent, blacks about 9 percent, and American Indians somewhat under 1 percent.[4] These very broad reporting categories only begin to suggest the diversity of California's K–12 educational cohort; the state's Department of Education lists fifty-eight primary languages spoken by California's K–12 students. These figures also do not illustrate the staggering growth of this educational cohort. Projections suggest the number of public high school graduates in California, just under three hundred thousand in 1997, will increase by 50 percent before the year 2005 (California Senate Select Committee, 1998).

These data also demonstrate the burgeoning "pipeline" challenge facing California's education policymakers as they endeavor to improve ethnic diversity in higher education. The disparity in percentage of high school graduates relative to K–12 attendees reflects both the large number of K–8 students in the Hispanic cohort and differential high school graduation rates for the various groups (Table 6.3).

Eligibility for Entry to California's Public Higher Education Institutions

Virtually all California high school graduates are eligible for admission to one of the state's 106 community colleges, yet black and Latino students form a smaller percentage of the community college population than of the statewide high school graduating class (Table 6.4). This is also a factor in the extremely low number of students in underrepresented groups transferring from community colleges to the state's public four-year schools. Despite a 1997 enrollment of nearly 1.5 million students in California community colleges, only 33,000 of those students transferred to the CSU system, fewer than 10,000 of them from underrepresented minority groups. Just over 8,600 stu-

Table 6.4. Enrollments in California Community Colleges, Fall 1998 (Percentage)

Racial/Ethnic Group	Enrollments	All High School Graduates
American Indian	0.8%	0.9%
Black	4.8	7.7
Latino	17.4	30.5
Asian	10.4	14.7
White/other	35.1	46.3

Source: California Community College Chancellor's Office (1999).
Note: Column percentages may not sum to 100% because the race of some students is unknown and other students are multiracial.

dents transferred from community colleges to UC campuses in the fall of 1997, with some 1,400 from underrepresented minority groups (California Postsecondary Education Commission (CPEC), 1997).

CALIFORNIA STATE UNIVERSITY

The eligibility of high school graduates for admission to the CSU and UC systems is a complex phenomenon and a significant factor limiting access to California higher education. The California Master Plan for higher education recommends that CSU set its eligibility criteria so that the top one-third of California's high school graduating class is eligible to enroll. Those wishing to be eligible for CSU must complete a prescribed sequence of fifteen courses and maintain a 3.0 grade point average in their final three years of high school. Eligibility can also be earned by completing the course sequence with a lower GPA if the student achieves a compensatory score on either the SAT 1 or ACT. Under the prevailing formula for 1996, the year of the most recent CPEC eligibility study, only 29.1 percent of the state's high school graduates were eligible for CSU admission, a decline of 14 percent from the 1990 level of 34.6 percent.[5] Nor were the eligible students distributed evenly across ethnic groups. Shown in Table 6.5 is the percentage of CSU-eligible public high school graduates from various racial/ethnic groups in 1990 and 1996. In 1996, Asians (54.4%) and whites (36.3%) had the highest cohort eligibility rates, with blacks (13.2%) and Latinos (13.4%) having significantly lower rates.

Taking into account the difference in numbers of students in each ethnic cohort, the data in Table 6.6 show the ethnic composition of the total pool of public high school students eligible for admission to the CSU system in

Table 6.5. Eligibility Rates for the California State University System, by Racial/Ethnic Group, 1990 and 1996 (Percentage)

Racial/Ethnic Group	1990	1996
Black	18.6%	13.2%
Latino	17.3	13.4
Asian	61.5	54.4
White	38.2	36.3

Source: California Postsecondary Education Commission (1999).

Table 6.6. Eligibility Pool for the California State University System, 1990 and 1996

Racial/ Ethnic Group	Racial/Ethnic Group as Percentage of all CSU-Eligible Students		Racial/Ethnic Group as Percentage of All High School Graduates (1996)
	Fall 1990	Fall 1996	
Black	4.4%	3.7%	7.7%
Latino	11.6	13.5	30.5
Asian	24.5	26.2	14.7
White	59.6	56.6	46.3

Source: California Postsecondary Education Commission (1999).

1990 and 1996. In 1996, blacks represented just 4 percent of the total pool of CSU-eligible students, Latinos 14 percent, Asians 26 percent, and whites 57 percent. Whites and Asians were eligible for entry to CSU in percentages greater than their representation in California's high school graduating class, but Latinos and blacks in considerably lower percentages.

UNIVERSITY OF CALIFORNIA

A similar though more extreme picture emerges in looking at the rates of eligibility of California's high school graduates for admission to the University of California. The Master Plan recommends that UC set its admissions criteria so that the top 12.5 percent of the state's high school graduating class is eligible to enroll. Students wishing to be eligible are required to maintain a 3.3 GPA for a prescribed sequence of fifteen courses. They also must take the SAT 1 or ACT and three SAT II subject examinations. Students with GPAs between 2.82 and 3.29 in the required courses can also become el-

Table 6.7. Eligibility Rates for the University of California, by Racial/
Ethnic Group, 1990 and 1996 (Percentage)

Racial/Ethnic Group	1990	1996
Black	5.1%	2.8%
Latino	3.9	3.8
Asian	32.2	30.0
White	12.7	12.7

Source: California Postsecondary Education Commission (1999).

Table 6.8. Eligibility Pool for the University of California,
1990 and 1996

Racial/Ethnic Group	Racial/Ethnic Group as Percentage of All UC-Eligible Students	
	Fall 1990	Fall 1996
Black	3.3%	2.0%
Latino	7.1	9.9
Asian	35.2	37.1
White	54.4	51.0

Source: California Postsecondary Education Commission (1999).

igible by achieving compensatory scores on the SAT 1 or ACT. In 1996 the overall eligibility rate was 11.1 percent, nearly 15 percent below the Master Plan's recommendation. Shown in Table 6.7 are the eligibility rates for public high school graduates from various ethnic groups in 1996. The eligibility rates for Asians (30%) and whites (12.7%) were considerably higher than those for blacks (2.8%) and Latinos (3.8%). As shown by the data in Table 6.8, the percentage of the total eligibility pool comprised by each racial/ethnic group in 1996 ranged from 51 percent for white students to 2 percent for black students.

As problematic as these eligibility numbers were for admissions officers hoping to admit diverse pools of students, the passage of Proposition 209 made things considerably more difficult. Neither the CSU system nor California's community colleges had been using affirmative action in their admissions practices, yet both were concerned about a possible decline in the enrollment of racial/ethnic minority students after Proposition 209. Their concern was

Table 6.9. Freshman Enrollments at California State University, by Racial/Ethnic Group, 1996 to 1998 (Percentage)

Racial/Ethnic Group	Fall 1996	Fall 1997	Fall 1998
American Indian	0.9%	1.0%	0.8%
Black	8.3	8.1	6.9
Latino	24.9	24.8	23.7
Asian	20.6	21.2	21.3
White	35.8	34.6	36.3
Unknown	9.5	10.3	10.9

Source: California State University Office of the Chancellor (1999).
Note: Column percentages may not sum to 100% owing to rounding.

due to the perception by high school graduates of a hostile climate for racial/ethnic minority youth in higher education, generated by passage of 209. As Christopher Cabaldon (1997), vice-chancellor for governmental and external affairs in the California community college system, testified during a senate hearing,

> Many students and their families still believe that our admission requirements have been constrained so they can't come to our colleges, and it's not true. But in outreach and in admissions, the perception is far more important than whatever regulations and policies and statutes are in place. So we do face a challenge. If students don't believe that those opportunities are available to them, they won't prepare themselves to come to any post-secondary institution, including the community colleges. So we see an impact of Proposition 209 in that area and all of the other ancillary policy debates that have been occurring and we think it is going to be important for us to step up our outreach programs. (p. 91)

Shown in Table 6.9 are freshman enrollments at CSU by racial/ethnic groups from 1996 to 1998. The percentage of enrollees from underrepresented racial/ethnic groups declined slightly in each of the two classes admitted after passage of Proposition 209.

Proposition 209 and University of California Admissions

The effects of Proposition 209 on UC admissions became apparent in the fall of 1997 when the first cohort of applicants to the university's graduate and professional schools was admitted without consideration of race and gender.[6] The university endured two waves of negative publicity, the first when the admissions figures were published and a second when actual en-

Table 6.10. Resident Freshman Enrollments at the University
of California, by Racial/Ethnic Group, 1996 to 1998 (Percentage)

Racial/Ethnic Group	Fall 1996	Fall 1997	Fall 1998
American Indian	1.0%	0.8%	0.7%
African American	3.8	3.9	3.0
Chicano	10.1	9.8	8.9
Latino	3.8	3.4	3.0
Asian	33.9	34.2	33.1
White	40.3	41.7	34.7
Unknown	4.5	3.3	13.8

Source: University of California Office of the President (1998).
   Note: Column percentages do not sum to 100%; race/ethnicity of remaining students is "other".

rollments were revealed. As one particularly devastating example, the number of African American students who chose to register at UC Berkeley's Boalt Hall Law School declined from twenty in 1996 to only one in 1997. A number of other UC professional schools suffered significant declines, and 1997 minority admissions at UC's medical schools were at twenty-five-year lows (Rice, in press).

The data in Table 6.10 show freshman enrollments for various racial/ethnic groups in the UC system. The fall 1998 figures reflect the first undergraduate cohort enrolled without the use of race or gender as admissions criteria. Systemwide, the number of enrollees from underrepresented racial/ethnic groups decreased: American Indians by 8.2 percent, African Americans by 19.4 percent, Chicanos by 4.9 percent, and Latinos by 8.6 percent. The largest percentage increase was among those who declined to state ethnicity ("unknown" in Table 6.10). Early UC estimates indicate that the group not declaring an ethnicity contained fewer students from underrepresented groups than the overall enrolled cohort.

Significant media and legislative concern was generated by release of the fall 1998 enrollment figures for the UC system's flagship campus, UC Berkeley, where declines in enrollments of students in underrepresented racial/ethnic groups were far more dramatic (Table 6.11). Berkeley's overall enrollment of these students declined by 46 percent from 1997 to 1998. Initial figures for student admissions at UC Berkeley had predicted a more substantial decline in underrepresented minority students. Subsequent rounds of the admissions process and a successful campus effort to increase yield rates among admitted applicants ameliorated the initial predictions. Nonetheless,

Table 6.11. Resident Freshman Enrollments at the University
of California, Berkeley, by Racial/Ethnic Group, 1997 and 1998
(Percentage)

Racial/Ethnic Group	Fall 1997	Fall 1998
American Indian	0.6%	0.4%
African American	7.8	3.7
Chicano	12.0	5.7
Latino	2.6	2.3
Asian	42.3	44.0
White	28.3	28.2
Unknown	4.6	14.6

Source: University of California Office of the President (1998).
   Note: Column percentages do not sum to 100%; race/ethnicity of remaining
students is "other."

the furor over the declines had significant political and policy consequences
at the state and national levels.

University of California Policy Responses:
Enhanced Outreach and Coordination

More than a year before passage of Proposition 209, in the aftermath of
the regents' approval of SP-1 and SP-2, members of the state legislature and
leaders of the three higher education sectors began developing strategies for
increasing diversity without using race and gender as factors in admissions
decisions. Central to those strategies was increased outreach to the state's
nearly six million K–12 students. The UC and CSU systems and California's
community colleges had long practiced a significant degree of outreach and
educational partnership. The Early Academic Outreach Program at UC,
which endeavors to increase eligibility in communities with low eligibility
rates, was instituted in 1975. By 1996 it had become a collaboration between
eight UC campuses and more than 130 school districts. Similarly, CSU's College Readiness Program was founded in 1986 to partner CSU campuses with
targeted high schools in order to increase the enrollment of first-generation
and low-income ninth grade students in college-preparatory courses. For the
last ten years, the California community college chancellor's office has ad-
ministered the Middle College program, a collaboration between community colleges and high school districts to increase high school graduation
rates and college enrollments among high-risk students (CPEC, 1997). These
are just a few of many programs targeting outreach and academic develop-

Table 6.12. Selected Characteristics of Top and Bottom Quintiles
(Based on Schoolwide Average SAT Scores) of California
Public Schools

Characteristics of Schools (N = 151)	Top Quintile	Bottom Quintile
Average SAT score (combined)	1007	715
Urban	12%	54%
Suburban	69	19
Rural	19	27
Students receiving Aid to Families with Dependent Children	5	28
Students with limited English proficiency	7	31
Students with father having high school diploma or higher	90	36
"a–f" enrollment rate	61	48
Seniors taking SAT	56	33
Students scoring 900+ on SAT	43	6
Students scoring 3 or more on Advanced Placement exams	27	6
High School graduates attending University of California	15	4
Combined Hispanic, African American, and American Indian	17	79

Source: University of California Office of the President (1997).

ment in the three higher education sectors. At the time of passage of Proposition 209, UC alone was devoting nearly $60 million a year to outreach.

Early in 1997, the University of California Office of the President (UCOP, 1997) presented the findings of a comprehensive outreach taskforce report. The taskforce pointed to a significant "educational disadvantage" for particular groups of California's school children. "Review of performance indicators, school-by-school, shows a continuing pattern of differing outcomes for racial and ethnic groups in California's school system, with groups least represented in higher education remaining most concentrated in the lowest-performing schools. Almost four out of every five students in these schools are either African-American, American Indian, or Latino—groups with historically low rates of UC eligibility and enrollment" (p. 1).

Table 6.12 presents some of the correlates of educational disadvantage and differential prospects for high school students attempting to enter the state's public universities. The table includes data for the top and bottom quintiles of California's public high schools, based on schoolwide average SAT scores. Students at schools in the bottom quintile are least likely to go on to higher education. UC's Outreach Task Force (UCOP, 1997) suggested that such factors as the four-year completion rate, percentage of seniors tak-

ing the SAT, and percentage of students completing the "a–f" course sequence (a UC designation for the sequence of courses required for eligibility, used for computing GPA) could be used as indicators of where to focus
outreach efforts. A key challenge for California's public higher education in
the wake of Proposition 209 has been how to increase eligibility rates for underrepresented groups without offering preferential treatment on the basis
of race or gender. A number of legal arguments and rulings suggest that targeted outreach is sustainable under Proposition 209 (Rice, in press), but
efforts to publicize and strategize around the concept of educational disadvantage offered an effective tool for enhancing eligibility and access without
courting immediate legal challenge.

The UCOP taskforce recommended expansion of UC's existing outreach and partnership programs, a focus on the most educationally disadvantaged students, and expanded outreach services to students and families
as early as primary school. It also suggested closer coordination between the
three sectors of public higher education, particularly with regard to increasing transfer from the state's community colleges to UC. To that end, UC subsequently set a goal of increasing community college transfers to the university by 33 percent between 1995 and 2005, bringing the total of community
college transfers to nearly 15,000 per year. Early in 1998, UCOP developed an
Outreach Action Plan incorporating many of the taskforce's recommendations. The plan called for an investment of new money totaling $60 million
annually over a five-year period. The primary focus of this funding was to
increase the development, recruitment, and retention of teachers in low-per-
forming schools.

Legislative Policy Responses

The passage of Proposition 209, publication of CPEC's 1996 eligibility
study, and revelation of the decline in minority admissions to UC's professional programs prompted strong reactions in the state capitol. In remarks
prepared for a state senate hearing on access, Senator Teresa Hughes (1998)
noted that "if such enrollment numbers continue to persist, California will
move toward a segregated society with non-college educated blacks and Latinos filling the underclass and whites and Asians disproportionately represented in middle and upper classes" (p. 2).

The state senate and assembly higher education committees held hearings on a number of issues related to access, eligibility, admissions requirements, outreach, and coordination. In November 1997, the senate Select
Committee on Higher Education Admissions and Outreach and the assembly Higher Education Committee held a joint hearing on outreach and eli-

gibility. The hearing centered on CPEC data demonstrating both the promise and the limitations of outreach as a tool for promoting access and diversity in California's higher education. For the year 1994–95, the rate of college attendance for students who had participated in Student Academic Development Programs, a set of outreach initiatives by the three public sectors serving some 120,000 students at a cost of about $20 million, was 64.5 percent. This was in contrast to the college attendance rate for all California students of 53.2 percent and the rate for students from groups with low eligibility rates, 42.6 percent. The CPEC assistant director, Penny Edgert, noted the limited scale of the outreach challenge. The Student Academic Development Programs served only 3.8 percent of students in grades 7–12, fewer than 10 percent of the students in groups with low college-going rates, and operated in only 7.5 percent of the state's schools (CPEC, 1997).

The challenge to increase diversity through outreach and intersectoral coordination following Proposition 209 was translated into new legislation and increased financial commitments. Bills were drafted to facilitate specific outreach initiatives, including a bill by Senator Vasconcellos that would have amended the Education Code to require CSU and request UC to adopt a systemwide program for outreach partnerships with each of the high schools in California to improve college preparation for pupils from socially or economically disadvantaged environments. The bill passed the senate but failed to make it out of the assembly. Several other outreach bills were vetoed by Governor Wilson, but a significant number were signed into law. Successful legislation included a bill that established regional academic partnerships between school districts and the three higher education sectors to support improvement of K–12 schools. Funds were earmarked for students in high schools where the percentage of graduates enrolling in public universities was below the state average, and the bill required notification of the parents of all eighth grade students in these schools of the course prerequisites for university admission. As a signal of ongoing legislative commitment to outreach, legislation was also passed creating a permanent authorization for one of the state's largest outreach programs, the California Student Opportunity and Access Program (Cal-SOAP), which previously required renewal every five years. Cal-SOAP incorporates school districts, all three public higher education sectors, and a large consortium of independent colleges to increase enrollment in higher education.

Other bills provided $10 million in matching funds for school districts to provide low-income high school students with college admission test preparation, and funding to enable school districts to waive advanced placement examination fees for economically disadvantaged students. Legislation also created new summer academies to increase math and science training for high school students in disadvantaged communities.

The 1998–99 general fund budgets for each of the three higher education sectors also included major increases for outreach, partnerships, and academic development activities. These increases were reflective of both increased legislative commitment to access and diversity and one of the largest overall budgets in California history. The 1998–99 budget provided the largest increases for higher education in more than twenty years, allowing major increases in student financial aid, fully funded enrollment growth in all three sectors, and doubled funding for outreach programs. Increases in outreach funding included more than $30 million for UC outreach programs and some $6 million for additional outreach programs for CSU. The community colleges also received significant general fund increases, as did the K–12 system. Governor Wilson vetoed $30 million budgeted for college-preparation programs at the K–12 level. The initial budget proposal of Governor Davis presented early in 1999 offered smaller increases in a number of higher education sectors, but it maintained a robust commitment to outreach and the improvement of transitions from K–12 schools to higher education. The legislature also continued its interest in supporting enhanced outreach and coordination. A number of bills introduced early in the 1999–2000 session offered support for intersectoral outreach and coordinating efforts.

New Approaches to Admissions Criteria

Despite the importance of Proposition 209 in shifting the political awareness of higher education in California and in awakening legislative interest in outreach, one could argue that its most lasting effect on California's higher education will be a reshaping of the construction of admissions criteria. As was the case with outreach, a number of factors, including publication of CPEC's eligibility report and the drop in minority enrollments, built legislative interest in the criteria shaping the eligibility requirements for UC and CSU. Perhaps the key contributor to legislative action on admissions criteria in California was passage by the Texas state legislature in early 1997 of House Bill 588, known as the Top 10 Percent Plan. The Texas plan, signed into law in May 1997, required public higher education institutions to consider eligible for admission all students who graduated in the top 10 percent of their high school class, regardless of performance on standardized tests (Chapa, 1999). (See Chapter 5 for more on the Texas plan.)

Shortly after passage of the Texas statute, Senator Teresa Hughes, chairwoman of the California senate's Select Committee on Higher Education Admissions and Outreach, began a campaign to provide similar guarantees in

California. The senator introduced a bill to amend the California constitution to make the top 12.5 percent of the graduating class from each high school automatically eligible for admission to UC. The bill would also have made the top one-third of the graduating class from each high school automatically eligible for admission to CSU.[7]

The issue of standardized tests as an obstacle to diversifying admissions also moved to the fore of the institutional and legislative debate. The role of standardized tests had earlier achieved prominence in California during the UC regents' debates over SP-1 and SP-2, and again when the sharp declines in minority student admissions to UC professional schools were announced. In August 1997, less than a year after passage of Proposition 209, the University of California Latino Eligibility Task Force (1997) added to the controversy with a report stating that "UC eligibility of Latino students can be greatly increased by eliminating the SAT. According to a simulation of eligibility relying only on Grade Point Average (GPA) requirements, without aptitude test scores, the proportion of Latino high school graduates achieving eligibility would rise by 59 percent (from 3.9 percent to 6.2 percent). Overall eligibility would also rise, but not as steeply, to 16.9 percent which is above the current master plan limit of 12.5 percent. However, the startling increase for Latinos illustrates the magnitude of the negative impact of the SAT on Latino student eligibility" (p. 18).

The suggestion that UC might move away from the SAT requirement engendered swift and polarized reaction. A number of regents questioned whether the university could maintain quality without standardized tests, and legislative and institutional leaders and representatives of the major testing services also weighed in publicly on the issue.

Throughout 1997, hearings were held in the senate and assembly to discuss standardized testing and test preparation, as well as various levels of admissions guarantees. Representatives from the three public higher education sectors, the California independent colleges and universities, K–12 institutions, CPEC, civil rights organizations, testing services, union organizations, and a wide variety of political leaders engaged policy questions that had long been the domain of the higher education institutions.

Legislative intervention on the issue of testing raised the stakes considerably, because the institutions themselves were divided on the issue. The chairman of UC's Latino Eligibility Task Force, Dean Eugene Garcia, suggested eliminating the SAT as a determinant of eligibility. Keith Widaman (1998), chair of UC's Board of Admissions and Relations with Schools (BOARS), argued for the SAT as a reasonably good predictor of UC applicants' success at the university. He also noted that under Master Plan guidelines, dropping the SAT would have little effect on the eligibility of under-represented groups. The lack of consensus on standardized testing returned legislative attention and institutional focus to guaranteed admissions. While Senator Hughes's "12.5 percent plan" initially garnered limited support in the capitol, an amended version offering guaranteed admissions to the top 4 percent attracted considerably more interest. The UC system was moving concurrently in the same direction.

In February 1998, Dr. Widaman, on behalf of UC BOARS, presented for the regents' consideration a program to guarantee admission to UC for students ranking in the top 4 percent of each high school in the state, a plan Widaman called "the most radical re-definition of eligibility criteria at the University of California in the last thirty years" (p. 103). Unlike Texas, where guaranteed admission was not tied to a distinct course sequence, for UC purposes the top 4 percent were to be drawn mainly from the ranks of those in each high school who completed UC's prerequisite course sequence. Although a number of regents initially expressed reservations about the 4 percent plan, the proposal received the endorsement of a key political actor on the board, Lieutenant Governor Gray Davis.

State Capitol Endorsements

As an ex officio regent in 1995, Lieutenant Governor Davis had voted to preserve affirmative action at UC, and he had also opposed Proposition 209. By the time the 4 percent plan was presented to the board of regents, Gray was a candidate for the Democratic party's nomination for governor. Over the next seven months he campaigned across the state on a platform laden with proposals for reform and improvement in California education. Davis included the 4 percent plan as one of his planks, and he stressed the need to improve the geographic distribution of students admitted to UC. Nearly one-third of the state's 863 high schools, disproportionately those in inner cities and in the state's Central Valley, sent few if any students to UC.

After Davis was elected governor in November 1998, he presided over a political summit quite different from the one he had witnessed as a regent in 1995. Davis brought together the newly elected lieutenant governor, the state superintendent of schools, the senate majority leader, and UC President Richard Atkinson for an announcement of his endorsement of a 4 percent plan for admissions to UC. The regents passed that plan in March 1999. Governor Davis also endorsed two other changes proposed to the regents by UC BOARS, one to deemphasize the impact of the SAT on campus admissions, the other to lower the influence of advanced-placement test scores.

Implications of the Changes in California's Access Policy

In the wake of the political struggles over access and diversity in California's higher education, a number of implications emerge that require further research and contemplation. Three in particular deserve increased attention: shifts in institutional autonomy in policymaking, increased resource allocation for outreach, and new methods for determining eligibility and admissions policy.

Regent Ward Connerly was the author of the regents' proposals SP-1 and SP-2 and a pivotal figure in the passage of Proposition 209. Before passage of the regents' proposals, he was aware of the risk of upsetting the decision-making balance between the university and the legislature. Connerly (1998) recalled a conversation with then UC President Jack Peltason before the votes. "Jack said, 'look, we've got a legislature to deal with that's really, that really has yes or no over our budget.' The code for everything that he was saying is that it's a Democratically controlled legislature, Willie Brown was the speaker, and John Vasconcellos was chairing the Budget Committee, and John took a real interest in the University. So Jack's concerns, legitimate concerns, were that, 'God, we're going to run into a buzz saw here,' and looking out for the best interests of the University, don't rock the boat."

With the luxury of hindsight, we can see that Connerly, while no stranger to California politics, misjudged the effect of Proposition 209 on higher education governance and policymaking. Like many others, Connerly apparently did not appreciate the degree to which SP-1 and SP-2 would shift the norms of governing board confirmations, nor did he or Governor Wilson suspect how quickly the political landscape would shift in the wake of Proposition 209. As the fund-raising chairman of the California Republican party in 1998, Connerly was at ground zero of the blast that hit the party in the November elections. Some of that electoral debacle should be attributed to a backlash against the Republicans' attacks on affirmative action.[8] The flurry of legislative hearings and bills on access, eligibility, and diversity, as well as the various legislative efforts to amend the constitution to remedy some of Proposition 209's effects, point to an increased legislative role in making higher education policy. In a similar fashion, Governor Davis's campaign for guaranteed admissions helped shift the UC regents' stance toward the 4 percent plan advocated by BOARS from initial caution to near unanimous support. Gubernatorial intervention, whether to ban affirmative action or remedy the effects of the ban, presents a continuing challenge to institutional leaders and planners.

Governor Davis's appointments to the governing boards of the three public higher education sectors will change the composition of those boards, though whether they (particularly the UC regents) will be less partisan or simply reflect a different partisan ideology remains to be seen. Governor Davis has served as both a CSU trustee and a UC regent, and he brings to the governor's mansion strong connections to the CSU system. And Barry Munitz, who served as director of the governor's transition team, is a former chancellor of the CSU system. Rebuilding the institutional-legislative working relationship has been a goal of state political and higher education leadership since the passage of Proposition 209. We have yet to see whether the emerging initiatives are harbingers of a new harmony or are a changing of the guard in a continuing interest-group struggle that will leave campus leaders increasingly beholden to the governor and the legislature.

Governor Davis also has an unprecedented opportunity to provide support for proposals and funding to increase outreach and partnerships between California's higher education and K–12 systems. He is likely to sign a number of outreach and partnership bills vetoed by Governor Wilson, and he may support comprehensive partnership bills that failed to achieve bipartisan support in earlier legislative sessions.

Despite the new legislative interest, significant obstacles to increasing access and diversity remain. The rapid increases in outreach funding since passage of Proposition 209 only begin to address the magnitude of the challenge, and signs already indicate that the impressive state revenue growth since 1995 will be considerably constrained over the next few years. Further, higher education institutions will have to compete with the K–12 system for funding and control of preparatory improvement, and such programs are presently at a low ebb. For 1996–97, California ranked forty-first in the nation in per-pupil spending at the K–12 level (EdSource, 1998). Despite Governor Davis's campaign pledges to improve the state's educational system, the situation is not likely to improve soon. As one long-time observer of the California political dynamic recently observed, "If California seemed to be a national model of high civic investment and engagement in the 1950s and 1960s, so it has become the lodestar of tax reduction and public dis-investment of the 1980s and 1990s" (Schrag, 1998, p. 275).

Although the attention generated by legislative hearings on the low rates of eligibility to the UC and CSU systems has spurred political and policy shifts, the task at hand, again, is enormous. The "radical" shift to a 4 percent admissions guarantee will initially lead to only minor increases in the number of underrepresented students at UC—by one estimate as little as 1 percent (Hamburg, 1998). It will have little impact on competition for spaces at UC Berkeley and UCLA, a contest that was central to the fight over SP-1 and SP-2. Further, improved eligibility rates may exacerbate the capacity crisis predicted for UC, which by some accounts will enroll sixty thousand new students by 2010 (Breneman, 1995; UCOP, 1999).

The degree of long-term popular support for efforts to increase outreach and eligibility for the educationally disadvantaged is also unclear. Near the end of the UC regents' tortuous deliberations over SP-1 and SP-2, Regent William Bagley offered a simple amendment that was incorporated into the initiatives despite resistance from Regent Connerly and Governor Wilson. It became the final paragraph of the regents' initiatives. "Believing California's diversity to be an asset, we adopt this statement: Because individual members of all of California's diverse races have the intelligence and capacity to succeed at the University of California, this policy will achieve a UC population that reflects this state's diversity through the preparation and empowerment of all students in this state to succeed, rather than through a system of artificial preferences" (University of California Office of the Secretary of the Regents, 1995, p. 3).

While the Bagley amendment has added legitimacy to UC's efforts to achieve diversity without using race or gender as criteria, no such proactive commitment was evident in the language of Proposition 209. Unknown as yet is whether the popular support and legislative action needed to pursue this sort of egalitarian effort throughout the higher education system will continue when the California economy slows.

Perhaps the most powerful finding to emerge in the aftermath of passage of Proposition 209 is that the racial/ethnic demographics of access and opportunity in California's higher education increasingly seem to bear little relation to the broader racial/ethnic demographics of the state. In 1970, 78 percent of the state's 20 million residents were white and 12 percent were Hispanic. By 1996, only 52 percent of the nearly 32 million residents were white and 30 percent were Hispanic (Schrag, 1998). Yet, in a state known for innovation and progress, a hallmark of its higher education sectors in the 1990s was the decreasing eligibility rates among the state's underrepresented minority students, and the most widely heralded electoral initiative of the 1990s was the elimination of affirmative action.

Just a decade ago, the report of a legislative committee reviewing the California Master Plan for higher education began this way: "Education has been the heart of California's productivity, the source of much of our inspiration, and the hope of our many and diverse peoples. Built on the commitments of generations of Californians, our schools, colleges, and universities offer a message of opportunity and freedom" (Joint Committee for Review of the Master Plan, 1989, p. i). Despite the promise inherent in this statement, emerging patterns of access and diversity in California's higher education offer faint hope to many of the state's diverse peoples. In the wake of Proposition 209, it is not clear whether initiatives to increase access and diversity are harbingers of a renewed commitment to an egalitarian higher education system or how much they will accomplish. What has become clear is how much remains to be done.

Notes

1. Interviews varied in length from forty-five minutes to nearly three hours.

2. The governor's advisory board on UC regent confirmations has had a desultory history; there is no evidence that it plays a significant role in nominations.

3. Underrepresentation occurs when the percentage of high school graduates from a particular racial/ethnic group eligible for admission to the CSU or UC system is below the state's average eligibility rate for all high school graduates for each system. In 1996, black, Latino, and Native American students were underrepresented at CSU, and Native American, African American, Chicano, and Latino students were underrepresented at UC.

4. The reporting categories *Chicano*, *Latino*, and *Hispanic* are used somewhat differently both across and within higher education institutions and agencies in California. Whenever possible, UC disaggregates *Chicano* and *Latino*, with *Chicano* referring to individuals whose families originated recently or historically in Mexico, and *Latino* to those whose families originated recently or historically in Central or South America or the Caribbean. However, on occasion UC has also aggregated individuals in these two groups under the broader category *Latino*. The California Postsecondary Education Commission uses the category *Latino* to encompass both *Chicano* and *Latino*, and the California Department of Education uses the category *Hispanic* to aggregate approximately the same two groups in reporting data for the K–12 system. Different systems and agencies also vary somewhat in applying the category labels *Asian* and *Asian American* and *black* and *African American,* and in use of the terms *Native American* and *American Indian.* In presenting data in this chapter, I maintain the categories and terms used in the original sources.

5. The decline in eligibility rates for admissions to CSU and UC from 1990 to 1996 was primarily due to increased course requirements.

6. Given the timing of the passage of SP-1 and SP-2 by the UC regents, the restriction on the use of race and gender in admissions took effect for graduate admissions in fall 1997 and for undergraduates in fall 1998.

7. The Hughes Bill, SCA 7, was introduced on February 28, 1997.

8. Governor Davis carried more than 75 percent of racial/ethnic minority vot-

ers; his opponent, Republican Dan Lungren, polled far fewer minority voters than he had in 1990 when he was elected attorney general.

References

Atkinson, R. C. (1996, November 6). *Letter from President Richard C. Atkinson to the University community re: passage of Proposition 209.* Oakland: University of California Office of the President.

Bagley, W. T. (1998, June 1). Interview by author. San Francisco.

Baldridge, J. V. (1971). *Power and conflict in the university: Research in the sociology of complex organizations.* New York: J. Wiley & Sons.

Berdahl, R. (1971). *Statewide coordination in higher education.* Washington, DC: American Council on Education.

Breneman, D. (1995). *Tidal wave II: An evaluation of enrollment projections for California higher education.* San Jose: California Higher Education Policy Center.

Cabaldon, C. (1997, November 18). Hearing transcript. Sacramento: California Senate Select Committee on Higher Education.

California Community College Chancellor's Office. (1999). *Management information services statistical library* [On-line]. Sacramento: Author [Producer and Distributor]. Available: http://misweb.cccco.edu/mis/statlib.htm

California Department of Education. (1999). *California basic educational data system, public school summary statistics* [On-line]. Sacramento: Author [Producer and Distributor]. Available: http://www.cde.ca.gov/demographics/reports/

California Postsecondary Education Commission. (1997, November 18). *Collaborative student academic development programs* [Hearing transcript]. Sacramento: Senate Select Committee on Higher Education Admissions and Outreach & Assembly Higher Education Committee.

California Postsecondary Education Commission. (1999). *Eligibility of California's 1996 high school graduates for admission to the state's public universities.* Sacramento: Author [Producer and Distributor].

California Senate Rules Committee. (1999). *Appointments archives* [On-line]. Sacramento: Author. Available: http://www.cpec.ca.gov/reports/96elig

California Senate Select Committee on Higher Education Admissions and Outreach. (1998, February 5). *Validating standardized testing: The role of the SAT and ACT in undergraduate admissions* [Hearing transcript]. Sacramento: Author.

California State University Office of the Chancellor. (1999). *Analytic studies statistical reports* [On-line]. Long Beach: Author [Producer and Distributor]. Available: http://www.co.calstate.edu/asd/Fsr.html

Chapa, J. (1999, January 14–16). *Hopwood effects and responses.* Paper presented to American Council on Education Research Conference, Washington, DC.

Chavez, L. (1998). *The color bind.* Berkeley: University of California Press.

Connerly, W. (1998, March 27). Interview by author. Sacramento.

del Junco, T. (1998, May 26). Interview by author. Los Angeles.

Douglass, J. A. (1992). Creating a fourth branch of state government: The University of California and the constitutional convention of 1879. *History of Education Quarterly, 32,* 31–71.

EdSource. (1998, November). *Expenditures per pupil: California and the U.S.* Palo Alto, CA: Author.

Ellis, V., & Frammolino, R. (1996, March 22). UC admissions code of ethics is proposed. *Los Angeles Times,* p. A3.

Fitzgibbon, R. H. (1968). *The academic senate of the University of California.* Oakland: University of California Office of the President.

Gardner, D. P. (1967). *The California oath controversy.* Berkeley: University of California Press.

Gladieux, L. E., and Wolanin, T. R. (1976). *Congress and the colleges: The national politics of higher education.* Lexington, MA: Lexington Books.

Gumport, P., & Pusser, B. (1997). Restructuring the academic environment. In M. Peterson, D. Dill, & L. Mets (Eds.), *Planning and management for a changing environment.* San Francisco: Jossey-Bass.

Hamburg, L. (1998, December 11). UC plan to broaden admissions wins key faculty endorsement. *San Francisco Chronicle,* p. A1.

Hammond, T. H., & Hill, J. S. (1993). Deference or preference? Explaining senate confirmation of presidential nominees. *Journal of Theoretical Politics, 5,* 23–59.

Hardy, C. (1990). Putting power into university governance. In J. C. Smart (Ed.), *Higher education: Handbook of theory and research.* New York: Agathon Press.

Hearn, J. C., & Griswold, C. (1994). State-level centralization and policy innovation in U.S. postsecondary education. *Educational Evaluation and Policy Analysis, 16*(2), 161–190.

Hughes, T. P. (1998, February 5). *Validating standardized testing: The role of the SAT and ACT in undergraduate admissions.* Background paper, California Senate Select Committee on Higher Education Admissions and Outreach. Sacramento: Author.

Joint Committee for Review of the Master Plan for Higher Education. (1989, March). *California faces California's future, final report.* Sacramento: Author.

Jones, G. A., & Skolnik, M. L. (1997). Governing boards in Canadian universities. *Review of Higher Education, 20*(3), 277–295.

Kamena, S. (1995, October). *Berkeley Counterpoint,* pp. 1–3.

Karabel, J. (1996, February 20). *University governance and the crisis at UC* [Hearing transcript]. Sacramento: California State Senate Select Committee on Higher Education.

Kerr, C., & Gade, M. L. (1989). *The guardians: Boards of trustees of American colleges and universities.* Washington, DC: Association of Governing Boards of Colleges and Universities.

Kingdon, J. W. (1984). *Agendas, alternatives, and public policies.* Boston: Little, Brown.

Lockyer, W. (1997, June 23). Hearing transcript. Sacramento: California State Senate Rules Committee.

Masten, S. E. (1995). Old school ties: Financial aid coordination and the governance of higher education. *Journal of Economic Behavior and Organizations, 28,* 23–47.

McCubbins, M. D., Noll, R. G., & Weingast, B. R. (1987). Administrative procedures as instruments of political control. *Journal of Law, Economics and Organization, 3,* 243–277.

Millett, J. D. (1984). *Conflict in higher education: State government coordination versus institutional independence.* San Francisco: Jossey-Bass.

Moe, T. M. (1995). The politics of structural choice: Toward a theory of public bureaucracy. In O. Williamson (Ed.), *Organization theory: From Chester Barnard to the present and beyond.* Oxford: Oxford University Press.

Peterson, M. W. (1996). Images of university structure, governance and leadership: Adaptive strategies for the new environment. In D. Dill & B. Sporn (Eds.), *Emerging patterns of social demand and university reform: Through a glass darkly.* Oxford: Pergamon Press.

Poole, K. T., & Rosenthal, H. (1987). Analysis of congressional coalition patterns: A unidimensional spatial model. *Legislative Studies Quarterly, 12,* 55–76.

Pusser, B. (1999). *The contest over affirmative action at the University of California: Theory and politics of contemporary higher education politics.* Unpublished doctoral dissertation, Stanford University.

Pusser, B., & Ordorika, I. (2000). Bringing political theory to university governance: the University of California and the Universidad Nacional Autónoma de México. In N. P. Stromquist (Ed.), *Higher education: Handbook of theory and research.* New York: Agathon Press.

Regents of the University of California. (1999, January 15). *Minutes.* Oakland: Author.

Rhoades, G. L. (1992). Beyond "the state": Inter-organizational relations and state apparatus in post-secondary education. In J. C. Smart (Ed.), *Higher education: Handbook of theory and research.* New York: Agathon Press.

Rice, C. (in press). *Affirmative action in the post–Proposition 209 era.* Washington, DC: American Council on Education.

Schrag, P. (1998). *Paradise lost: California's experience, America's future.* New York: New Press.

Slaughter, S. (1993). Retrenchment in the 1980s: The politics of prestige and gender. *Journal of Higher Education, 64,* 250–282.

Slaughter, S., & Leslie, L. L. (1997). *Academic capitalism.* Baltimore: Johns Hopkins University Press.

Stadtman, V. (1970). *The University of California 1868–1968.* New York: McGraw Hill.

Trombley, W. (1995). *Ambitious reform agenda: Restructuring in Virginia higher education* (CrossTalk Vol. 3, No. 3). San Jose, CA: National Center for Public Policy and Higher Education.

University of California Latino Eligibility Task Force. (1997, July). *Latino student eligibility and participation in the University of California. ¡YA BASTA!* Oakland: Author.

University of California Office of the President. (1997, July). New directions for outreach: Report of the University of California Outreach Task Force. Oakland: Author.

University of California Office of the President. (1998). *Campus admissions office, OA & SA files.* Oakland: Author.

University of California Office of the President. (1999, February 22). UC prepares for growing enrollments. *Office of the President News* (Oakland).

University of California Office of the Secretary of the Regents. (1995, July 12). *Regents SP-1.* Oakland: Author.

Vasconcellos, J. (1995, July 21). *Letter to the University of California regents.* Oakland: Author.

Weingast, B. R., & Marshall, W. J. (1988). The industrial organization of congress; or, why legislatures, like firms, are not organized as markets. *Journal of Political Economy, 96,* 132–163.

Widaman, K. (1998, February 5). Hearing transcript. Sacramento: Senate Select Committee on Higher Education Admissions and Outreach.

Wilson, J. Q. (1989). *Bureaucracy: What government agencies do and why they do it.* New York: Basic Books.

Young, C. E. (1998, May 19). Interview by author. San Jose, CA.

Zusman, A. 1986. Legislature and university conflict: The case of California. *Review of Higher Education, 9,* 397–418.

III   ACCOUNTABILITY

7 Public Policy and Accountability in Higher Education: Lessons from the Past and Present for the New Millennium

WILLIAM ZUMETA

Accountability is a word not usually associated with academic endeavors, which have generally been thought of as necessarily freewheeling and unconstrained. Indeed, for much of their history in the United States, public academic institutions were treated with unusual deference by their state sponsors, who were often content to "leave the money on the stump" with few questions asked (Trow, 1993). Elected officials and those who worked for them were frequently perplexed and even intimidated by the "learned men" of academe and their doings and by their claims of a special need for autonomy and academic freedom. Thus, the officers of the state were usually deferential. When they concerned themselves with higher education, it was mostly with rather traditional political matters such as allocation of enrollments, tuition rates, location of campuses, and the size of capital budgets.[1]

Similarly, with the notable exception of the Morrill Act land grants to the states in 1862, the federal government (unlike most national governments in the developed world) paid little attention to higher education until World War II and its aftermath. Even in the Morrill Act, the federal government did little to control how the grants were used, and in its post–World War II forays into large-scale research funding and student aid, it imposed remarkably few conditions on the institutions. Indeed, in debates on the initial terms for providing major federal financing for research and student aid, a central notion was that government should, as much as possible, leave institutions' core academic functions alone (Keppel, 1987; Trow, 1993). In short, higher education had the respect and trust of government officials, and academic institutions were thought to function best when granted substantial autonomy.

The picture is much different today. Public universities and colleges face unprecedented external demands. Plainly, the halcyon days of academic autonomy were left behind after World War II as higher education grew in social and economic importance and in its budgetary impact. In the late 1990s, however, we seem to be witnessing the initial phases of a sharp, historically significant ramp-up in the degree of government involvement in academic matters. In the name of greater accountability to taxpayers and their representatives, public universities and colleges not only are being asked to provide more data about their operations and the results achieved ("outcomes" in the current jargon), but in an increasing number of states are also finding some of their state appropriations linked to measured performance on the state's list of priorities (Burke & Serban, 1997, 1998). Significantly, these priorities no longer are limited to the number of students enrolled or to tuition policy, but range well into the traditional realm of academic decision making.[2] In some cases, states have mandated "efficiency" or performance goals such as improving graduation rates, increasing faculty time in teaching undergraduates, raising transfer rates between community colleges and four-year institutions, and showing improvements in graduates' scores on standardized tests of learning (Burke, 1997b).

This shift in states' expectations of and relations with colleges and universities is significant not only for academe's own interests but, as I seek to show in this chapter, for important societal values. The historic shift also highlights the general problem of *democratic accountability* of academic institutions: public colleges and universities are legally creatures of the state and are substantially supported by tax revenues, but they differ from other state-funded sectors such as state prisons or highway departments. Virtually all would agree that they function best when given some autonomy from direct state control, but how much autonomy and how to assure an appropriate balance between autonomy and accountability to the public's elected representatives are complex questions, answered differently in various periods of American history.

Here I survey some critical aspects of this history, with the primary goals of shedding light on the special features of the present era and suggesting key desiderata for a constructive and workable new balance of autonomy and accountability. My basic argument is that the present context is historically different: more explicit accountability is required from public higher education than in the past, but a long experience with the relation of higher education to its state sponsors is embodied in valuable principles and institutional structures that should not be lightly discarded. Rather, we will be best served by building upon the principles and structures that have evolved over the years.

The chapter begins with an explanation of the recent origins of the increased accountability demands on higher education and shows how these demands are linked to current expectations for other publicly funded activities and current practices in the business sector. I then present a historical sketch of American approaches to the problem of democratic accountability of public higher education and consider how historically evolved ideas and institutions now operate. I argue that these mechanisms are less able to secure accustomed levels of academic autonomy than in the past. A survey of states' recent accountability initiatives provides a concrete sense of the issues currently at stake.[3] Profiles of recent steps and their associated experiences in several states seem to suggest broader lessons.

Finally, having concluded that the current era presents academe with some new, irresistible, and, in an important democratic sense, politically legitimate demands for accountability, I offer some building blocks for a contemporary synthesis of concepts of academic autonomy and accountability that provide some hope of meeting current demands while preserving what is crucial about academic autonomy. This discussion is the centerpiece of the essay.

Origins of Demands for Heightened Accountability in Higher Education

Higher education has faced gradually increasing scrutiny from government since World War II, but a clear increment in this scrutiny occurred in the 1990s. Much of the explanation lies in economics. The economic pressures brought about by rapid technological change and globalization have led to extensive corporate downsizing and firms' closer attention to costs, both in their own enterprises and in public sector enterprises supported by their taxes. These pressures have also caused business leaders to pay more attention to education and its products since education is increasingly seen as the key to business and economic competitiveness (Marshall & Tucker, 1992). Thus, business leaders have applied pressure to universities, directly and through the political process, to "streamline their production processes" as they themselves have done. Business leaders want educational institutions to pay more attention to quality control, customer satisfaction, and other "outcomes" of their activities. In short, private sector management ideas have permeated the public sector, and a large quasi-governmental function such as public higher education could not expect to be exempt from this trend.[4]

Extreme financial pressures on states during the economic slowdown of the early 1990s were followed closely by the mid-decade tax revolt and Republican electoral ascendancy. The resulting squeeze on public spending has led state policymakers to look especially closely at higher education. Certainly, any large, state-supported function would be subject to scrutiny in such circumstances, but higher education has some special vulnerabilities, a key one being built into the structure of state budgets. Other major functions supported by states' general funds—in order of proportion of the general-fund total nationwide: elementary and secondary education, Medicaid, corrections, and welfare—are driven either by federal or judicial mandates not subject to much state budgetary control or by caseload demands that are nearly impossible to resist.[5] (See Chapter 2 for more on state budget spending for different priorities.)

In higher education, by contrast, "caseloads" (enrollments) are regarded as discretionary and thus subject to postponement when state finances are tight. Higher education is also seen as uniquely able to mitigate the effects of budget cuts by tapping other sources of revenue such as tuition increases, grants, and private donations. Thus, higher education experienced three years of absolute decreases in state appropriations during the economic slowdown of the early 1990s, and the more recent recovery in its state funding occurred more slowly than in past periods of prosperity, evidently owing to the ascendancy of fiscal conservatism in most state capitals (Zumeta & Fawcett-Long, 1997). Truly drastic budget cuts may be in store when the next recession arrives, because demands from the other major state-supported functions tend to grow during economic slumps.[6]

Several other factors are pushing policymakers to look more closely at how higher education operates and why it costs so much. Partly in response to weaker state support, public colleges and universities have been raising their charges to students (in real terms) for many years.[7] While tuition levels remain far below those of private institutions—whose generally more affluent clientele have been helped by bullish stock market growth, growth in the availability of federal student loans, and sophisticated, though little understood, price discounting schemes—the growth in public college prices, greatly in excess of the growth in typical middle- and working-class incomes, has not gone unnoticed. Public opinion data show that citizens are more concerned than ever about assuring access to higher education, which they see as essential in the modern economy, but are resistant to paying much more for education in tuitions or taxes. Their responses indicate a desire for institutions to become more efficient.[8]

Thus, in the last few years, governors and legislators have pressed public colleges and universities to hold the line on tuition and have become more inclined to tell them how this might be achieved through internal efficiency measures—since elected officials are unwilling to appropriate more state funds. Policymakers in many states are also very concerned about the fiscal implications of the maturing of the "baby boom echo" generation of potential college students. Numbers of high school graduates are projected to grow more than 20 percent in sixteen states and more than 10 percent in fifteen more in the next decade (Western Interstate Commission on Higher Education & College Board, 1998). Large increases are expected in as many eastern as western states, and the ten-year gains are estimated at more than 50 percent in populous California and Florida and ranging up to 80 percent in

Nevada. This represents a substantial and potentially costly pressure on states' higher education capacity, given that many of these high-growth states are already at or near the limits of their current facilities, at least using current assumptions about capacity. Thus, absent drastic efficiency measures, more students mean high costs for expansion.

Finally, higher education seems a particularly inviting target to many in power today. A tension has always existed between some of academe's values and pursuits and the populist strains in American politics (Hofstadter, 1963), most notable in recent times in the McCarthy era and the Vietnam War period. But generally, American politicians have been remarkably little inclined to involve themselves in the operations of academe in any systematic way, even as the enterprise has grown quite large and costly. Now, though, what might be termed *cultural critiques* of higher education seem to mesh neatly with fiscal pressures and broader political forces to facilitate public officials' criticisms of higher education and, by extension, to exert pressure on higher education to toe a line closer to the desires of elected officials. In the last decade or so, we have seen an unusual number and intensity of published critiques of the fundamental values and practices of modern higher education. Critics, including some insiders, have excoriated universities for setting weak academic standards; for bending too far to embrace multiculturalism in the academic canon and in discourse (termed "political correctness"); for unfairly accepting allegedly ill-qualified minority students over better qualified others in the name of affirmative action; for neglecting undergraduates in favor of sometimes esoteric research and an apparent excess production of PhDs; for permitting faculty workloads perceived to be light, unbalanced (away from undergraduate teaching), and generally unmonitored; and for administrative bloat.[9]

Adding to higher education's problems with the public's, and particularly elected officials', perceptions has been a stream of press reports about abuses: the charging of costs to government grants; end runs around established peer-review processes in the pursuit of research and capital grants; and numerous reported instances of misconduct by scientists in reporting research results, including cases of apparent conflicts of interest in industry-supported research. This broad litany of criticisms meshes with the efficiency and effectiveness concerns that are part of the new accountability thrust and may well make legislators less willing to abide by traditional norms of academic autonomy vis-à-vis government. Some particulars resonate with certain legislative critics, other particulars with other critics, but together they provide significant ammunition for those who conclude that public higher education's priorities and values are out of line with the values of those who pay much of the bill.

Accountability in Higher Education: Historical Overview

Public colleges and universities are creatures of the state and, ultimately, of the people who pay taxes to support them. Over time, the United States has evolved structures for managing the delicate problem of academic accountability in the democratic context. In thinking about current problems and possibilities, we need to understand both what we are building upon and how it might match present needs and demands. In general, the problem of academic accountability is a difficult one, perhaps especially for a democracy with high aspirations for higher education and populist tendencies—not to mention current problems of constrained public resources. Defining accountability and balancing this appropriately with academic autonomy probably cannot be accomplished once for all time. As with other social and political arrangements, periodically it may be necessary to redefine terms, rewrite social contracts, and rework institutional arrangements as circumstances and expectations change. The present may be such a time, but to appreciate this we first need to understand the major features of the American experience with public governance of higher education.

As in many other countries, accountability issues in the United States were for a long time related more to higher education's relations with the church than those with the state. The religiously oriented colleges of the colonial era and the early nineteenth century had state charters, often had legislative appointees on their boards, and episodically received state funds, usually for endowments and buildings, but they were more likely to be called to account by churchmen concerned about doctrinal rectitude or student behavior than by elected officials (Trow, 1993). However, much changed after 1819 when the state of New Hampshire sought to enforce substantial changes in direction at state-chartered Dartmouth College, and the trustees resisted; this led to a U.S. Supreme Court decision affirming the college's autonomy from the state under the rather broad terms of its charter. Such schools as Dartmouth, Harvard, and the College of New Jersey (Princeton), though state-chartered and earlier supported by the state, evolved toward what we now call private colleges and universities. After the *Dartmouth* case, as states became more interested in expanding opportunities for higher education— particularly after the Morrill Act land grants to the states for this purpose in 1862—they saw virtue in creating institutions that were more clearly state-controlled, what we now call public colleges and universities.

Yet, by and large, states did not generally involve themselves deeply in the affairs of their academic creations. They were normally satisfied to let academics decide most policy matters about what to teach and study, who was qualified to teach and enroll, how many courses to require for a degree, and how the academic enterprise was organized. Institutions did not always get all the state money they sought, but this was more a constraint on their overall rate of growth than an excuse for state inroads into internal decision making (e.g., by reducing or eliminating individual programs or mandating heavier faculty teaching assignments to reduce costs).[10]

Why did legislators and governors leave the internal workings of these public institutions largely alone for much of their history? Early on, political leaders tended to be somewhat in awe of highly educated men. They were very proud of their state's collegiate creations and eager to see them develop and achieve greatness—at least as much greatness as those of neighboring states—and they saw them as engines of economic and social development to be encouraged rather than highly regulated. In short, they *trusted* academic leaders to lead the schools in the broad directions both parties wanted to go. Moreover, most state governments had little capacity for more than occasional, fairly limited involvement in academic affairs (e.g., aiding the admission of a well-connected student or pushing for creation of a new law school or medical school) or for serious critical oversight, even had they been so inclined.

There was also some awareness of the dangers of political interference with what would now be called academic freedom. The concept of the academy as a "marketplace of ideas" has a very American ring. Academic freedom does not fit well into a governance regime that lacks substantial institutional autonomy from government. States expected the land-grant institutions to serve state needs in agriculture and other "practical arts," as the Morrill Act called for, but beyond this broad mission, many recognized that if a university were to be first-rate intellectually and open to new ideas, it needed considerable latitude from its state sponsors. Influences from Europe, particularly from the emerging German research-oriented universities, played an important role in refining, elaborating, and strengthening earlier ideas about academic freedom and institutional autonomy (Veysey, 1965). The Universities of California and Michigan, perhaps the most distinguished American public universities today, in the mid-nineteenth century were given an autonomy explicitly recognized in the state constitutions (Glenny & Dalglish, 1973). Many other public institutions bore with more detailed direction from their state sponsors, but California and Michigan set an important standard.

Role of the Lay Board of Trustees

Another reason why state leaders were willing to keep some distance (most of the time) from their academic creations lay in the respect accorded to an important American invention in higher education: the lay board of trustees. The idea of appointing leading citizens who were not academics as the legal governing body for an academic institution dates back to the colonial era and is at variance with European guildlike traditions of faculty control. Before any clear distinction between private and public institutions, many college boards were an amalgam of legislative appointees (who might include legislators), churchmen, and other leading citizens who had initially formed the college and sought its charter from the state (Trow, 1993). As the private and public sectors of higher education went their separate ways after *Dartmouth,* private boards no longer included legislative appointees, and public institutions' boards could be appointed by the governor or by the governor and the legislature or even elected by the state citizenry (Glenny & Dalglish, 1973). A mechanism thus existed for ensuring some accountability of the academic enterprise to lay judgment and the public will through elections, whether directly or indirectly. To be sure, board members were generally among the more educated of the citizenry and had to accept their responsibility as volunteers, and thus most were favorably disposed toward higher education—a disposition that the institutions' leaders sought to reinforce wherever possible.

Thus, lay governing boards have tended to provide a benevolent and generally not very intrusive oversight of their charges. The experiences of thousands of institutions over more than two centuries vary, of course, but the boards have tended to focus on providing their charges with political and fund-raising support, have taken some interest in the "business side" of the institutions (an area in which laymen feel they have most expertise), and have attended fairly closely to the hiring and oversight of presidents. This last is clearly a necessary and potentially potent governance function, but boards have generally delegated broad authority to the president, once hired, for the president is the school's chief academic and is the logical liaison with the faculty, who carry on its primary academic business. Presidents are on occasion fired or eased out for poor performance or corruption by trustees. The arrangement has been similar in many ways to the traditional relationship of corporate boards of directors to their chief executives, except that the chief academic executive is less likely to influence board appointments and senior members of academic administrations do not normally sit on the board. Thus, the academic boards have been, if anything, more independent of the administration than are many corporate boards.

Only recently has this traditional pattern begun to change significantly (Association of Governing Boards, 1998). Boards of trustees have sometimes been criticized for being too pliant and unwilling to ask difficult questions about academic policy matters in a time of constrained resources. Now they are more prone to question administrators about issues at the intersection of academic and fiscal policy, such as whether new buildings or proposed new programs (or all academic programs now offered) are really necessary, and even whether tenure arrangements should be rethought to ensure adequate flexibility in an era of limited funds and rapid changes in demands. Some are showing interest in the same types of efficiency and performance indicators advocated by states.[11] This is not surprising, given that many trustees are from business backgrounds where these concepts are now pervasive.

Beyond this "natural" development, recently some governors have moved aggressively to appoint ideological allies to the boards of trustees, appointees who may push for drastic internal restructuring, cost cutting, and a rather simplistic quantification of outcomes (Healy, 1997; Magner, 1999). If many trustee appointments become politicized and boards get very aggressive in their demands for "more efficient" academic management, we could see great pressure not only on administrative functions but also on traditional forms of academic organization, personnel and curricular decision making, and resource allocation, with the faculty's role substantially circumscribed (Miller, 1998; Richardson, 1999; Stimpson, 1998). Direct threats to academic freedom are also possible (Healy & Schmidt, 1998).

Although this somewhat extreme scenario is not yet apparent in most states, the lay board of trustees composed of leading citizens and business people will most likely provide a less robust defense of academic autonomy than in the past, simply because these cadres of society feel less deferential to academe in an era of widespread emphasis on organizational efficiency and "quality management." Business leaders believe their experiences in managing large enterprises are relevant to the governance of the institutions on whose boards they serve. Moreover, at a time of more intense political and ideological partisanship than in much of U.S. history, appointed trustees may feel, or be pressured to feel, more loyalty to the agendas of the elected officials who appointed them. Finally, of no small significance is business and government leaders' recognition of education, at both the elementary and secondary and the college levels, as more important than ever to the economy. Many see education as "too important to be left to educators," who may be seen as self-serving, complacent, and unresponsive to modern realities. Trustee appointees may increasingly reflect such attitudes.

Role of State Higher Education Boards

Another American innovation that has traditionally buffered higher education against the political and other demands of the state is the citizen state higher education board. After World War II, when demand for and public spending on higher education grew dramatically, the academic enterprise attracted a good deal more attention from state leaders. As states tried to respond to the burgeoning demand for enrollment in the 1950s and 1960s, many found themselves poorly equipped to plan rationally and efficiently for expansion of their public higher education systems. Indeed, the word *system* is a misnomer since institutions generally operated quite independently and expansion efforts tended to be driven more by the aspirations of individual institutions and the efforts of district-based politicians and local boosters than by any systematic state planning (Berdahl, 1971; Glenny, 1959). Largely to avoid some of the potentially ruinous costs and obvious inefficiencies caused by politically driven expansion, the states, in rapid succession, developed what proved to be a significant addition to the higher education policy arena: the state higher education board or commission. This board was to plan for, rationalize, and generally oversee the expansion of public higher education (Berdahl, 1971).

Various structural mechanisms for performing these functions were tried and indeed remain today. The two major forms of state-level governance of higher education are (1) state *coordinating boards*, which seek to mesh the efforts of separate institutions or multicampus systems using only limited powers beyond data collection, planning and analysis, and access to institution and state policymakers for purposes of persuasion (e.g., California, Illinois, Washington); and (2) state *governing boards*, with line management authority over all public institutions in the state, functioning as a "super" board of trustees (e.g., North Carolina, Wisconsin).[12] The primary aim in either case is to rationalize the efforts of the individual campuses. Although assessments of the overall effectiveness and efficiency of the different arrangements vary, both types do serve to buffer the institutions and their decisions against the unfiltered scrutiny—and the potential for politically or ideologically motivated interference—of the legislature, governor, and state budget officials.

These state higher education boards are composed entirely or mostly of citizens not directly affiliated with the institutions, and they traditionally have been chaired by a leading citizen with an established interest in higher education. As with individual institution boards, citizens who seek state board appointments (usually made by the governor) are likely to have an interest in and some knowledge of the higher education field; they have been, broadly speaking, more supporters than critics of the enterprise they oversee. The boards are served by a usually influential staff cadre, led by senior executives with PhDs and some knowledge and credibility in academic matters and higher education policymaking. Many senior staff members have faculty and university administrative experience. The influence of this staff group, filtered to a varying extent through the citizen board, thus tends to impart considerably more rational planning, continuity, and policy analysis to state policymaking than would strictly legislative direction, and it has less potential for troublesome micromanagement, which could threaten managerial efficiency and perhaps academic freedom as well. Yet, it also provides some expert perspective independent of an institution's administration, potentially serving as both a safeguard for autonomy and a useful mechanism for accountability to the legislature and the citizenry.

Relationships between these citizen higher education boards and state policymakers are complex and difficult to characterize. Although the boards have long been seen as primarily institution-dominated—some originated as coordinating bodies of institutional representatives—this is by no means always the case. These bodies, especially the coordinating boards (the agency type, which lacks line management authority), occupy a rather precarious position with heavy responsibilities, conflicting expectations from their institution and state constituencies, and limited resources other than whatever strategic analysis and persuasive abilities their incumbents may possess.[13] Board and executive turnover is high, and reorganizations of board structures and powers are fairly common as an agency is identified either (by state officials) as too close to the institutions or (by some in the higher education community, who carry their complaints to elected officials) as too hard on or too biased toward certain institutions. Most important in the present context, a determined governor or legislative majority usually has the necessary powers—in particular, appointive powers and control over the agency's budget and ultimately its existence—to bend a higher education board to its wishes, although these powers have not often been assertively and persistently used in this way. Thus, the traditional buffering role of state higher education boards, like that of trustees, seems to be weakening. Increasingly, the boards are being used as instruments in states' efforts to enforce more business-like accountability standards on institutions. Still, the higher education community is likely to have more influence in states where the state board plays a leading role in an accountability regime than in those where elected officials dominate directly (empirical evidence for this is presented in the next section).

In summary, in the United States we have established several mechanisms for filtering state-elected officials' wishes about what should be done in higher education, and how it should be done. Early reticence by state leaders to involve themselves in higher education policy has been replaced by a greater salience and concern, as the economic and social importance of higher education grows, state government's capacity for data collection and analysis increases, and elected and appointed officials with a college or more education show less deference toward or trust in the learned souls of the academy. Much of this shift in attitudes has been gradual, with the pace picking up noticeably in the 1960s and then again in the late 1980s and the 1990s as data-processing capabilities surged forward and economic changes induced more widespread concern with efficiency, performance, and their measurement. Because these concerns are so pervasive and because determined state leaders hold the trump cards in terms of ability to influence oversight boards and their values, the traditional structural sources of protection for academic autonomy are now considerably weakened. Circumstances in individual states, such as a strong state economy, a governor with other policy priorities, or particularly skillful institutional or board leaders, may temporarily blunt the pressures for more narrowly conceived efficiency and performance measurement, but a significant reversal in the near future seems unlikely.

This is the environment in which public higher education finds itself today. The public and those it employs to make policy decisions expect higher education to be efficient and accountable for its spending and its outcomes. Policymakers are no longer hesitant to advance proposals for ensuring such results. If the academic community is not to be forced to operate under regimes devised entirely by others—in other words, if it is to retain some autonomy—it must join the debate and the search for sensible, balanced indicators of, and arrangements to ensure mutually acceptable visions of, efficiency, quality, responsiveness, and accountability. In short, if the academy is to retain much control of its destiny, it must seek a new balance between the concepts of academic autonomy and democratic accountability that recognizes the realignment of forces and priorities in higher education's political environment. This does not mean that older ideas and arrangements are irrelevant, but new thinking about how to make them work in the present context is clearly necessary.

Recent Accountability Initiatives

Recently, ideas about appropriate accountability of higher education to government and the public have moved beyond the traditional reliance on delegation to the judgment of specialized citizen oversight bodies (though these remain in the picture) to a focus on "objective" information and explicit financial incentives. For several years in the 1980s and early 1990s, the main emphasis in state accountability policy was on information: increased reporting of data on institutional operations and results to state agencies, the legislature, and the public, in what was often called an institutional "report card" (Ruppert, 1994).[14] Although much of this continues, policymakers have generally been unsatisfied that reporting alone leads institutions to *fully* accountable behavior, that is, to changes in their operations to produce what the overseers consider improved performance.

In the last few years, therefore, the stakes have been raised: public colleges' and universities' state budget allocations have been related in some fashion to their performance on accountability measures. Explicit linkage of state dollars to measured performance on specific indicators is termed *incentive funding*, or more commonly, *performance funding*.[15] Note that it implies a greater role for policymakers outside the higher education board–institution nexus, such as the governor, executive budget office, and legislature, since these actors either specify the measures employed or can readily use them in attempts to directly influence institutions' priorities and behavior. Previously, as described above, states had typically depended much more on the good judgment of citizen trustees and higher education boards to monitor institutions' activities in the broad public interest. State dollars for public higher education were usually linked to very broad aggregates, such as enrollments, expected ratios of faculty to students, and price indices for library books, staff salaries, and the like.[16] These traditional budget drivers remain, but they are being supplemented by much narrower indicators that state policymakers consider more indicative of efficiency or desired *outcomes*, or both.

Recent national surveys give a good picture of the scope of accountability reporting in higher education and the use of performance-based funding approaches in particular. From a 1997 survey of states' higher education agency heads, Melodie Christal (1998) found that 37 states reported using performance measures in higher education policymaking, and 23 reported using them in the budgetary process. Eight of the latter 23 states reported a direct linkage between an institution's "score" on performance measures and part of its state budgetary allocation (performance funding, as defined earlier). In 23 of the 37 states, performance measures were mandated by legislation; and 16 of the 23 states using performance measures in budgeting were following a legislative mandate.

Using slightly different definitions and a survey conducted in mid-1998, Joseph Burke and Andreea Serban (1998) identified 26 states that used performance indicators in the state budgeting process for higher education, including 13 that used performance funding. These figures were up noticeably from a similar 1997 survey by these authors, in which 16 states were using performance budgeting and 10 performance funding.[17] Significantly, Burke and Serban's respondents in 12 of the 13 performance-funding states in 1998 said this budgeting approach was likely to continue, and respondents in an additional 12 states said that adoption of performance funding within the next five years was likely or highly likely in their state. So, performance funding—the explicit linking of state funds to college and university performance on specified measures—appears to be the leading edge of the movement for greater accountability, was in place in about a dozen states by the end of the 1990s, and seems likely to spread to a substantial additional group in the near future.[18]

Burke and Serban's studies show that most states using performance funding do not at this point tie a large share of their higher education budget strictly to performance measures. The proportion ranges from less than 1 percent to as high as about 4 percent in Tennessee (and perhaps somewhat more in South Carolina). Because most states have not used performance funding for long, there is no definitive evidence that the proportion of funding linked to performance necessarily increases over time, but the survey respondents tended to believe that it would increase in the future (Serban, 1997, p. 13).[19] Also, even the current small percentages represent a much larger fraction of the *incremental* annual funding provided to colleges and universities, so the small aggregate proportions are somewhat misleading. Given the pressures on institutions' overall budgets described earlier in this chapter, the amounts seem large enough to get the attention of academics and are likely to influence behavior if the arrangements persist. Of special interest is South Carolina, where legislation passed in 1996 mandates that, by 2000, the *entire* state allocation to higher education will be driven by thirty-seven performance measures (Schmidt, 1996). This experiment is being watched with considerable interest elsewhere (Schmidt, 1997; Trombley, 1998). If the results are found satisfactory, this will almost certainly provide impetus for expansion of performance-funding components in state budgeting arrangements for higher education elsewhere. (South Carolina's performance-funding effort is described later in the chapter.)

Measures of Accountability

Burke and Serban have done extensive research on the measures of accountability used in states employing performance funding (Burke, 1997a, b; Burke & Serban, 1997; Serban, 1997),[20] and they have provided a taxonomy of measures that illuminates what is actually going on (Burke, 1997, pp. 35–36). The taxonomy distinguishes *input, process, output,* and *outcome* measures. To summarize briefly, the rhetoric of the current accountability and quality-improvement movement in business, government, and higher education calls for a refocusing of attention, particularly in resource allocation, on *outcomes* of activities or programs, ideally in relation to explicit goals, rather than the traditional focus on *inputs* (Osborne & Gaebler, 1992). Thus, policymakers are urged to link resources to—and so direct institutions' attention to—matters such as whether students graduate, how much they learn, and how they are received by the outside world (outcomes), rather than strictly to counts such as how many students are enrolled and how many books are in the library (inputs). Not surprisingly, Burke found that only 13 percent of the indicators used in the performance-funding states fall in the input category; but more surprising was the finding that only 18 percent could be classified as outcome measures.[21] A slightly higher percentage of the measures (21%) were classified as *output* indicators—for example, numbers of graduates, counts of publications, sponsored research funds secured, planning targets achieved, and the like—which are usually thought of as measures of volume of activity plausibly related to desirable outcomes, although the link is often tenuous in the absence of verification.[22]

The largest share (42%) of the indicators used to drive state funding in the eight performance-funding states are, in Burke's classification, *process* indicators. Process measures provide an indication of *how* resources are allocated, not how much is produced (output) or the social value of the output (outcomes). Many of these process measures are old standbys in higher education budgeting, such as measures of faculty teaching loads, various measures of class size (e.g., average class size, proportion of full-time faculty teaching undergraduates, proportion of very large classes), and counts of institutions' cooperative efforts. Popular process measures of more recent vintage include proportion of courses or of faculty using new technologies and measures of whether student learning is formally assessed beyond the classroom setting (e.g., by standardized tests). Within the context of the accountability and quality-improvement logic, at least some of these process indicators are seen as proxies for difficult-to-measure outcomes, and often as provisional until better ways can be devised to assess outcomes (e.g., a measure of whether increased use of technology in classes produces superior educational results). Sometimes they are seen simply as indications of the use of "best practices," at least best in the view of state-level policymakers. In fact, most of the process indicators identified by Burke are efficiency-oriented in a quite narrow sense—teaching load, average class size, program "duplication" indicators—although some appear to reflect notions about quality improvement (e.g., whether the institution provides for independent assessment of student learning and whether it has a process for reviewing the performance of tenured faculty).

In Burke's view, the substantial focus on process and output measures (63% of all the measures identified fell in these two categories) reflects both states' demands for indicators that are readily measurable and understandable for budget decision making and business and government's focus on apparent quality and "best practices" when outcomes are difficult to measure. Yet, as the obvious limitations of some measures suggest, these foci are not necessarily always consistent with strategies to improve outcomes across the full range of institutional purposes, which include graduate education and research, intellectual innovation, independent social criticism, excellence in artistic endeavors, and so forth, not just educating undergraduates.

According to Burke's (1997a) report, the most common performance indicator across the eight performance-funding states was undergraduate "retention/graduation rates" (used in all eight). Next were professional licensure test scores or pass rates, transfers from community colleges to the baccalaureate sector, use of technology or distance learning in teaching, and faculty teaching load measures—all used in four of the eight states. Another twelve indicators were used in three states: credits at graduation or time required to obtain a degree; faculty/staff diversity indicators; indicators of a typical student's (economically) feasible choices among colleges; job placements after graduation; preparation levels of entering students; noninstructional cost as a share of all costs; program duplication across campuses; survey results on satisfaction (of alumni or employers); sponsored research funds obtained; indicators of institutional involvement in improving teacher education; student learning measures (test scores); and workforce training/ development indicators. This list indicates the nature of the accountability measures to which public colleges and universities are now being held through fairly powerful fiscal incentives.[23]

Source of the Accountability Initiative and Its Significance

Burke makes a useful distinction between states where the legislature initiated the performance-funding program and those where the higher education coordinating board was the prime mover (significantly, in no case was an institution the initiator). Among states with a legislative mandate for performance funding, he further distinguishes between those where the legislature prescribed all or most specific measures and those where the coordinating board largely negotiated specific measures with the institutions. As might be expected, this categorization tends to correlate fairly well with the focus of the indicator set on external accountability versus internal notions of improvement (the more state prescription, the more the focus on external accountability) and with the extent of institutions' involvement in designing specific indicators (the more state prescription, the less institutional involvement).

Overall, Burke found that external concerns dominated the selected measures. Although the external stakeholders might well claim that they too are concerned with institutional improvement (Serban, 1997), their ideas are likely to differ from those on campus, and they cannot participate directly in or learn from efforts at implementation. The predominance of external visions is a clear indication of the practical effects of reduced institutional autonomy.

Burke also classifies the performance indicators according to their focus on *efficiency, quality, equity,* and *choice.* Efficiency was the dominant value in states where a state mandate prevailed; in two of the three states lacking such a mandate, quality was the dominant value. Overall, in the eight states, efficiency-oriented indicators dominated, but quality indicators were second in frequency and a number of indicators appeared to reflect both efficiency and quality (Burke, 1997a, pp. 39–41). Indicators focusing on equity or choice were relatively rare. The researchers also found that only in states where the performance regime was not state-mandated (in particular, Tennessee and Missouri) did the traditional academic "model of excellence," based on *resources and reputation,* have much prominence.[24] In states operating under legislative mandates, other models of excellence prevailed, what Burke calls the *strategic investment* or *cost-benefit* model, which emphasizes indicators of returns on the state's investment (basically, the extent to which explicit state goals are met), and the *client/customer-centered* model, which emphasizes students' and other clients' satisfaction (pp. 41–43). If the researchers' taxonomies and interpretations are accurate and generalizable, these findings seem to reinforce the unsurprising suggestion that academics can better influence this wave of change by moving out in front of it than by ignoring it. They also suggest that the lack of congruence between the values of academe and those of state policymakers is substantial.

Implementation Considerations

Burke and Serban's survey evidence and Lambert's research point to several, quite predictable difficulties in the implementation of performance funding (see especially Lambert, 1997; Serban, 1997). Some states have emphasized interinstitutional comparisons within the state in their use of performance measures, which predictably heightens conflict. This should be easily correctable, and the researchers note that most of the performance-funding regimes now emphasize improvements in an institution's performance over time or toward preestablished goals—sometimes supplemented by comparisons with peer institutions in other states—rather than divisive within-state, interinstitutional comparisons. Another widespread problem has arisen in balancing the desire of state officials for uniform or similar measures across institutions with the need to reflect the diversity of institutional missions, aspirations, and circumstances. Measures tend to reward outputs or outcomes (e.g., standardized test results, graduation rates, postgraduation success) without adequate consideration of differences in inputs, such as preparedness of incoming students or base resource levels, which may have powerful effects on these results. But appropriate adjustments are difficult and controversial to calibrate. Also, current indicators tend to be heavily focused on undergraduate education, usually the primary concern of the state's elected officials, and thus run the risk of distorting incentives of institutions whose missions include an important graduate education and research component. The fundamental tension here seems to be that state policymakers tend to value these other missions substantially less than do most academics.[25]

Finally, the choice of specific indicators, success thresholds, and weights in allocating state dollars has proved difficult and controversial. This is hardly surprising. The goals and priorities of the various stakeholders differ significantly, and the stakes are large and tangible. A considerable degree of judgment remains in most scoring systems because justifying or getting agreement on rigid formulas is difficult, but subjectivity inevitably means at least a modicum of criticism and controversy after annual weighty judgments have been rendered. Given higher education's still considerable political clout in most states, these implementation difficulties could undermine the performance-funding regime over time, if a sufficient number of influential oxen are gored as resources are reallocated based on the measures and if new state leadership emerges that may be less committed to the basic idea. A continued robust economy may also take the edge off the pressures for tying accountability to funding. At this point, however, it seems unlikely that the tide will turn very dramatically or for long.

Profiles of Accountability Regimes in Four States

Here I further explicate the nature and evolution of current performance-funding regimes in higher education by profiling four of the more significant cases: Tennessee, Missouri, South Carolina, and Washington.[26]

The Tennessee Experience

Tennessee's performance-funding program, initiated in 1979 by the Tennessee Higher Education Commission, was the first in the nation and has influenced other states' ideas, particularly in recent years. Interestingly, the program was initiated largely in response to concerns that the existing enrollment-driven funding model would no longer fund institutions adequately as enrollments began their predicted decline in the 1980s. From the beginning, Tennessee's performance-funding program placed a special focus on a perennial concern of the legislature: the quality of undergraduate education. Over the years, the performance measures have been broadened somewhat (through five major revisions) and the institutions have played a substantial partnership role in refining the indicators and how they are used; the legislature, though broadly supportive, has stayed largely in the background. The periodic revisions have refined the rather complex scoring procedures; intensified and specified the focus on assessments of student learning; shifted the overall emphasis somewhat away from external reporting and toward internal improvement;[27] tried to take differences in institutional missions more fully into account; and sought to allow for innovative efforts that do not have immediately measurable results.

Institutions' overall performance scores are based on a variety of indicators, with some variation by type of institution. The basic categories are (1) graduates' tested academic performance on nationally normed tests of general education outcomes and evidence of innovative efforts to improve general education assessments (plans, progress reports, etc.); (2) graduates' tested performance in their major field, maintenance of program accreditation (where applicable), or scoring (according to established standards) on program-quality reviews conducted by out-of-state experts; (3) student retention relative to institution-established goals, student and alumni satisfaction survey results, and (for two-year career programs only) job placement results; and (4) progress toward goals identified in state and institutional strategic plans.

The Tennessee Higher Education Commission has always described performance funding as an incentive supplement to an institution's budget base, but initially the funds were redirected from base funding. And the funds have been part of the fiscal picture for so long that institutions now expect to receive some funding from this source. Initially, the maximum performance funding available to an institution was set at 2 percent of its instructional budget, but this has grown to more than 5 percent. The link to the institution's budget base means that the performance-funding dollar amount goes up (or down) with the base and that institutions are not in direct competition with each other for these funds. In fiscal year (FY) 1997, $25 million was available statewide for performance funding, about 4 percent of total higher education appropriations, the highest such percentage in the nation that year. The program appears to be well accepted by the major stakeholders and, at this point, most tinkering with the program takes place at the five-year assessments. Thus, performance funding seems to be well institutionalized in Tennessee.

Assessments of the program point to its increasing attention to under-graduate general education and its measurable outcomes (e.g., tested read-ing, writing, computing, and critical thinking skills), but significantly, the ev-idence of improvements in students' performance in these areas over the years is "scant" (Banta, Rudolph, Van Dyke, & Fischer, 1996). Two long-time participants in the performance-funding effort who are now observers of the state system question whether faculty behavior has been changed much by the emphasis on student assessment. There is solid evidence of improve-ments in student and alumni satisfaction with both academic programs and student services, in job placement rates for graduates of two-year college ca-reer programs, and in the proportion of accreditable programs that are ac-credited. Also, our sources indicate that support for higher education in the business community seems to be enhanced by the perception that colleges and universities are seeking to improve their performance and are being held accountable.

Missouri's Two-Tiered Approach

Missouri's performance-funding program, Funding for Results (FFR), is the next oldest after Tennessee's; it dates back to 1989, but was not imple-mented until FY 1994. As in Tennessee, the initiative came from the higher education agency, the Missouri Coordinating Board for Higher Education. Some Missouri colleges had long had an interest in student assessment, and the board decided that, in an era of constrained resources, a visible move to-ward a more cost-effective higher education system focused on quality would be prudent. Many believe the Coordinating Board's initiative forestalled a legislatively mandated accountability program.

The Missouri performance-funding arrangement now has two tiers: a state-level goals tier and a campus-level tier. Some of the state goals are differ-entiated by sector (type of institution). Over the few years of FFR's existence, some of the goals have moved appreciably toward the output/outcome end of the performance measurement continuum. For example, the number of graduates achieving threshold performance levels on various assessments has replaced the number tested, and for two-year colleges, the number of transfer students *who graduate from four-year schools* has replaced the num-ber who transfer. Student assessments include nationally normed tests of general education learning and of achievement in the major subject; for ex-ample, the proportion scoring above the fiftieth percentile on a GRE field achievement test, pass rates on national certification and licensure exams (in fields that have these), and in other fields, graduates' receipt of competitive awards.

The FFR program rewards institutions for meeting graduation-time or graduation-rate goals that are differentiated by type of institution[28] and for improvements in this area over time, and it provides additional rewards for timely graduation of minority and financially disadvantaged students. Graduate programs are rewarded for the tested quality of students admitted. Teacher education receives special emphasis in that institutions are rewarded for high percentages of entrants in the upper third on national tests and for 80 percent or more of graduates at or above the fiftieth percentile on the National Teacher Examination. Two-year colleges are rewarded for the number of certificates and associate degrees awarded and for the number of vocational-program graduates placed in jobs six months after graduation, in addition to the number who transfer to and graduate from four-year schools.

The campus-level tier of the FFR program is particularly popular with the institutions and is less score-oriented. Campuses set their own goals for teaching/learning projects[29] under a grantlike funding arrangement and are rewarded for satisfactory progress reports. The projects are supposed to be related ultimately to improving performance on the state goals, but the linkage is sometimes loose.

State funding for the FFR program grew from about $3 million in FY 1994 to a peak of $12.6 million in FY 1997, before falling to $7.5 million in FY 1998. The funds provided are especially valuable to the institutions because they are discretionary and become part of the school's base for calculating future budgets. The proportion of total state appropriations represented by FFR remains low—less than 2 percent of state support for higher education at the high-water mark in 1997—but it is a significant share of the new money available in most years.[30] It seems to be enough to get institutions' attention.

Missouri's public colleges and universities were, in general, not initially enthusiastic about the FFR program when it involved only performance indicators established at the state level, but they have participated extensively in the program's ongoing design and refinement. Their influence has increased the emphasis on improvements over time rather than interinstitutional comparisons and on differentiation of some indicators by type of institution. The institutions are particularly supportive of the campus-level tier of the program with its locally generated goals and projects. Overall, they seem to appreciate the program's symbolic significance in demonstrating accountability and are pleased about the discretionary funding it has produced. The program's support seems to be fairly broad and stable.

Interestingly, the objective results of the FFR effort appear somewhat mixed. Graduation rates, including those of minority students, and graduates' pass rates on licensure exams have improved since FFR was introduced (although the causal nexus is not fully established), community college graduates' job placement rates have risen somewhat, and many of the campus-level projects have shown progress. But the proportion of graduates scoring above the fiftieth percentile on nationally normed tests of general education and both the entry and exit test results of teacher candidates fell slightly through 1997.

The South Carolina Experiment

South Carolina's performance-funding effort is of more recent origin than those of Tennessee and Missouri, and much more far-reaching in its intent. In 1996 the legislature declared its intention to shift from a fairly traditional enrollment- and need-driven funding model for public higher education to an *entirely* performance-driven approach. The performance-based system was to be fully in place by FY 1999–2000, and implementation efforts have been under way since 1996. The governor has been supportive, but much of the impetus has come from the state's business community—which believes that its high-technology strategic direction calls for a stronger, more responsive, more cost-effective higher education system—and its legislative supporters. Both the business community and the legislature have been heavily involved in the complex implementation process (Christal, 1998, pp. 24–25).

The unusually specific initiating legislation called for state resources to be allocated to colleges and universities according to their performance on indicators (some with multiple parts) in thirty-seven specific areas, most of them from a business-oriented taskforce report. Implementation planning efforts have been somewhat contentious (Schmidt, 1997; Trombley, 1998). The South Carolina Commission on Higher Education, anticipating legislative concerns, essentially rejected the recommendations of the first round of plans prepared by sectoral committees[31] composed of institutional representatives, coordinating commission members, and business leaders. The operative plan was then devised by the Commission on Higher Education, after careful consultation with key figures in the legislature and business community. The commission plays a key role in approving institutions' annual targets on each indicator, scoring each school's performance, and setting longer-range targets for "continuous improvement." The plan called for a steadily increasing proportion of the state's higher education appropriations to be allocated according to the performance-funding scheme, reaching 100 percent by 1999–2000.

Although the legislation touts an entirely performance-driven budgeting method as its goal, an important role remains for institutional "needs" as determined by a sector-specific formula based on national comparisons to similar institutions, modified by the amount the legislature elects to allocate to higher education (e.g., it might fund only 80 percent of formula-determined needs in a given year). Essentially, each college or university receives a percentage of its total potential funding for that year based on its overall score on the indicators for the previous year's performance. For example, if a university's score is 90 percent of its potential score on the performance indicators—all of which are weighted equally because of sharp differences over alternative weightings—it receives 90 percent of its potential funding for the year. In addition, a small amount of performance funding is set aside for improvement grants, for which institutions compete within their sector. Apparently as an equity measure, schools with lower scores on the performance indicators are given some preference in this competition.

South Carolina's numerous performance indicators are organized into nine broad areas: "mission focus"; quality of faculty; instructional quality; institutional cooperation and collaboration (among institutions and with outside partners such as business organizations); administrative efficiency; entrance requirements for students; graduates' achievements; "user friendliness"; and research spending. Most of the individual indicators are, in Burke's (1997a) classification, input or process indicators; only a few are outcome or even output indicators. The indicator set appears to be primarily oriented toward ensuring that institutions are producing and following mission statements and strategic plans consistent with the state's vision and toward monitoring fairly traditional input and process indicators—for example, faculty credentials; whether faculty performance reviews follow "best practices"; class size; average credit hours taught by faculty; program accreditation; entry qualifications of students; proportion of state-resident students; transferability of student credits; ratio of indirect to total costs; and use of "best practices" in administration. There is also considerable focus on evidence of cooperation with other institutions and with business, especially on efforts to improve teacher education. Measurements of outputs and outcomes are limited to counts of public service activities; research grants secured; graduation rates; graduates' rates of employment; measures of employer satisfaction with graduates (not yet complete); pass rates on certification and licensure tests; and numbers of graduates going on to advanced study. Little effort is apparent in focusing on direct assessment of student learning or on the impacts of faculty research.

Participants in and close observers of the South Carolina performance-

funding initiative report that the colleges and universities are paying attention to their scores on the mandated indicators. But the challenges of data
collection and interpretation in such a complex system are prodigious and
in some cases quite costly, and many in higher education continue to protest
to influential supporters in government about aspects of the program, on
both philosophical and technical grounds. This response is likely to escalate
as the budgetary stakes grow. At some point, if well-connected institutions
fare poorly under the new system, it will surely be tested in the political arena.
Indeed, even strong supporters of the new approach may be taken aback by
instances in which it leads to reduced funding for institutions already poorly
funded (Trombley, 1998).[32] The system's sheer complexity and the unpre-
dictability it creates for institutions' fiscal planning suggest that some rethinking will be necessary. Yet, the new approach carries powerful symbolic
meaning and has tenacious support from influential quarters, thus it is less
likely to be overthrown than modified and blunted by compromises in implementation that can be camouflaged in technical budgetary language.

There are signs that policymakers are beginning to recognize these realities. In early 1999 the claim persisted that 100 percent of the state's higher
education funding in the next budget would be driven by institutions' scores
on the thirty-seven performance indicators. But the main implementer, the
Commission on Higher Education, has responded to criticism by moving to
reduce duplication and contradictory incentives among the numerous sub-
indicators and has modified institutions' targets ("benchmarks") and sim-
plified the scoring system (reducing the number of potential scoring points
per indicator from six to three). These changes were evidently intended to
dampen potential swings in institutions' funding from year to year.[33] Also,
the commission recommends creating an explicit "performance improvement pool" of funds that appears to be the real performance-funding
pot. This would be a sizable amount—1.75 percent of an institution's cur-
rent-year allocation, plus half its potential next-year funding under the need-
driven formula, plus the opportunity to compete for funds unclaimed within
its sector from the latest round of performance scoring—but it is far from
100 percent. How the legislature will respond to these proposals is not clear,
but some compromise seems inevitable.

The Washington State Initiative

Washington's performance-funding initiative is one of the newer ones,
postdating initiation of the Burke research project in 1996. After years of a
"report card" approach to accountability, which some legislators found frus-
trating for its lack of clear influence on institutions' behavior, the 1997 legis-

lature specified that about 1 percent of the state's budgetary allocation to public higher education for the 1997–99 biennium (about $10.7 million for the six four-year colleges and universities)[34] would be "reserved" subject to satisfaction by the institutions of two contingencies. First, to release funds for 1997–98 (about 40% of total performance-linked funds for the biennium), the institutions would have to submit satisfactory accountability plans. Second, to release funds for 1998–99 ($6.4 million), they would have to show they had achieved the performance targets for 1997–98 codified in the plans. Although this concept of reserved funds is ambiguous, all parties in the state regarded these funds as coming from an institution's "base" state funding.

The legislation specified long-term numerical goals in three areas, all applicable to undergraduate students only: five-year graduation rate, year-to-year retention rate, and the "graduation efficiency index," a measure devised to assess the relationship of credits accumulated to number needed to graduate (with separate goals for "native" first-year and transfer students). These goals were to be achieved by 2004–5. To take account of differences in institutional missions and student populations, goals for graduation and retention rates were set at a higher level for the two research universities than for the four comprehensive institutions. In addition, the legislation specified that the Higher Education Coordinating Board (HECB) and the institutions were to develop a fourth measure—a faculty productivity measure for each institution—and a fifth measure of the institution's choosing, reflecting its mission and subject to HECB approval. The latter two measures were permitted to have up to four sub-indicators. The HECB was to negotiate the long-term goals for each measure with the institutions. For all five measures, baseline data were computed (based on 1995–96 figures) and the HECB established a timetable of interim targets for each year that would move an institution steadily from its baseline level to the final goal by 2004–5. The assumption was that funds would continue to be held in reserve each year to enforce continued progress toward these goals. The expected progression for the legislatively specified measures for each of the six four-year institutions is summarized in Table 7.1. Finally, the legislature expressed its desire that the HECB and the institutions look into ways of assessing student learning outcomes that could be built into the performance-funding arrangement.

A number of criticisms have been, or could be, raised about this arrangement—of interest because many of them apply to similar performance-funding schemes emerging elsewhere. First, the goals (especially those set by the legislature) are generally arbitrary and fail to give credit for prior improvements—which some institutions could show—or to take into account

Table 7.1. Schedule of Performance Targets and Goals for Washington State Higher Education, 1998–2005

Institution[a]	1995–96 Baseline	Statewide Goal[b]	Gap[c]	1998[d]	1999	2000	2001	2002	2003	2004	Goal 2005
Measure 1a: Graduation Efficiency Index (Freshman Students)											
UW	89.1	95.0	5.9	89.51	89.99	90.69	91.52	92.35	93.17	94.06	95.0
WSU	89.6	95.0	5.4	89.96	90.39	91.04	91.80	92.56	93.32	94.13	95.0
EWU	93.2	95.0	1.8	93.33	93.47	93.69	93.94	94.19	94.44	94.71	95.0
CWU	89.8	95.0	5.2	90.16	90.58	91.20	91.93	92.66	93.39	94.17	95.0
WWU	85.0	95.0	10.0	85.70	86.50	87.70	89.10	90.50	91.90	93.40	95.0
TESC	91.3	95.0	3.7	91.56	91.86	92.30	92.82	93.34	93.85	94.41	95.0
Measure 1b: Graduation Efficiency Index (Transfer Students)											
UW	80.4	90.0	9.6	81.07	81.84	82.99	84.34	85.68	87.02	88.46	90.0
WSU	79.8	90.0	10.2	80.54	81.36	82.58	84.00	85.42	86.85	88.37	90.0
EWU	85.3	90.0	4.7	85.63	86.01	86.57	87.23	87.89	88.54	89.25	90.0
CWU	83.3	90.0	6.7	83.77	84.31	85.11	86.05	86.99	87.92	88.93	90.0
WWU	77.2	90.0	12.8	78.10	79.12	80.66	82.45	84.24	86.03	87.95	90.0
TESC	89.1	90.0	0.9	89.16	89.24	89.34	89.47	89.60	89.72	89.86	90.0

Measure 2: Undergraduate student retention

UW	86.7%	95.0%	8.3%	87.28%	87.95%	88.94%	90.10%	91.27%	92.43%	93.67%	95.0%
WSU	84.6	95.0	10.4	85.33	86.16	87.41	88.86	90.32	91.78	93.34	95.0
EWU	86.5	90.0	3.5	86.75	87.03	87.45	87.94	88.43	88.92	89.44	90.0
CWU	74.4	90.0	15.6	75.49	76.74	78.61	80.80	82.98	85.16	87.50	90.0
WWU	79.7	90.0	10.3	80.42	81.25	82.48	83.92	85.37	86.81	88.35	90.0
TESC	73.0	90.0	17.0	74.19	75.55	77.59	79.97	82.35	84.73	87.28	90.0

Measure 3: Five-year graduation rate

UW	61.7%	65.0%	3.3%	61.93%	62.20%	62.59%	63.05%	63.52%	63.98%	64.47%	65.0%
WSU	55.2	65.0	9.8	55.89	56.67	57.85	59.22	60.59	61.95	63.43	65.0
EWU	32.4	55.0	22.6	33.98	35.79	38.50	41.67	44.83	47.99	51.38	55.0
CWU	40.0	55.0	15.0	41.05	42.25	44.05	46.15	48.25	50.35	52.60	55.0
WWU	50.0	55.0	5.0	50.35	50.75	51.35	52.05	52.75	53.45	54.20	55.0
TESC	48.0	55.0	7.0	48.49	49.05	49.89	50.87	51.85	52.83	53.88	55.0
Yearly gap closure target[e]				7%	8%	12%	14%	14%	14%	15%	16%

Source: Washington State Higher Education Coordinating Board (1997).

[a] Institutions: UW, University of Washington; WSU, Washington State University; EWU, Eastern Washington University; CWU, Central Washington University; WWU, Western Washington University; TESC, The Evergreen State College.

[b] Statewide goals are to be achieved by 2004–5 (FY 2005).

[c] The gap is the difference between an institution's goal for 2004–5 and its baseline year (1995–96) performance. Performance levels to be achieved in intervening years, shown by institution for each measure, are the prospective targets to which performance funds are linked.

[d] All years given are fiscal years.

[e] The yearly gap closure target is the percentage of the total gap to be closed in each intervening year. Note that the gap closure targets become more demanding over time.

what is achievable in the light of national benchmarks vis-à-vis peers. Although comparable peer data to support benchmark analysis are far from perfect, some of the long-term goals seem unrealistic, so much so that in instances where institutions have made substantial improvements after years of effort, additional efforts may not be cost-effective. This also suggests that goals should be more differentiated by individual institution, since not all institutions within the broad categories are similarly situated in terms of students or prior efforts.

Some of the measures may create undesirable incentives. For example, the most direct way to increase student credit hours per faculty full-time equivalent (FTE) is to enlarge classes, which is probably not what most policymakers, citizens, or students want. Similarly, "graduation efficiency" can be improved by limiting students' options in exploring courses and shifting majors, but it is hard to justify the stringent goal that 95 percent of students' credits should count directly toward their ultimate major or other course requirements.

Beyond this, in large, complex institutions, institutionwide aggregate measures such as research funding per faculty member, overall retention rate, and students' evaluations of courses are very hard to affect directly, certainly in a way that will produce steady year-to-year improvements. For example, the ups and downs in federal research funding are not much subject to institutional control, so why would the state want to penalize its universities because the federal government chooses to cut research and development spending? Similarly, overall undergraduate retention rates are subject to a host of external forces in students' lives and finances that institutions cannot control. If anything in this sphere is to be monitored, the monitoring of major checkpoints in the undergraduate career might make more sense, such as freshman attrition or bottlenecks at the point of selecting a major and gaining access to courses that might be subject to assessable policy intervention by the institution. One must also wonder about expending resources to change aggregate averages of students' course-evaluation scores. In the University of Washington data, the baseline value on this indicator is 94.5 percent, which shows that a very high percentage of students rated their courses at 3.0 ("good") or better on a five-point scale. What is the value of raising this already high number to 98 percent, as the goals call for?[35]

The indicator set could also be criticized as too narrowly (though not entirely) focused on undergraduate education and for giving no attention to states' access or diversity goals.[36] Most importantly perhaps, the assumption built into the year-to-year targets of *continuous* improvement toward the goals seems highly problematic. Interestingly, the institutions' performance "scorecards" for 1997–98 allowed them to claim from 64 to 90 percent of the funds reserved for 1998–99, in all, $4.9 million of the $6.4 million available (Washington State Higher Education Coordinating Board, 1998).[37] Although the universities may have breathed sighs of relief after this first year, their ability to keep up the pace of continuous improvement expected by the state seems unlikely, given the considerations outlined above. This concern is all the more real because the HECB's schedule of targets progressing toward the 2004–5 performance goals is nonlinear, with the smallest amount of improvement generally called for in the early years. It will be interesting to see how policymakers respond if many of the institutions begin to "hit the wall" in terms of their ability to meet the escalating expectations for continuous improvement and thus to claim the performance portion of their base funding. The result could be a backlash against the performance-funding program.

The performance-funding and accountability regime contemplated when the legislation was passed in 1997 was substantially compromised during the 1999 session of the Washington legislature. The session was complicated by an unusual 49–49 tie between the political parties and thus split control of the House. Only a limited legislative agenda could be passed in this delicate situation. In higher education, only major priorities (such as overall state support, salary and tuition increases, and a few special projects) received attention from the full House. Although continuation of the established performance-funding program had influential legislative supporters (as well as strong opponents), and even the institutions were reluctantly supporting a modified approach linking some funds to the indicators, interparty brinkmanship bargaining near the end of the session's legally mandated deadline left no time for resolving differences over what was seen as a relatively minor issue. The hasty compromise on performance funding provided for continuation of institutional reporting on the performance targets through the HECB, but no funds were tied to performance.

Although supporters of performance funding promised that the issue was not settled, the initiative's momentum may have been permanently broken. This remains to be seen. The broader lesson may be that, for a modest program of performance funding (such as exists in all states using performance funding save South Carolina), changes in legislative priorities from session to session and turnover in key supporters are crucial problems unless the program can garner true institutional commitment such as seems to have been achieved in Tennessee and Missouri.

Having used these mini–case studies to clarify some of the realities and pit-falls of policy implementation in this area, we can examine how a viable new balance might be struck between the twin imperatives of academic auton-omy and democratic accountability of public higher education in contem-porary American society.

Academic Autonomy and Accountability: Elements of a New Balance

The elements of a new synthesis between the autonomy and account-ability concepts can only be sketched here, but perhaps this sketch could help start a discussion on further conceptual development around this issue. This field should not be left, on the one side, to those with an essentially business-based perspective and, on the other, to academics who see no need to alter long-established ways in response to potent new challenges.

First, a bedrock principle must be the effective protection of academic freedom, both in the classroom and in research topics and scholarly writings. This is a widely acknowledged value (American Association of University Professors, 1986; O'Neil, 1997). Without it, academic institutions have little hope of sustaining intellectual diversity and vitality or responsiveness to changing societal needs and trends. As suggested earlier, the need to safe-guard academic freedom argues strongly for substantial autonomy of col-leges and universities from direct control by state political authorities, and so against the most intrusive forms of academic micromanagement.

Second, and more generally, the prevailing view in management theory is that highly centralized management (i.e., decision making from the top about all important and many less important matters) is generally ineffec-tive and inefficient in rapidly changing environments such as those faced by organizations in the "knowledge industry," of which colleges and universities are a leading example. Rather, those closest to the market and production processes are likely to have the best information and ideas about what direc-tions to take or changes to make, and how to do this in a timely fashion (Drucker, 1985; Marshall & Tucker, 1992).[38] Their efforts can be usefully guided by budget discipline—that is, an overall spending target—and by in-dicators of movement toward desired results, but such indicators should be oriented toward measuring total spending and its results (outcomes) rather than a particular input or the ways in which resources are deployed by the units (such as institutions and departments) nearest to the market and the production process. Within this framework, process measures depicting how resources are employed, such as those Burke finds to be dominating the cur-rent accountability and performance-funding scene in higher education, are sometimes used as proxies for outcomes where these are difficult to measure. There is a real danger, however, that reifying today's "best practices" not only may be off the mark but may stultify innovation.[39] Thus, an accountability program should strive to monitor performance and total cost but should not focus on *how* money is spent—most of the wisdom on such matters is not likely to reside at the top of the system hierarchy—or how results are achieved, save to help improve truly unsatisfactory performance (as determined by careful comparisons with peer institutions over time).

A third key principle is that, clearly, everything important in such a complex enterprise as higher education cannot be measured, so we should avoid seeking to drive all or most resource allocation according to what can be measured. If we ignore this maxim, we will surely induce serious goal displacement and other distortions as participants respond to powerful fiscal incentives by focusing inordinately on what is measured and rewarded. For example, if we reward colleges and universities too aggressively for how rapidly students attain their degrees and how few drop out, institutions will be pushed to relax standards for degrees while taking fewer risks in admitting students on any grounds other than prior academic performance. If resources are driven largely by students' test results at graduation, admissions may be similarly affected and course content may shift to focus on immediately testable elements rather than on the more subtle aspects of preparing students for the challenges of later life (or anything not readily testable in a standardized way). Similarly, excessive focus on students' "relevant" job placements and earnings may work against otherwise worthy fields not readily linked to the job market at the baccalaureate level.

Fourth, another serious problem with excessive reliance on measurable performance to drive a substantial part of budget allocations is that this is likely to create budget instability. Gains in such indicators as graduation rates or average success of graduates in the inevitably cyclical labor market are unlikely to be steady and sure, despite an institution's best efforts, owing to many uncontrollable factors. Even with multiple measures, substantial year-to-year instability is a strong possibility and is potentially destructive of successful planning and sustained support of steps toward improvement. More sensible would be performance indicator schemes that reward improvements on agreed-on measures with enough resources to ensure attention but with base resource allocations not so heavily weighted toward these indicators as to distort institutional priorities and disrupt essential organizational stability.

As a fifth principle, academic values may count for more in this debate than many think. Elected officials are generally proud to see their state's institutions score highly in national rankings of quality, which are largely driven by academic and research reputation, and are happy to welcome the inflow of federal and private research and development dollars and economic development spinoffs that often accompany universities' research efforts. Most important, citizens and their children "vote with their feet" by flooding the most highly regarded colleges and universities with applications for admission. These customers of public higher education, who are also citizens, voters, and taxpayers, are unlikely to be altogether pleased by a forced refocusing of much of their institutions' attention away from traditional notions of academic quality and toward values such as cost control, efficiency, truncated time-to-degree, and so forth. The public still seems to value quality in higher education, more or less as traditionally defined (Immerwahr, 1997), as the sales of college and graduate school ratings guides attest. To the extent that the two types of goals are compatible (in particular, when a performance-funding program rewards traditionally defined quality, along with other goals), there may be no problem, but if measured accountability becomes so important that traditional dimensions of quality are threatened, states that push accountability the hardest could well see a backlash.

Sixth, state policymakers, as well as academics, would do well to appreciate and try to strengthen rather than undermine the roles of boards of trustees and state higher education boards. These citizen bodies provide an important type of *democratic accountability*, that is, accountability of academe to citizens' views and perspectives. The boards are usually appointed by elected officials for fixed terms, so they are accountable in this sense as well. Yet these citizen boards have the advantage of generally being more knowledgeable about higher education and more stable and less politicized in their views than are elected officials, as the latter have generally recognized in establishing these boards and deferring to them on many matters in the past. Thus, if legislators want more closely calibrated accountability from higher education institutions, they would be wise to say so in general terms and leave the details to the state higher education board and its expert staff, which has experience working with the institutions and their boards. After all, it is the educators who provide the performance data and have most to say about what they mean, and the educators who must implement sensible steps to improve results.

This line of thinking is closely tied to the final and most important point. If a contemporary but balanced accountability regime is to be developed, more *trust* must be built and sustained among the key players: faculty, institutional administrations, governing and coordinating boards, elected policymakers, state budget officials, the media, and ultimately the public. Of course, this is more easily said than done. Legislators and the public are suspicious of academics for a variety of reason. At bottom, academic values and public values are at variance on some points. The public sees the main purpose of state colleges and universities as teaching students, especially state-resident undergraduates, well and efficiently. Employers want graduates who are dependably trained and broadly knowledgeable. Thus, they and their elected representatives question academic practices that seem to deemphasize teaching and undergraduates, avoid independent assessment of student learning, and pay little attention to costs to students and taxpayers.

If they are to win back some measure of public trust, crucial to maintaining autonomy in the long run, academics must be willing to convince state leaders and the public that they care about and will act upon more of what the public values. To overcome current negative perceptions, institutions may well have to accept indicators that legislators see as capturing the public's concerns, even if some are output or process indicators with little real connection to outcomes. These may do relatively little harm, yet they can be helpful symbolically if the dollars tied to them are not large or if they are adequately counterbalanced by measures that are more outcome-oriented and more comprehensive across higher education's multiple missions.

Even problematic process indicators can sometimes be improved upon after analysis, perhaps analysis jointly undertaken by state and institutional staffs. For example, in Washington State a proposed, legislatively mandated measure of average time-to-degree for undergraduates has been replaced by a measure of "excess" credit units.[40] This avoids penalizing the institution for lengthy times to graduation due simply to students' financial difficulties, while encouraging careful advising of students and scheduling of the courses they need to graduate.[41]

Also in Washington, institutions have persuaded state officials to shift from their typical focus on faculty teaching loads—a true micromanagement type of process indicator—to the broader measure of student credit units generated per faculty FTE, which at least allows for different approaches to teaching and learning by different disciplines or by innovative departments.[42] Another possibility would be to adjust widely used measures of graduation rates (and, as yet less used, student learning) for the characteristics of entering students so that institutions with less well-prepared students are not disadvantaged and public institutions are not pressed to improve their measured performance by simply narrowing their admission criteria.

The current interest in student learning assessment should be welcomed by all sides in the accountability debate. This is a potential vehicle for enhancing mutual trust, as long as assessments are not too heavily weighted to the immediately measurable, given what we know about the limitations and biases of standard tests. Indicators of alumni and employer satisfaction and graduates' graduate school and employment success are, if not too short-range and not too heavily weighted in driving resource allocations, valuable sources of outcome-oriented information that can also provide data to aid in making improvements. Documenting alumni and employer satisfaction should also help build a sense that institutions are concerned with what the public wants from them.

In the area of balance across missions, the present interest in outcomes provides a good opportunity to document the impacts and benefits of academic research and public service (by students as well as faculty). This may present further opportunities to identify societal benefits not yet widely appreciated. Finally, the performance-indicator movement could even be a vehicle for bolstering the case for diversity efforts in higher education (an area in which most states' indicators are notably silent according to Burke's data), if it can be shown that more diverse student populations and faculty cadres have beneficial educational and attitude-changing effects in our increasingly diverse society.

Conclusion

In this chapter I have sought to shed some light on the contemporary movement to hold public higher education to rigorous accountability standards devised by state policymakers and increasingly tied to budget allocations. The main ideas and forces driving this accountability effort are not unique to higher education—indeed, they permeate current society; but higher education cannot expect to be exempt. The pervasiveness and likely persistence of these forces, together with some self-inflicted damage to higher educations' public image in recent years, have resulted in a weakening of traditional buffers against direct state influence: the independent institutional governing board and state-level citizen coordinating board and the deference and general good will of the public and legislators. These changing circumstances call for public higher education to rethink its responses to the polity's expectations.

Institutions can sustain their treasured autonomy, essential to the realization of core values such as academic freedom, responsiveness to changing societal needs, and commitment to high quality in the generation and transmission of knowledge, only if they meet new public expectations for accountability. This seems possible and acceptable after a reasoned dialogue between public higher education and its state sponsors, under the following conditions:

- Academic freedom is adequately secured.
- The parties give their major attention to results—in particular, results over which institutions can exercise substantial control—rather than to mandating processes for achieving them.
- The parties recognize the logic of keeping most key *process* decisions in the hands of those best situated to make them.
- Policymakers do not become carried away with measurement and with linking large amounts of resources strictly to measurable results.
- Some balance is assured across higher education's societal missions in what is measured and what is rewarded.

Here, as in the exercise of independent judgment on matters of what is to be measured and with what consequences, the continued strong role of citizen governance bodies (boards of trustees and state higher education boards) is essential.

Historically, higher education has served the nation well. To continue to do so, the enterprise needs to respond to new challenges in affordability, access, and accountability, the tripartite theme of this book. The three are inextricably linked. Public institutions will surely be held accountable by the public and its elected representatives for providing affordable access to the growing numbers seeking the benefits of higher education. Public higher education must respond to demands for places in the system and concerns about the price paid (as well as the quality of the education). The accountability imperative is powerfully reinforced by an acute awareness of the limits of public willingness to provide tax-derived funds to higher education (or other public functions) without some understandable accounting of what the resources are producing and whether they are used efficiently. Higher education can respond to these challenges and serve society even better if the parties to policymaking remain true to the essential principles of autonomy and social responsibility (read, democratic accountability) that only together can preserve and sustain high quality in the public academic enterprise.

Notes

The author acknowledges valuable help in the research for this chapter from Mary Beth Lambert and Joseph Burke, but the responsibility for all assertions and conclusions herein rests solely with the author. An earlier, condensed version of this chapter appeared in *Policy Studies Review* (Zumeta, 1998).

1. There were exceptions, notably in the McCarthy era of the 1950s; see Hofstadter and Metzger (1955) and Hofstadter (1963).

2. For example, state priorities cover such matters as which programs are expendable, how teaching is to be done (e.g., face-to-face or by distance learning), and how resources are allocated between teaching and research.

3. The focus here is on the accountability claims of states rather than those of the federal government. Even today, federal concerns are largely limited to rather specialized matters such as accounting for research expenditures, breaches of research integrity, student loan collections, equal-opportunity regulation, and campus crime reporting. Because of states' nominal "ownership" of public institutions and greater financial role in their basic support, states' accountability claims cut closest to the heart of academe.

4. Osborne and Gaebler's *Reinventing Government* (1992) was a seminal contribution to thinking on the application of business ideas to government for simultaneously improving quality and results while reducing costs through *restructuring* or *reengineering* of operations. This type of thinking is daunting and bewildering to most in higher education, who have always seen higher quality as inevitably implying higher costs.

5. Higher education was for many years the second largest function supported by states' general funds, but was surpassed in the early 1990s by Medicaid, an *individual entitlement* program to which states must contribute for each eligible enrollee. Both elementary and secondary education and corrections caseloads must be funded by legislatures, often under pressure of judicial mandates. The largest welfare program, Aid to Families with Dependent Children (AFDC), was a federally mandated expenditure for states until 1997.

6. Although welfare is no longer an individual entitlement (meaning that, in an economic downturn, states will not be required by federal law to respond to increased needs for assistance), under current law states will face full political responsibility for responding to their citizens' needs without any increase in federal assistance. As a practical matter, in many states this will put an even greater squeeze on funding for other state functions such as higher education than did the old federal-state partnership arrangement.

7. Over the two decades from 1975 to 1994, the average price of four years of tuition, fees, and room and board at a public college or university in the United States, measured in 1994 dollars (i.e., adjusted for general price inflation), more than doubled (+134%) (Institute for Research in Higher Education, 1997), while median household incomes grew hardly at all in real terms. Tuition increases were more moderate in the late 1990s, but still substantially exceeded inflation and growth in family incomes (College Board, 1998, p. 5). (See Chapter 1 for more on the rising tuition costs in public higher education.)

8. According to a Public Agenda Foundation survey of Californians' attitudes on higher education, the public wants to see "more effective use of facilities," more use of new technologies, more use of private colleges and universities to meet ac-

cess demands, and more emphasis on support of students rather than of institutions (Immerwahr, 1997, p. v). In another poll in Washington State, the public called for reducing administrators and "increasing the number of classes each professor teaches" rather than limiting enrollments (MGT & Elway Research, 1995, p. iii).

9. For critiques ranging from the strictly ideological to the mainly managerial, see Anderson (1992), Bennett (1987), Bloom (1987), D'Souza (1991), Huber (1992), Smith (1990), and Zemsky and Massy (1990).

10. For exceptions, see Glenny (1976), Glenny and Dalglish (1973), and Rudolph (1962).

11. See reports on recent events in New York (Healy & Schmidt, 1998), California (Selingo, 1999), and Florida (Lively, 1999).

12. Individual campuses may or may not have their own boards. Some states have separate governing boards for two-year and four-year institutions. For a description and appraisal of the various structures, see McGuinness (1997).

13. A former, very experienced head of a state higher education coordinating board pointed out to the author that the state board had no loyal alumni to call on for political support and no grand prizes such as football tickets to distribute (J. K. Folger, personal communication, 1986).

14. Data were typically reported on such measures as graduation rates, time required to graduate (time-to-degree), numbers and proportions of students completing community college degrees and transferring to baccalaureate institutions, ethnic diversity measures for students and faculty, and various types of cost indicators.

15. When these types of indicators are used in the budgeting process but the linkage to dollar allocations is not formulaic but more judgmental and inclusive of nonmeasured elements, the approach is called *performance budgeting* (Burke & Serban, 1998).

16. Capital funding has generally been even more loosely determined, based on a general showing of need by institutions and their long-trusted overseers, the campus trustees and state higher education boards, subject of course to the general availability of funds and policymakers' judgments about priorities.

17. The 1997 figures are revised from figures published earlier by the same authors (Burke & Serban, 1997).

18. Burke and Serban (1998, pp. 12–13) also point out that eight of the thirteen states using performance funding to allocate part of their budget for higher education also employ performance budgeting.

19. The proportion of the state higher education budget involved in performance funding has generally grown modestly over the years in the two states with the longest history of such funding, Tennessee and Missouri (Lambert, 1997).

20. The published studies were conducted in 1996 and 1997 and focus on the eight states employing performance funding at the outset of the research. All the publications originate from the Public Higher Education Program at the State Uni-

versity of New York (SUNY), Albany, which Burke directs. Burke was formerly provost and acting chancellor of the SUNY system.

21. Examples of indicators classified as outcome measures are graduate job placements (used mostly for two-year institutions); pass rates or scores on professional licensure tests; faculty/staff diversity measures (rarely used); results of satisfaction surveys of students, alumni, or employers; standardized test results purporting to measure students' learning (in place in only two states but much talked about); and graduate or professional school continuation rates for those with baccalaureate degrees (Burke, 1997a, pp. 48–49). Note that even these measures of underlying outcomes are rather crude and far from comprehensive, such as standardized test scores to measure students' learning gains from general education and first job placements as a proxy for higher education's value in careers.

22. These kinds of output counts are not a great stretch from traditional practice in higher education, though using them to drive state funding is new. Plainly, the questions remain as to whether graduates are *well* prepared for careers and other aspects of life, whether research funds produce results, whether publications are significant, and so forth. The answers would fall in the realm of *outcomes*.

23. Christal (1998, p. 5) provides a list of "commonly reported performance measures" drawn from all thirty-seven states that in her survey reported using performance measures in higher education. The most common measures were graduation rates (32 states); transfer rates from two-year to four-year institutions (25 states); faculty workload or productivity measures (24 states); follow-up satisfaction studies (23 states); sponsored research funds secured (23 states); pass rates on licensure exams (21 states); remediation activities and their effectiveness (21 states); degrees awarded (20 states); job placement for graduates (19 states); admission standards and measures (18 states); total student credit hours (18 states); and number of accredited programs (13 states).

24. *Resources and reputation* is Burke's term for the traditional approach to assessing quality in academe according to resources available and the scholarly and professional standing of the faculty and academic programs.

25. Alternatively, state policymakers may assume that these other missions are in little danger of being underemphasized by academics.

26. The profiles of Tennessee, Missouri, and South Carolina are based primarily on research conducted by Mary Beth Lambert (under supervision of the author) in the summer and fall of 1997, using telephone interviews with principals and knowledgeable observers and review of documents. The information was updated in early 1999 by Zumeta, with the aid of Joseph Burke. The Washington profile was developed by Zumeta in March 1999, based on research conducted over 1997–1999.

27. This assessment of the revisions by one of our sources is echoed in Banta, Rudolph, Van Dyke, & Fischer (1996).

28. For example, the six-year graduation-rate goal for full-time freshman students ranges from 75 percent at the most selective universities down to 45 percent for open enrollment institutions.

29. Examples include efforts to improve sophomore retention rates, projects to incorporate new technologies into teaching, and innovative approaches to student outcomes assessment.

30. This proportion grew steadily until 1998 when a substantial state initiative to invest in new technology in higher education took priority and the share devoted to performance funding fell.

31. In South Carolina, public higher education is officially categorized into four sectors: research universities, teaching universities, regional campuses, and technical colleges.

32. Many measures used in the system tend to reward institutions based on, for example, their attracting academically able students and the students graduating expeditiously. Some institutions are, at the outset, much better suited than others to achieving these goals (even within broad categories of schools). As the new system rewards the "winners," less fortunate institutions may simply be further impoverished and hampered in their efforts to do better. Such a pattern will surely lead to demands for revisions from local interests affected and perhaps from those who want to see improvements in the entire state system.

33. In general, the commission's scoring in the first few years of performance funding has been characterized as fairly generous and not very discriminating across institutions, probably because of the concern about year-to-year swings in funding.

34. Another $6.8 million for the state's thirty-two community and technical colleges was similarly reserved, contingent upon performance. Administration of the funds for the four-year institutions was delegated to the Higher Education Coordinating Board and responsibility for the two-year schools to their statewide board (with a different set of measures). For the sake of brevity, the focus in the text is on the four-year schools' portion.

35. This point is reminiscent of economists' critique of the original Clean Water Act, which called for ridding the nation's waterways of 100 percent of pollution by a fixed date. At some point as we approached 100 percent, the economists pointed out, residual pollution would be very costly to remove, and probably not very harmful. Moreover, in the case of higher education, placing too much emphasis on improving students' evaluations of courses could have undesirable side effects.

36. Enrollments are funded elsewhere in the budget, however. In the area of diversity goals, Washington's recent passage of an initiative outlawing affirmative action makes the state's goals very hazy at present.

37. The board had earlier released all the funds for 1997–98 following approval of the institutions' accountability plans.

38. The "new public management" paradigm in public administration/management holds many of the same tenets. See the recent symposia on new public management and related topics that were the subject of two entire journal issues (Nagel, 1997; Terry, 1998).

39. Examples of process measures widely used in higher education include faculty's weekly class hour counts, measures of how extensively "new" technologies are used in the classroom, and measures of average class size. Presumably, the value of such process indicators lies in their assumed relationship to outcomes such as student learning and preparation for the contemporary workplace, though some clearly have other symbolic purposes as well. But, to the extent possible, why not measure and provide incentives for the desired results directly rather than using imperfect proxies that are prone to obsolescence?

40. The new indicator is the Graduation Efficiency Index (GEI), which relates the number of credits a student accumulates to the number required for the degree (Gillmore & Hoffman, 1997).

41. The graduation efficiency target can even be designed to allow for a "reasonable" number of credits beyond the minimum needed for the degree.

42. Of course, one might ultimately wish to see a less input-driven indicator than student credits per faculty, but persuading state participants on such a symbol-laden topic is likely to be an extended process.

References

American Association of University Professors. (1986, January/February). 1940 statement of principles on academic freedom and tenure (Reprinted). *Academe*, pp. 52–54.

Anderson, M. (1992). *Impostors in the temple: American intellectuals are destroying our universities and cheating our students of their future.* New York: Simon & Schuster.

Association of Governing Boards. (1998). *Statement on institutional governance.* Washington, DC: Author.

Banta, T., Rudolph, L., Van Dyke, J., & Fischer, H. (1996). Performance funding comes of age in Tennessee. *Journal of Higher Education, 67*(1), 23–45.

Bennett, W. (1987, February 18). Our greedy colleges. *New York Times*, p. A31.

Berdahl, R. O. (1971). *Statewide coordination of higher education.* Washington, DC: American Council on Education.

Bloom, A. (1987). *The closing of the American mind.* New York: Simon & Schuster.

Burke, J. (1997a). *Performance-funding indicators: Concerns, values, and models for two- and four-year colleges and universities.* Albany: State University of New York, Rockefeller Institute of Government.

Burke, J. (1997b, July 9). *Performance funding for state colleges and universities: Review and recommendations.* Paper presented at an Education Commission of the States workshop, Providence, RI.

Burke, J., & Serban, A. (1997). *State performance funding and budgeting for public higher education: Current status and future prospects.* Albany: State University of New York, Rockefeller Institute of Government.

Burke, J., & Serban, A. (1998). *Current status and future prospects of performance funding and performance budgeting for public higher education: The second sur-*

vey. Albany: State University of New York, Rockefeller Institute of Government.

Christal, M. (1998). *State survey on performance measures, 1996–97*. Denver, CO: State Higher Education Executive Officers.

College Board. (1998). *Trends in student aid*. New York: Author.

Drucker, P. (1985). *Innovation and entrepreneurship: Practice and principles*. New York: Harper & Row.

D'Souza, D. (1991). *Illiberal education: The politics of race and sex on campus*. New York: Free Press.

Gillmore, G., & Hoffman, P. (1997). The graduation efficiency index: Validity and use as an accountability and research measure. *Research in Higher Education, 38*, 677–698.

Glenny, L. (1959). *Autonomy of public colleges: The challenge of coordination*. New York: McGraw-Hill.

Glenny, L. (1976). *State budgeting for higher education*. Berkeley: University of California, Center for Research and Development in Higher Education.

Glenny, L., & Dalglish, T. (1973). *Public universities, state agencies and the law: Constitutional autonomy in decline*. Berkeley: University of California, Center for Research and Development in Higher Education.

Healy, P. (1997, March 21). Virginia board members urged to become activists. *Chronicle of Higher Education*, pp. A35–A36.

Healy, P., & Schmidt, P. (1998, July 10). In New York, a 'standards revolution' or the gutting of public colleges? *Chronicle of Higher Education*, pp. A21–A23.

Hofstadter, R. (1963). *Anti-intellectualism in American life*. New York: Vintage Books.

Hofstadter, R., & Metzger, W. (1955). *The development of academic freedom in the United States*. New York: Columbia University Press.

Huber, R. (1992). *How professors play the cat guarding the cream: Why we are paying more and getting less in higher education*. Fairfax, VA: George Mason University Press.

Immerwahr, J. (1997). *Enduring values, changing concerns: What Californians expect from their higher education system*. San Jose: California Higher Education Policy Center.

Institute for Research in Higher Education, University of Pennsylvania. (1997). Adding it up: The price-income squeeze in higher education. *Change, 29*, 45–48.

Keppel, F. (1987). The higher education acts contrasted, 1965–1986: Has federal policy come of age? *Harvard Educational Review, 57*(1), 49–67.

Lambert, M. (1997). *Performance funding: State profiles*. Unpublished manuscript, University of Washington, Graduate School of Public Affairs.

Lively, K. (1999, February 26). U. of Florida's 'bank' rewards colleges that meet key goals. *Chronicle of Higher Education*, pp. A35–A36.

Magner, D. (1999, June 18). Battle over academic control pits faculty against governing board at George Mason U. *Chronicle of Higher Education*, pp. A14–A16.

Marshall, R., & Tucker, M. (1992). *Thinking for a living: Education and the wealth of nations*. New York: Basic Books.

McGuinness, A. (1997). The functions and evolution of state coordination and governance in postsecondary education. In Education Commission of the States (Ed.), *1997 state postsecondary education structures sourcebook*, (pp. 1–48). Denver: Education Commission of the States.

MGT & Elway Research. (1995). *Washington state residents' views of higher education*. Olympia: Washington State Higher Education Coordinating Board.

Miller, M. (1998, September 4). Speed up the pace of campus governance, or lose the authority to make decisions. *Chronicle of Higher Education*, pp. B6–B7.

Nagel, J. H. (Ed.). (1997). *Journal of Policy Analysis and Management, 16*(3).

O'Neil, R. (1997). *Free speech in the college community*. Bloomington: Indiana University Press.

Osborne, D., & Gaebler, T. (1992). *Reinventing government: How the entrepreneurial spirit is transforming the public sector*. New York: Penguin.

Richardson, J. (1999, February 12). Centralizing campus governance isn't simply wrong; it's bad business, too. *Chronicle of Higher Education*, p. B9.

Rudolph, F. (1962). *The American college and university*. New York: Vintage Books.

Ruppert, S. (Ed.). (1994). *Charting higher education accountability: A sourcebook on state-level performance indicators*. Denver: Education Commission of the States.

Schmidt, P. (1996, May 24). Earning appropriations: States link spending on colleges to progress in meeting specific goals. *Chronicle of Higher Education*, pp. A23–A24.

Schmidt, P. (1997, April 4). Rancor and confusion greet a change in South Carolina's budgeting system. *Chronicle of Higher Education*, pp. A26–A27.

Selingo, J. (1999, February 5). Plan to reshape California State U. disturbs many faculty members. *Chronicle of Higher Education*, pp. A32–A33.

Serban, A. (1997, June). *Performance funding for public higher education: Views of critical stakeholders*. Paper presented at the American Association for Higher Education, Assessment and Quality Conference, Miami Beach, FL.

Smith, P. (1990). *Killing the spirit: Higher education in America*. New York: Viking.

Stimpson, C. (1998, January 16). Activist trustees wield power gone awry. *Chronicle of Higher Education*, pp. B4–B5.

Terry, L. D. (Ed.). (1998). *Public Administration Review, 58*(3).

Trombley, W. (1998). Performance-based budgeting: South Carolina's new plan mired in detail and confusion. *National CrossTalk, 6*(1), 1, 14–16.

Trow, M. (1993). Federalism in American higher education. In A. Levine (Ed.), *Higher learning in America, 1980–2000*. Baltimore: Johns Hopkins University Press.

Veysey, L. (1965). *The emergence of the American university*. Chicago: University of Chicago Press.

Washington State Higher Education Coordinating Board. (1997, June). *Guidelines for higher education accountability plans.* Olympia: Author.

Washington State Higher Education Coordinating Board. (1998, December). *Performance funding and accountability: Current status and recommendations for the future.* Olympia: Author.

Western Interstate Commission on Higher Education & College Board. (1998). *Projections of high school graduates by race/ethnicity 1996–2012.* Boulder, CO: Western Interstate Commission on Higher Education.

Zemsky, R., & Massy, W. (1990). Cost containment: Committing to a new economic reality. *Change, 22,* 16–22.

Zumeta, W. (1998). Public university accountability to the state in the late twentieth century: Time for a rethinking? *Policy Studies Review, 15*(4), 5–22.

Zumeta, W., & Fawcett-Long, J. (1997). State fiscal and policy climate for higher education: 1996. In H. Wechsler (Ed.), *The NEA 1997 almanac of higher education* (pp. 83–112). Washington, DC: National Education Association.

8 A Study in Tension:

State Assessment and Public Colleges
and Universities

MICHAEL NETTLES AND JOHN COLE

Today, as we perceive this elemental paradox in the tensions between the academy and the state, it is useful to keep in mind its generic quality. For at heart we are dealing, I submit, with a dilemma we cannot rationally wish to resolve. The public interest would not . . . be served if the academy were to enjoy an untroubled immunity. Nor could the public interest be served by the academy's being subjected to an intimate surveillance . . . Whatever our current discomforts, because of a sense that the state is crowding us a bit, the underlying tension is benign . . . the academy is for the state a benign antibody and the state is the academy's legitimator, benefactor, and protector. Both perspectives are valid. May they remain in tension. (Bailey, 1974, pp. 5–6)

Stephen Bailey got his wish. Since 1974, the tensions between states and institutions of higher education have remained a dominant feature of the public higher education policy landscape. In many states, the tensions have increased over the last quarter-century as state policymakers called for colleges and universities to be more accountable and a smaller proportion of institutional revenues came from state appropriations. Institutions now chafe under tightening budgets and perceived encroachments on their autonomy. The tensions between states and higher education institutions take a variety of forms, ranging from student financial aid policies and campus crime to faculty tenure and student access. Exacerbating these myriad tensions is the increasing competition for state funds between higher education and other state functions, such as health care, criminal justice, and elementary and secondary education (Zumeta, 1995; see Chapter 2 for more on the competition for state resources).

This chapter addresses another dimension of the tension between states and institutions: assessment, a relatively recent phenomenon in higher education. The need to assess institutions grew in concert with the explosion of government funding (both state and federal) for public higher education in the post–World War II era (Stevens & Hamlett, 1983). As president of a public university and later chancellor of the board of regents of a state university

198

system in the 1950s and 1960s, John Millett (1984) was well positioned to comment on this new trend in higher education. "State boards of higher education are going to hear a great deal about quality in the next several years. We have talked about quality in public higher education in the past, but I believe it is fair to say that at the level of state government our necessary preoccupation in the 1960s and 1970s was with quantity rather than quality. Now state governments will be told that it is time to give renewed attention to the quality of our higher education endeavors" (pp. x–xi).

With the large increases in state and federal funding for public higher education came a wave of national reports in the mid-1980s that hailed the need for substantive educational reform. Among the organizations producing such reports were the Association of American Colleges (1985), the National Institute of Education (1984), and the National Endowment for the Humanities (Bennett, 1984). Balancing these criticisms with a call to action on assessment was a paper by Peter Ewell (1985a), who argued that state governments should get involved in the assessment of undergraduate education because of states' significant financial investments in higher education and because successful higher education systems could contribute to other state policy objectives. Ewell's advice to state policymakers developing assessment policies included recommendations to recognize and preserve institutional diversity; to distinguish funding incentives for improvement from ongoing institutional funding mechanisms; and to give institutions discretion in achieving improvement but hold them accountable for regular demonstration of progress (Ewell, 1985b).

The states, in the form of the National Governors Association (1991), spoke out. In the report *Time for Results,* the governors made their position clear. "The public has a right to know what it is getting for its expenditure of tax resources; the public has a right to know and understand the quality of undergraduate education that young people receive from publicly funded colleges and universities. They have a right to know that their resources are being wisely invested and committed" (p. 3).

Thus the stage was set and all the players were assembled for the higher education policy drama about to unfold. The analogy between theater and higher education policymaking has been drawn most eloquently by Bruce Johnstone (1998). "Planning and decision-making [in higher education] are often exercised in a veritable cauldron of political theatre, posturing, and political agendas . . . Also cynical and ultimately injurious to the strategic planning process can be the purely political demand for a new strategic plan simply to discredit a current or past administration, or to take the credit for forcing the president or chancellor or governing board to do something rigorous and businesslike, with little regard for the output of the exercise. Thus, the theatre of strategic planning in the public sector" (p. 2).

We provide elsewhere a more detailed history of the evolution of the assessment movement at the levels of state government and regional accrediting associations from 1986 to the present, together with a review of the research on these topics (Nettles, Cole, & Sharp, 1997). The history and literature review are useful for understanding the context of this chapter, which explores in greater detail the relationship between state-level assessment policies and institutional assessment practices.

The chapter begins with a focused review of the literature on the role of the state in the governance of higher education, the relationship between state regulation and institutional autonomy, and the effects of differing state higher education governance structures on higher education policy. Following a synthesis of this review relating these broad topics to the more specific issues of assessment and accountability, we report the second- and third-year findings from our research project on state-level assessment, as part of our work with the National Center for Postsecondary Improvement. These findings are drawn from the thirty-eight responses to a questionnaire on state-level assessment policies sent to all fifty state higher education academic officers in late 1997. The chapter concludes with our interpretations of the data and suggestions for future research.

Research on the Governance Role of the State:
A Literature Review

In much of the scholarly literature, research on the role of the state in the governance of public higher education has focused on statewide boards of higher education. These boards are largely products of the last half-century. In 1940, thirty-three states had no statewide board or structure for coordinating higher education; by 1970, only two states lacked some kind of statewide governance structure (Berdahl, 1974). Much of the early scholarly treatment of statewide higher education boards featured efforts to define and categorize the various types of boards (Berdahl, 1971). By the early 1970s, a widely accepted taxonomy for the governance structures of the fifty states had been developed (Berdahl, 1974):

- States with no coordinating structure
- States in which institutions formed a voluntary association with varying degrees of coordinating activity
- States with advisory coordinating agencies, which were state-mandated and gave advice on policy matters but did not supersede the authority of institutional or system boards

- States with regulatory coordinating agencies with final approval on some policy matters
- States with consolidated governing boards

More fine-grained distinctions among statewide boards of higher education were offered by some scholars and practitioners. In particular, Millett (1974) addressed the distinction between coordinating boards and statewide governing boards. "There is a fundamental difference between a state coordinating board of higher education and a statewide governing board for institutions of higher education. The difference is essentially one of orientation: the state board of higher education is necessarily oriented toward state government. The statewide governing board is necessarily oriented toward state institutions of higher education. This difference is reflected in their activities as well as in the kinds of persons who are selected as their chief executive officer or professional administrator" (p. 61).

Millett elaborated on this difference in orientations. State coordinating boards are more involved with higher education policy issues that attract the interests of the governor and legislature, whereas governing boards are more concerned with policy issues not addressed by the governor or the legislature or those that the institutions would rather not have addressed by legislation. Another key difference is perspective: a state board "is concerned with a state government point of view to provide adequately but not excessively for higher education . . . Governing boards, on the other hand, want all the support they can obtain, are very mindful of the unfilled needs they would like to meet, are convinced of the particular capacity of their institution and campuses to provide educational service to the state, and seek to advance the prestige and status of their particular institution" (Millett, 1974, p. 65). Based on this observation, it is not unreasonable to see tensions not only between the state and the institutions but also among the institutions themselves as they compete for state support and public prestige.

Armed with this taxonomy, some scholars began the task of researching the actions, decisions, dynamics, and effectiveness of the state boards. The task was made formidable by a number of issues, among which was the role of individual personalities. "To keep things in perspective, one should acknowledge that the success or failure of state boards will normally be more dependent on the role of personalities than on the issue of structure or powers" (Berdahl, 1974, p. 4). Berdahl goes on to quote from Sam Gould at length, and Gould's eloquent and insightful observations are worth repeating here.

> The more subtle personal contacts . . . are the warp and woof of the fabric of the relationship [between state and university] . . . such contacts defy rules and de-

finitions and formulas . . . They are the true means by which the delicate balance
of authority, responsibility, and interdependence existing between the university and state government is maintained, or, when matters go awry, is upset. They
represent the interplay of personalities, the development of attitudes on the part
of these personalities reflecting a clear understanding of respective roles and
motivations, and most of all the creation of a climate of mutual trust and respect. (Gould, 1966, p. 4)

Another difficulty, perhaps related to the role of individual personalities,
is the power and influence of a state board relative to the authority granted
in its enabling legislation. "Some agencies have more power . . . because they
are heavy on informal power, influence, and 'credibility' with state officials
and the public . . . The web of informal relationships, communication, and
respect among legislators and the state agency is extremely important and is
often overlooked" (Miller, 1970, p. 49).

By the early 1980s, the literature on the role of the state in higher education policy was more mature, and this maturity gave scholars a chance both
to reflect on the development of the state's role (and the corresponding state
agencies) and to look ahead to its future. One critical observation, from a
structural perspective, addressed the potentially unchecked control many
state governments could exert over institutions of higher education. "State
legislatures and executive agencies can exercise virtually unlimited control
over the public colleges and universities in their state" (Glenny & Schmidtlein, 1983, p. 134). The notable exceptions to this rule were those states where
institutions or their boards, or both, were given special constitutional status
and thus (in theory) were not as vulnerable to state intervention or control.
Despite the potential in most states for unchecked intrusion into institutional affairs, Glenny and Schmidtlein were not fearful of the state's motives.
"There are many ways in which states can intervene in higher education, and
all of these usually are exercised to further legitimate state interests" (p. 134).

Glenny and Schmidtlein delineated the various roles of states in higher
education policy: access; instruction; research; public service; general support (i.e., budgeting); governance, coordination, and administration; and accountability (here the authors focused on the financial dimension of accountability, such as adherence to certain accounting procedures, auditing of
accounts, and rules for purchasing). For each of these policy areas, Glenny
and Schmidtlein spelled out some possible implications of state control, including the state's ability to fix the number, distribution, and qualifications
of admitted students; to eliminate academic program duplication; to require
certain state-relevant research and development activity; and to use bud-

getary procedures or funding levels to enforce policy agendas. Interestingly, and very significant to the topic of this chapter, Glenny and Schmidtlein reiterated the findings from earlier research indicating that political staffs are more important than politicians. As many research projects revealed, "in most states, state agency staffs involved with higher education have far more direct influence on policy and specific courses of action than do governors and legislators. Exceptions generally occur when an issue reaches high political salience" (p. 141).

Given these potential areas of greater state involvement in higher education and the possible implications of such involvement, Glenny and Schmidtlein then turned to a discussion about the future and the trends and issues likely to influence state roles and functions from 1985 to 2005. In the area of economics, they highlighted a growing competition for state funds, the rising cost of higher education (relative to the cost of living), and an inability to increase productivity; in the social sphere, they predicted declining public support for higher education and growing suspicion about its socioeconomic benefits. As for the effect these trends would have, Glenny and Schmidtlein expected states to scrutinize institutions and hold them more accountable, certainly in comparison to other competitors for shrinking state funds. "The anticipation of fiscal stringency is causing state governments to examine the productivity of higher education and its economic benefits . . . The growing familiarity of the public with higher education, together with its diminished role as a conveyor of social and economic status, no doubt will adversely affect its funding competition with other state programs" (p. 148). This was precisely the reality of state policy when examined by William Zumeta (1995) twelve years later.

A little more than a quarter-century after writing his landmark *Autonomy of Public Colleges* (1959), Glenny had the chance to reexamine the modern concept of state coordination of higher education. He concluded that "organizations and procedures for conducting coordination continue in a dynamic state. The less power the agency has, the more dynamic the operational milieu. The accelerating trend in the nation is for more centralization of public higher education" (Glenny, 1985, p. 18). Reviewing more than forty years of state coordination, he argued that state legislators used coordination to "try to bring order to the inevitable chaos of institutional parochialism in pursuing self-interests . . . All state leaders want outstanding institutions, thoroughly educated students, well-conducted research, and continued development of new knowledge. They believe these ends are better achieved through coordination and planning than by allowing each institution, at will, to create new centers, add new programs, and adjust admission standards and tuition as if such independent actions in the aggregate promote the best interests of the state" (p. 1).

Commenting on the relative strengths and weaknesses of state coordination, Glenny (1985) concluded that "coordination has been effective . . . As one examines the four major functions of coordination—planning, budgeting, program review, and policy analysis—the record is clear" (p. 11). On the subject of budgeting, Glenny's words foreshadowed the rise of performance funding. He advised states that, given the success of objective formula funding in contrast to a more subjective, political process, "supplementing formula budgeting with 'quality funding' should be done cautiously to prevent political power rather than academic merit from again becoming determinative" (p. 12).

Among the weaknesses in statewide coordination, Glenny (1985) saw an unwillingness by coordinating boards and staffs "to involve faculty members and administrators from the institutions in a full and open manner that leads to better and more acceptable policy recommendations" (p. 14). He also noted a communications gap between coordinating boards and state legislators: he saw "poor continuing contacts with legislators and their staffs on matters of importance, both during sessions and between them, thus failing to overcome the legislative view of the agency as one closely tied to the governor and his budget office" (p. 15). In a sense, Glenny envisioned the coordinating boards as inhabiting a no-man's-land between administrators and faculty on the one hand and legislators on the other, and as struggling to establish consistent, effective communication with either side. This breakdown in communication is a major impediment to the ultimate success of coordination. "By whatever agency performed, the most successful coordination involves widespread participation by faculty and administrators of the coordinated organizations, experts and lay people from the public and representatives of organizations interested in education" (p. 20).

From his perspective in 1985, Glenny looked ahead to issues that coordinating agencies would face in the late 1980s and beyond. One in particular deserves mention here: the measurement of educational progress. "Some states have adopted assessment exams at the postsecondary level. Some states apply similar tests to students and even to the instructors in teacher education programs . . . Though the results of applying such devices are mixed, the pressure will increasingly be on higher education to measure educational progress for college programs of all kinds. This is an area of public policy requiring coordination, at least among all the public institutions" (p. 17).

In the late 1980s the literature shifted again, this time from description, review, and evaluation to prediction and the correlation of governance characteristics with higher education policy behaviors. The pioneer in this field is James Hearn, who in 1996 coauthored a study of state tuition and student financial aid policies in the fifty states (Hearn, Griswold, & Marine, 1996). Among the findings from this study were statistically significant relationships between a variety of variables—including the geographic region in which a state is located, social and economic resources (e.g., state population, average disposable income, and high school graduation rate), and higher education governance structures—and the type of tuition and student financial aid policies at the state level.

Preceding the study of states' tuition and financial aid policies was a similar analysis by Hearn and Carolyn Griswold (1994) on the relationship between state-level centralization and innovations in higher education policy. Their definition of a policy innovation was a "qualitatively distinct action, not changes at the margins to existing structures and processes" (p. 165). One policy innovation included in the study was mandatory student assessment; Hearn and Griswold found that states with relatively centralized governance structures were more likely than other states to impose mandatory student assessment policies. The other policy innovations (the dependent variables) were whether "states required tests for teaching assistants, offered a tax-exempt college savings bond, offered a pre-paid college tuition plan, restricted or taxed college businesses, made vandalism of animal-research facilities a crime, allowed nontraditional paths for certification of K–12 teachers, and required that high school teachers not be education majors" (p. 165).

In outlining the conceptual framework for the study, Hearn and Griswold described the setting in which states and higher education institutions found themselves in the 1990s. "The context for postsecondary education in this era is arguably one both producing and calling for substantive policy change. Resources are extraordinarily tight, and higher education often represents the single largest item of discretionary spending in a state's budget. As a consequence, colleges are under increased scrutiny by the public and legislators. In many states, this context has led directly to substantive, novel policy action on a wide variety of fronts. For example, policymakers concerned over the quality of postsecondary graduates in their states imposed new outcome assessment programs on their public institutions in the 1980s" (p. 165).

Hearn and Griswold also attempted to describe the roles of various players in the higher education policy domain, acknowledging that governing and coordinating bodies are "only sometimes the originators or the driving forces behind breakaway innovations in postsecondary policy" (p. 165). Among the roles of higher education governance officials are "mediators, ne-

gotiators, analysts, 'fine tuners,' and facilitators" (p. 165). Governing and coordinating bodies "serve as active participants in policy debates, as significant agents in implementing policy, and, more generally, as important actors
in postsecondary policy contexts . . . It is no exaggeration to suggest that governance agencies can and often do help propel or block innovations. They
therefore must be viewed as potentially critical actors in a state's consideration of change in the postsecondary arena" (p. 165).

Ultimately, Hearn and Griswold chose John Kingdon's (1984) "policy
stream" framework as a means of conceptualizing their discussion of the
higher education policy process. "In keeping with Kingdon's view, we see
governance arrangements not as ultimately determining forces in rationally
organized political systems, but rather as potentially influential forces among
a welter of potentially influential forces" (Hearn & Griswold, 1994, p. 166).
Kingdon's study of how issues reached the policy agenda at the federal government level is a landmark in the political science and policy analysis fields.
Some of his insights have profound implications for state higher education
policy analysis, such as his conclusion that the federal government is an "organized anarchy" and that "separate streams run through the organization,
each with a life of its own. These streams are coupled at critical junctures,
and that coupling produces the greatest agenda change" (Kingdon, 1984,
pp. 90–91). Kingdon enumerated three "families" of processes in agenda setting at the federal level—problems, policies, and politics—and three major
process "streams"—problem recognition, formation and refining of policy
proposals, and politics.

> First, various problems come to capture the attention of people in and around
> government . . . Second, there is a policy community of specialists—bureau-
> crats, people in the planning and evaluation and in the budget offices, [Capitol]
> Hill staffers, academics, interest groups, researchers—which concentrates on
> generating proposals. They each have their pet ideas or axes to grind; they float
> their ideas up and the ideas bubble around in these policy communities. In a
> selection process, some ideas or proposals are taken seriously and others are dis-
> carded . . . Third, the political stream is composed of things like swings of na-
> tional mood, vagaries of public opinion, election results, changes of adminis-
> tration, shifts in partisan or ideological distributions in Congress, and interest
> group pressure campaigns . . . Each of the actors and processes can operate ei-
> ther as an impetus or as a constraint. (p. 92)

Given this description of an ever-changing policy landscape, Hearn and
Griswold (1994) pointed out that "it is rare for a given body or agency or interest to be able to claim a consistently preordained superior level of power

in public policy debates" (p. 166). Kingdon's examination of the federal-level policy process may be useful as a theoretical framework for considering the state-level assessment policy process and its streams.

Hearn and Griswold's basic hypothesis is that "policy innovation in postsecondary education will be associated with several interrelated factors: a state's size, region, educational development, and socioeconomic development, in addition to its postsecondary governance arrangement" (p. 166). They found mixed results, but two broad themes emerged. "First, governance structures are the most influential in the core educational activities of states' postsecondary enterprise: teaching, research, and the preparation of citizens and workers. Statewide governing boards and strong coordinating boards are positively associated with innovation in academic areas, *such as the assessment of undergraduates* . . . A second theme in the findings for governance arrangements is the striking absence of systematic differences in innovation patterns between states with consolidated governing boards and states with strong coordinating boards" (p. 183, emphasis added).

Isolating results from Hearn and Griswold's multiple regression analysis allows for a fuller picture of the relationships between their selected independent variables and the development of a mandatory state-level assessment policy. Larger states (in terms of population) were more "innovative" in their academic policies, but the difference between large and small states in requiring student assessment dropped out when confounding factors were controlled for. Along other dimensions, states in the southeastern United States (Alabama, Arkansas, Florida, Georgia, Kentucky, Louisiana, Mississippi, North Carolina, South Carolina, Tennessee, and Virginia) were most likely to require assessment. The percentage of a state's population with at least a high school education also had a positive relationship with a mandated assessment policy. None of the other independent variables, including higher education enrollment and wealth, were significant at the $p \leq 0.15$ level.

Hearn and Griswold concluded by raising a number of issues for future study, including the need to "identify successful and unsuccessful innovations, or hostile and friendly innovations, and relate these systematically to different kinds of state governance arrangements" (p. 184). Echoing the advice of Robert Berdahl, they stressed the importance of individuals in the policy process. "There can be no question that individuals play an important role in postsecondary reform as well. For example, a number of southern governors have been quite influential in developing assessment and teacher education reforms in their states. These individual efforts deserve consideration in serious analyses of innovation in postsecondary education" (p. 185).

Hearn and Griswold saw a "chicken and egg" dilemma here: does centralization produce innovation, or does innovation somehow bring about centralization? Finally, they recommended adding other contextual factors into the
state policy analysis, such as the existence of regional associations, the size of
governing or coordinating boards, the size of related professional staffs, the
number of institutions under the control of a state board, and the public-
private mix of institutions in a particular state.

Another natural direction for research on the state role in higher education is examination of the relationship between state regulation and institutional autonomy. This concern dates back to Glenny's first book on the
subject, appropriately entitled *Autonomy of Public Colleges* (1959), but more
empirical attempts have since been made to understand this vital ramifica-
tion of state governance.

J. Fredericks Volkwein (1987) examined the subject of state regulation
and campus autonomy, beginning with a brief review of the various conceptualizations of institutional autonomy. Berdahl (1971) distinguished between *procedural* and *substantive* autonomy; procedural autonomy is largely
administrative in nature, whereas substantive autonomy addresses academic
matters. Both the Carnegie Foundation's (1982) report on the governance of
American higher education and Daniel Levy's (1980) analysis of government's role in higher education in Mexico differentiated among three types
of autonomy: *academic, financial,* and *personnel,* which are self-explanatory.

Based on his research from the mid-1980s, and using these three types
of autonomy, Volkwein (1987) developed continua of academic and financial
centralization on which he placed the fifty states. On the academic dimension, the continuum runs from centralized (which he compared to a European ministry model of academic administration) to independent (which he
compared to a free-market model). On the financial dimension, the continuum runs from centralized (state agency) to decentralized (state-controlled
and state-aided) to independent (or corporate model). As of 1983, Volkwein
ranked no state as independent in either the academic or financial realms.

Summarizing the existing literature on state regulation in 1987, Volkwein
highlighted six main themes: (1) the amount of regulation had grown over
the preceding forty years; (2) regulation varied widely from state to state; (3)
greater regulation was seen as a disincentive to good campus management;
(4) state regulation was under criticism, especially in states with more centralized arrangements; (5) in general, universities' relationships with state
governments had remained fairly static; and (6) changes since the mid-1980s
had been more deregulatory in nature.

Volkwein then reviewed the literature on the various factors leading to state regulation of higher education, classifying them as socioeconomic and political. In the socioeconomic realm, he hypothesized that "to the extent that state regulation of public universities is a 'policy outcome,' the relative amounts of tax capacity and effort, urbanization, industrialization, population characteristics, and education levels in each state should be associated with university fiscal and academic autonomy" (p. 136). In the political realm, he highlighted the roles of governors, legislatures, political parties, and governance structure. He found, based on his literature review, that governors were "increasingly viewed as a dominant figure in public higher education . . . governors rarely intervene in regulatory policy issues but, instead, are likely to allow them to be handled by other state officers . . . Governors were likely to intervene directly when there was a strong relationship between an institution's programs and the political interests of the governor" (pp. 137–138). Volkwein also found a consensus that legislatures and their staffs had a significant influence on education policy, but the nature of the influence was not detailed. In terms of political parties, Volkwein reported that the "more a state is characterized by a pattern of elected Democrats and by a large number of government employees, the more likely it is to be active in educational policy" (p. 138). Finally, he reviewed much of the literature discussed above (Berdahl, 1971, 1974; Millett, 1974, 1984) that pointed to a relationship between governance structure and higher education policy.

    In his own research, Volkwein used multiple regression analysis to explore and quantify the relationships between various state characteristics and the three types of state regulation—academic, financial, and personnel. In terms of academic regulation, the most relevant for the purposes of this chapter, Volkwein found six state characteristics significantly predictive of academic regulation: (1) expenditures per capita for higher education, (2) population density, (3) public enrollment in higher education per thousand, (4) Democratic party strength, (5) number of government employees, and (6) ratio of private to public universities. Of these, expenditures per capita and public enrollment per thousand were negatively correlated with the amount of state regulation on academic issues. Overall, Volkwein's data revealed "neither consistent nor strong correlations between the amount of state regulation, on the one hand, and the major economic, social, and political variables, on the other. The low relationships suggest that regulatory controls may perhaps be more idiosyncratic, and therefore more easily changed, than commonly believed by many in higher education" (p. 140).

    Volkwein revisited this topic in a later article on the changes in state regulation of higher education from the mid-1980s to the mid-1990s. He and his coauthor found that, generally speaking, "a significant number of states have delegated increased authority to their university campuses since the early 1980s" (Volkwein & Malik, 1997, p. 18). This was the trend across all three areas of regulation—academic, financial, and personnel. Looking again at whether certain socioeconomic and political characteristics of states resulted in greater state regulation of higher education, they came to essentially the same conclusion Volkwein had reached a decade earlier. "We find modest, but hardly dramatic, evidence of a relationship between a state's characteristics and the administrative controls it imposes on public universities" (p. 32).

Implications for State Case Studies of the Research on State Assessment Policies and Practices

One important manifestation of states' roles in the governance of public higher education, and the focus of our research at the National Center for Postsecondary Improvement, is state-level assessment policy. At least one of the studies reviewed above (Hearn & Griswold, 1994) made explicit reference to assessment of undergraduates as an example of innovation in higher education policy; the other studies have important implications for case studies of state assessment policies and practices. The synthesis that follows explains these implications as a means of informing the development of state case-study research protocols.

Four broad categories of issues emerge from the literature, each with its own set of implications: *process, personality, context,* and, for want of a better word, *concerns.* In terms of process, some of the older literature on statewide governance, particularly Millett's (1974), makes clear the importance of considering the orientation of states' higher education governance structures when analyzing any state policy, including assessment. What is the political orientation of governing and coordinating boards in each of the case-study states? Does Millett's observation that governing boards are oriented toward institutions and coordinating boards toward the state government hold true? If so, what intervening or mediating effects do these bodies have on the creation and implementation of assessment policies? To what extent do these bodies serve the political agendas of governors, legislators, institutional administrators, and faculty, vis-à-vis assessment? Is one type of governance structure more likely to have a positive influence on the nature and extent of assessment requirements imposed on institutions?

Another critical element of process is communication, among all groups involved in the higher education policy arena. Glenny (1985) observed an unwillingness of some coordinating boards and staffs to communicate with administrators and faculty and to make them more equal partners in the policy process. Is this occurring with the assessment policy process? Does the communication gap work in the other direction, between boards and legislators? Can the communication process be seen as a triangle, with the legislature as one point, coordinating/governing boards as another point, and institutions as the third? If so, which lines of communication are open and which are closed? Does a lack of communication result in confusion or resentment over the perceived intrusiveness of state-mandated assessment requirements at the state level?

Finally, perhaps we can apply Kingdon's (1984) policy stream model as a way of understanding the state assessment policy process. Do the streams that Kingdon saw in the federal policy process—problems, policies, and politics—also run through the landscape of state assessment policy for public higher education? If so, where are the crucial junctures, and how does the coupling of these streams produce changes in a state's assessment agenda? What can we learn about the assessment policy process by looking at it from this perspective, and how might this perspective contribute to the creation of a policy model for improvement?

Beyond process there is personality. Discussions about the role of personalities in the policy arena go back at least as far as Berdahl (1974), who suggested that the ultimate success or failure of state governance structures depended more on personalities than on other considerations. James Miller (1970) also stressed the importance of individual personalities and "the web" of personal relationships, and reminded researchers that these relationships are largely neglected in most analyses. Personality is, by its nature, difficult to quantify, and tracing the influence of this nebulous factor on the development of assessment policy in public higher education will prove a daunting task. But by using case studies and semi-structured interviews with key persons in state higher education policymaking, we can make at least some progress toward understanding how personality affects policy.

Providing the backdrop for both process and personality are the contexts—social, economic, and political—and how they interact. Glenny and Schmidtlein (1983) forecast the growing competition for state funds between higher education and other state activities; in his review of state budgets and policy developments, Zumeta (1995) confirmed this competition as a reality in many states. In short, the economic context for higher education has been a difficult one and has resulted in greater demands for accountability and for evidence that state investment in higher education is justified. From this angle, state-level assessment policies were inevitable. In the social context, Glenny and Schmidtlein (1983) also pointed to the diminishing public trust and confidence in higher education, leading to a chillier political climate for colleges and universities in many state legislatures. As Howard Bowen (1977) observed in his book *Investment in Learning,* even in the 1970s the American public had become less deferential to higher education and increasingly doubtful that public investment in higher learning produced a return either sufficiently public or sufficiently good. This unfortunate trend of public skepticism about higher education has continued to the present day.

A more systematic analysis of the various contexts in which state higher education policy operates was presented by Hearn and Griswold (1994). They measured the correlations between a variety of socioeconomic and political characteristics of a state and its tendency to engage in higher education policy innovations, including assessment. While they found little evidence of a correlation between many characteristics and assessment, some—location in the southeastern United States and percentage of the population with at least a high school education—did prove statistically significant. Others, such as wealth and higher education enrollment, did not. Why are certain characteristics predictive of a state assessment policy and others not? Given that certain characteristics have an effect, *what* is the effect? Is there a regional effect in the southeast? Is this effect partly the result of individual personalities, such as those of governors, as Berdahl proposes? Are there substantial or interesting differences between assessment policies in the southeast and in other regions of the country?

Volkwein's (1987) results demonstrating a correlation between a variety of noteworthy characteristics and the amount of academic regulation in states addressed academic regulation more broadly, but state-mandated assessment policies could fit neatly as examples of academic regulation. What relationship, if any, exists between characteristics such as expenditures per capita for higher education or the ratio of private to public institutions and a state's tendency to require assessment? In other words, can Volkwein's findings be extrapolated from the general to the specific (from academic regulation to assessment)? If not, what makes assessment different from other types of state regulation?

A reading of the state governance literature raises other concerns related to assessment. Glenny (1985) argued that state legislators knew what they wanted in terms of higher education and their desires were compatible with the wants and needs of institutions. Is this true for assessment? When state legislators approve an assessment requirement for institutions, do they really know what they want this requirement to accomplish? Are some state legislators interested in assessment only as a tool of accountability? What happens when the interests of legislatures and universities collide? Does assessment promote a legitimate state interest? What balance should be struck between a state's interest in accountability and an institution's interest in autonomy?

Hearn and Griswold (1994) used the imposition of state-mandated assessment requirements as one of their higher education policy innovations, which they defined as "qualitatively distinct actions, not changes at the margins to existing structures and processes" (p. 165). Is assessment an innovation by this definition? Are some states using existing structures and processes to achieve assessment? If so, what degree of innovation is lost? Our work through the National Center for Postsecondary Improvement is looking closely at reforms and innovations in higher education.

Last, and perhaps most important, what is the nature of the tension between state-mandated assessment and institutional autonomy? Understanding how state regulation affected campus autonomy was one of Volkwein's (1987) chief concerns. However we envision autonomy—distinguishing between procedural and substantive autonomy, as did Berdahl (1974), or among academic, financial, and personnel autonomies, as did Levy (1980)—there can be little question that state assessment policies have some impact on institutional autonomy. This is perhaps the single largest source of controversy surrounding assessment, and it will likely remain the most pressing concern of faculty.

Preliminary Research Findings

In an initial attempt to explore a few of these issues, as part of our research through the National Center for Postsecondary Improvement at the University of Michigan we sent a questionnaire to all fifty state higher education academic officers. The questionnaire contained a range of items, some of them designed to elicit responses related to issues of process and personality, as discussed above. Here we outline some of the preliminary results.

Respondents were asked to rank the significance of twelve entities for each of five stages in the assessment policy process (the stages and their definitions are adapted from Anderson, Brady, Bullock, & Stewart, 1984):

Entities evaluated

- State legislature
- Governor/executive staff
- Executive agencies
- System boards of trustees/regents
- Campus executive officers
- Faculty
- External consultants
- Existing policies and practices on campuses
- Other state policies and practices
- Professional organizations
- Regional accrediting associations
- Disciplinary accrediting associations

Policy stages

- Problem formation
- Policy formulation
- Policy adoption
- Policy implementation
- Policy evaluation

The significance scale ranged from 1 to 4, with 1 representing not significant; 2, slightly significant; 3, moderately significant; and 4, very significant.

For *problem formation* (when the need for an assessment policy is expressed), respondents ranked system boards of trustees/regents as the most significant, followed closely by state legislatures and campus executive officers. At this earliest stage in the policy process, state legislatures enjoy their greatest significance, a finding that reinforces the widely held belief that the call for assessment in public higher education has been largely a political phenomenon, generated by legislators looking to hold institutions more accountable.

For *policy formulation*, when a variety of policy options are presented and considered, respondents reversed the order and scored campus executive officers as most significant, with system boards trailing slightly. State legislatures ranked third, but well behind system boards. Is this decrease in the role of the legislatures a symptom of the communication gap between institutions and legislatures? Could this be the stage when campus and system leaders try to wrest control of the assessment issue from legislators, in the hope of minimizing intrusion on campus autonomy?

Campus executive officers are also the most significant entities during *policy adoption*, when support forms, shifts, and re-forms around different options. Following campus executive officers in terms of significance are system boards, faculty, and existing campus policies and practices. The responses here seem to reflect the prevalence of campus-based entities, including faculty, in determining the "nuts and bolts" of the assessment policy. This makes intuitive sense, given that the campuses and faculty are ultimately responsible for whatever policy is finally developed.

During *policy implementation*, campus executive officers again rank as the most significant, followed closely by faculty and more distantly by system boards. Once more, campus-based entities—executive officers and faculty—are the leaders, on the front lines of the implementation effort. The lower significance scores of legislatures and governors may indicate that in most states, political interference from the state level is limited. Whether this is the result of the state's respect for institutional autonomy or campuses' precautions to protect their "turf" remains to be determined.

Finally, during *policy evaluation,* campus executive officers rank first yet again. System boards are second, and faculty finish third.

While these data are preliminary, they hint at some interesting issues that echo the literature and illuminate paths for case-study research. For example, in terms of campus executive officers, it will be interesting to explore how their personalities (à la Berdahl) influence the assessment policy process and how the web of relationships (à la Miller) between campus leaders and state legislators drives assessment policy decisions. On the topic of system boards, case-study research is needed to ascertain the political orientation of these boards (a factor stressed by Millett) and whether (and if so, how) orientation affects assessment policy.

These data would also seem to suggest four predominant entities in the assessment policy process: campus executive officers, system boards, faculty, and state legislatures. Some combination of these ranked as the three most significant entities during all five policy stages. Our data are based on the policy process framework developed by Anderson et al. (1984), and this model may be too rigid to capture the more fluid movements of other entities during the process. Perhaps Kingdon's (1984) policy stream model, by emphasizing problems, policies, and politics rather than stages, would provide a fuller, richer picture. For these and many other questions, only the case studies will tell.

Conclusion

Although states do not "practice to deceive," it is a tangled web they weave as they continue to develop and implement assessment policies and practices. Assessment remains a controversial and problematic issue for the entire higher education community, from regional accrediting associations and state legislatures to campus presidents and individual faculty members. This chapter has taken an important step toward untangling the web. Assessment will surely persist as a leading concern in higher education, and higher education researchers and policymakers should work together to ensure that this powerful policy tool is used properly to prepare and improve American higher education for the twenty-first century.

To some extent, the laudable goals of ensuring that a college education is both affordable *and* accessible—goals of public higher education in the United States since the 1960s—decreased in importance as accountability came to the fore in the 1990s. Interestingly, state policymakers are generally less concerned with access and affordability. Many have simply added accountability to their list of expectations: they want public higher education to be affordable, accessible, *and* accountable. As a result, tension between the state and higher education has increased. But how will this relatively new tension affect the longstanding, widely shared aims of affordability and access?

As Bailey (1974) implied, some tension between academy and state is healthy and desirable. In moderation, it can serve as a creative force for improvement and innovation. Among the standard dictionary definitions of *tension* are the following: "the interplay of conflicting elements" and "a balanced relation between strongly opposed elements." Key words in both of these definitions—*interplay* and *balanced*—suggest that tension can be positive when the elements are equal and when the interaction includes give and take from both elements to produce a reasonable compromise. Tension can quickly become unhealthy and disruptive when the elements are out of balance and one exerts a greater force on the other. In recent history, states have had to exert relatively little force on public higher education to ensure affordability and access because the state and the institutions shared these goals. (In recent years, in the wake of the affirmative action backlash, higher education has been exerting force on states to preserve access for underrepresented or disadvantaged populations.) In most cases, the tension worked at the margins, establishing the parameters within which states and institutions could operate effectively.

With the increasing clamor for accountability and the implementation of policies such as performance funding to hold higher education accountable, the tension in some states has reached a critical point. States and institutions do not necessarily share the goal of accountability, or at least they do not define accountability in the same way, and institutions are quick to defend their autonomy from invasive state-mandated assessment and accountability policies. And some in higher education argue that certain accountability measures result in *decreased* access, because institutions, especially those with missions to serve underprepared students, might be forced to raise admissions requirements to comply with state accountability standards—an essential response when state funding is linked to institutional success in meeting state-mandated performance criteria. Thus, even legislators deeply committed to maintaining affordability and access may undermine such goals by establishing accountability policies that have unintended or unforeseen consequence—all the more reason why state policymakers need to know and understand every strand and skein in the tangled web of state higher education policy.

References

Anderson, J., Brady, D. W., Bullock, C. S., III, & Stewart, J., Jr. (1984). *Public policy and politics in America*. Monterey, CA: Brooks/Cole.

Association of American Colleges. (1985). *Integrity in the college curriculum: A report to the academic community: The findings and recommendations of the project on redefining the meaning and purpose of baccalaureate degrees*. Washington, DC: Author.

Bailey, S. K. (1974). Education and the state. *Educational Record, 55*(1), 5–12.

Bennett, W. J. (1984). *To reclaim a legacy: A report on the humanities in higher education*. Washington, DC: National Endowment for the Humanities.

Berdahl, R. O. (1971). *Statewide coordination of higher education*. Washington, DC: American Council on Education.

Berdahl, R. O. (1974). Problems in evaluating statewide boards. In R. O. Berdahl (Ed.), *New directions for institutional research: Evaluating statewide boards*. San Francisco: Jossey-Bass.

Bowen, H. (1977). *Investment in learning: The individual and social value of American higher education*. San Francisco: Jossey-Bass.

Carnegie Foundation for the Advancement of Teaching. (1982). *The control of the campus: A report on the governance of higher education*. Princeton: Princeton University Press.

Ewell, P. (1985a). *Levers for change: The role of state government in improving quality of postsecondary education* (ECS Report No. PS-85-2). Denver: Education Commission of the States.

Ewell, P. (1985b, June). *The legislative role in improving postsecondary education*. Paper presented at the 1985 American Association of Higher Education Assessment Forum, Denver.

Glenny, L. A. (1959). *Autonomy of public colleges*. New York: McGraw-Hill.

Glenny, L. A. (1985). *State coordination of higher education: The modern concept*. Denver: State Higher Education Executive Officers.

Glenny, L. A., & Schmidtlein, F. A. (1983). The role of the state in the governance of higher education. *Educational Evaluation and Policy Analysis, 5*, 133–153.

Gould, S. (1966). The university and state government: Fears and realities. In W. J. Minter (Ed.), *Campus and capitol*. Boulder, CO: Western Interstate Commission on Higher Education.

Hearn, J. C., & Griswold, C. P. (1994). State-level centralization and policy innovation in U.S. postsecondary education. *Educational Evaluation and Policy Analysis, 16*, 161–190.

Hearn, J. C., Griswold, C. P., & Marine, G. M. (1996). Region, resources, and reason: A contextual analysis of state tuition and student aid policies. *Research in Higher Education, 37*, 241–278.

Johnstone, D. B. (1998, November). *Planning and change in public higher education*. Paper presented at the 1998 Meeting of the Association for the Study of Higher Education, Miami.

Kingdon, J. (1984). *Agendas, alternatives, and public policies.* Boston: Little, Brown.

Levy, D. C. (1980). *University and government in Mexico: Autonomy in an authoritarian system.* New York: Praeger.

Miller, J. (1970). New directions in statewide higher education planning and coordination. In *Proceedings of the Southern Regional Education Board 19th legislative work conference.* Atlanta: Southern Regional Education Board.

Millett, J. (1974). State coordinating boards and statewide governing boards. In R. O. Berdahl (Ed.), *New directions for institutional research: Evaluating statewide boards.* San Francisco: Jossey-Bass.

Millett, J. (1984). *Conflict in higher education.* San Francisco: Jossey-Bass.

National Governors Association. (1991). *Time for results: The governors' 1991 report on education.* Washington, DC: Author.

National Institute of Education. (1984). *Involvement in learning: Realizing the potential of American higher education: Final report of the Study Group on the Conditions of Excellence in American Higher Education.* Washington, DC: U.S. Department of Education.

Nettles, M., Cole, J., & Sharp, S. (1997). *Benchmarking assessment: Assessment of teaching and learning in higher education and public accountability* (NCPI Technical Report No. 5-02). Palo Alto, CA: National Center for Postsecondary Improvement.

Stevens, J., & Hamlett, B. D. (1983). State concerns for learning: Quality and state policy. In J. R. Warren (Ed.), *Meeting the new demands for standards.* San Francisco: Jossey-Bass.

Volkwein, J. F. (1987). State regulation and campus autonomy. In J. C. Smart (Ed.), *Higher education: Handbook of theory and research.* New York: Agathon Press.

Volkwein, J. F., & Malik, S. M. (1997). State regulation and administrative flexibility at public universities. *Research in Higher Education, 38,* 17–42.

Zumeta, W. (1995). State policy and budget developments. In *The 1995 NEA almanac of higher education.* Washington, DC: National Education Association.

9 The Call for Public Accountability:

Rethinking the Linkages to Student Outcomes

EDWARD P. ST. JOHN, KIMBERLY A. KLINE,
AND ERIC H. ASKER

Given the call for accountability in public higher education, we need to rethink the linkages between the use of accountability measures and the outcomes of higher education. Accountability measures are increasingly used in allotting supplemental funding to public universities, now an important issue to universities because of the erosion of state funding. State funding per full-time equivalent (FTE) student enrolled in public universities declined nationally in the last two decades (St. John, 1994b). By reaching agreements with state agencies about criteria for supplemental funding—in the guise of accountability—some public research universities have been able to increase their funding (Weerts, 1999). However, these new developments do not necessarily provide a sound basis for public policy, especially if the goals of access and affordability are to be maintained. Indeed, the use of accountability measures as currently constructed in many states can erode equal opportunity and diversity, especially if these measures were constructed without an understanding of student choice.

A rethinking of the ways in which accountability measures link to student-choice processes and higher education outcomes is in order. In this chapter we suggest an alternative way of viewing the linkages between accountability measures and student-related outcomes of higher education. First, we compare the dominant views on student outcomes (the developmental and change theories) with an alternative that bases accountability measures on a research-based understanding of how college students make educational choices. After providing a more detailed explanation of the student-choice perspective, we use this understanding to reexamine the links between student outcomes and the public accountability process and review recent developments in two states to illustrate how our alternative perspective might inform practice. The chapter ends with some suggestions about steps that states might take to refine their approaches to accountability and finance in higher education.

Evolving Policy Perspectives on Student Outcomes

During most of the twentieth century, taxpayers supported expanding access to state systems of higher education through direct subsidies to institutions, a strategy consonant with the general egalitarian goals of the progressive period. In the mid-1960s, the federal government began to make a substantial investment in student grants, improving affordability and emphasizing equal opportunity by providing a chance for all qualified students to attend college. These investments were rationalized by arguments about economic development and human capital (Slaughter, 1991). This strategy held together liberal interests (i.e., equal opportunity) and conservative interests (i.e., economic development) in support of public higher education systems for most of the century. It was also compatible with theories of student development widely used through the 1970s.

In the early 1980s, new conservative critiques of higher education began to push for greater accountability as a means of reducing the costs associated with the apparently inefficient public finance strategy. Efficiency became a central concern in the policy arena. After decades of valuing quality and opportunity as goals in the development of public systems, accountability became one widely used method of promoting efficiency within these systems. The new student-change theories were somewhat compatible with this new wave of policy, and attempts were made to illuminate these linkages.

However, tension between old progressive values and new pressures for accountability and control complicated efforts to manage and finance public higher education. Underlying assumptions about the goals of higher education were discarded in favor of indicators of quality not sufficiently linked to social goals. A third perspective, viewing students as educational choice makers, merits consideration. States could use this approach to focus more explicitly on social goals while responding to students' interests.

Developmental Theories and Equal Opportunity

Providing qualified students with the opportunity to develop personally, within the time-honored structure of the academy, was the vision of student outcomes most evident in higher education policy discourse through the 1970s. A set of developmental theories about college students evolved (e.g., Chickering, 1969, 1976; Perry, 1970), providing a basis for working with college students that was consonant with the liberal arts tradition. Most of these theories were initially based on studies of traditional college-age male students, such as William Perry's theory of college student development derived from a study of college men at Harvard. The theories dealt with both academic and student life experiences and supplied a basis for a discourse between faculty and the new professionals in student affairs.

As colleges and universities expanded and became more diverse, attempts were made to adapt these base theories to include female, minority, and older students. Research testing these theories assessed changes in students over time, using developmental schemes to interpret data. Initially the schemes were based on individual case studies, but a second wave of theories on ego development (Loevinger, 1976) and moral development (Kohlberg, 1981) used standardized instruments with measurable sequences of development.

These theories and related measurement instruments provided a way of focusing discourse in the academic community on student development but little opportunity to measure how academic practices and state subsidies influenced these outcomes. However, when developmental theories were influential in higher education research, public funding tended to be enrollment-driven and thus there was little reason to be concerned about this incongruity. The opportunity for individuals to develop may be a noble social goal, but it does not provide a basis for responding to new public concerns about accountability.

Change Theories and Accountability

A competing view of student outcomes gained broad acceptance in the 1980s, especially among state and federal policymakers. The change theories, originating with the work of Alexander Astin (1975, 1993), focused on the explicit empirical links between college experiences and student outcomes. The emerging theories of college choice (Hossler, Braxton, & Coopersmith, 1989; Jackson, 1978; Paulsen, 1990) and persistence (Bean, 1990; Tinto, 1987)—students' continued progress in attending college—provided well-specified ways of linking academic experience to student outcomes. Further, national longitudinal databases were used to test models linking finance policy to student outcomes—access (Jackson, 1978; St. John, 1990a, 1991), choice of college (Jackson, 1978; Manski & Wise, 1983; Tierney, 1980), and persistence (St. John, 1990b; St. John, Andrieu, Oescher, & Starkey, 1994; Terkla, 1985). These newer analytical models provided a better empirical basis for evaluating the effects of student aid programs.

These models were also much tighter in their conceptualizations of the linkages between higher education experiences and student outcomes. Gregory Jackson's (1978) research on access and college choice was an important conceptual and empirical breakthrough. He supplied not only a new conceptualization of the choice process but also a rationale for using student aid as an integral part of enrollment management. Ernest Pascarella and Patrick Terenzini's (1979, 1980, 1991) research on persistence was the foundation for another breakthrough. They used structural equation models to test Vincent Tinto's (1987) persistence theory, providing more systematic methods of linking college experiences to persistence. These new, tighter models gave researchers a foundation to explore; building better models became a preoccupation, a way of providing information that fueled a new academic discourse about the effects of college on students.

This structured way of thinking about the links between academic practices and student outcomes seemed more compatible with the new concerns of conservative policymakers of the 1980s about efficiency and accountability in higher education. Some advocated the idea of routinely assessing the outcomes of higher education and developing funding strategies to promote the desired outcomes (e.g., Astin, 1993). Despite some successful examples of state performance funding, such as Tennessee's efforts to enhance learning outcomes (Banta, Rudolph, VanDyke, & Fischer, 1996), state political coalitions have had difficulty holding together, in part because of ambiguities about outcomes (Hearn & Anderson, 1995). (See Chapter 7 for more on performance funding.)

The problems encountered with federal efforts to use default rates as a central outcome measure for the regulation of federal loans and other student aid programs are illustrative (St. John, 1994b). Research on loan default consistently indicates that students' background characteristics, rather than institutional practices, are the best predictors of default (Flint, 1997; Wilms, Moore, & Bolus, 1987). Eliminating Title IV funding because of high default rates, an approach taken in the 1980s and early 1990s, essentially penalized schools that served low-income students (St. John, 1994b). The federal government also required institutions to report persistence rates, and some states adopted the use of these measures in their accountability systems.

These initial efforts to use outcomes as a basis for public funding became problematic for at least two reasons. First, the conceptualization of student outcomes embedded in the new market approach carried forward a higher education–centered perspective that did not adequately consider diverse groups. For example, the use of performance-funding measures such as high rates of persistence to graduation or high scores on standardized admissions tests could bias results in favor of selective institutions with traditional clienteles (see Chapter 3 for more on this issue). It could also provide an incentive for these institutions to increase their selectivity. Ironically, only after higher education was extended to more students from diverse backgrounds in the 1960s and 1970s did states begin experimenting with the use of student outcome measures as a basis for funding. Many of the measures selected in these accountability efforts had this unintended bias in favor of selectivity.

Second, the change theories adapted for use in the new accountability models also carried forward a conventional set of assumptions about college students. Research on college students has focused nearly exclusively on traditional college-age students (Pascarella & Terenzini, 1991). A more explicit focus on how different measures might reward institutions serving nontraditional students (especially older students and students of color) was needed if these new accountability measures were to support the goals of expanding access and diversity. Thus, although student-change theories were more compatible with the new market-oriented policies aimed at promoting accountability and improving efficiency, they were adapted to inform new public policy initiatives that rewarded traditional patterns. These new initiatives may have discriminated against those most at risk of not gaining entry to college in the first place.

Student-Choice Theory

Investigating how students actually make educational choices provides an alternative to the two competing perspectives on student outcomes. Student-choice theory is based on critical reviews of sociological, economic, and educational (developmental and change) theories (e.g., Hossler, Schmit, & Vesper, 1999; St. John & Hossler, 1998; St. John, Paulsen, & Starkey, 1996). These reviews focused on the factors influencing students to make a sequence of choices that result in greater educational attainment. Rather than uncritically carrying forward progressive notions, the reviews examined outcomes from diverse racial/ethnic and ideological perspectives in an attempt to identify factors that influence attainment. In other words, the idea of diverse paths of educational attainment is integral to the student-choice construct. The basic principles of the construct are as follows:

1. *Students follow a sequence of choices.* The sequence includes the formation of higher education and career aspirations, the opportunity to attend college (access), the choice of college, the choice of major, the choice to persist, and choices about graduate education.
2. *Diverse patterns of choice are possible.* Because students of different backgrounds face different choice sets, we must consider how different groups (e.g., racial/ethnic, age, gender groups) make educational choices.
3. *Students make choices in "situated" contexts.* The sequence of choices can follow traditional or nontraditional patterns; in either case it results in gains in both attainment and employability. However, all the educa-

tional choices are situated within students' values and beliefs and can be constrained by financial means and enabled by financial incentives.

Given these principles, we can envision how theory and research on student choices could inform a refinement of finance and accountability policies in higher education. The theory and practice of enrollment management (Hossler, 1984; Hossler, Bean, & Associates, 1990) have demonstrated how research on college choice and persistence could be used to build more integrated institutional strategies. As a parallel development, the student-choice construct provides a more integrated way of viewing the linkages between student outcomes and institutional, state, and federal policies on quality, access, and affordability. A new balance is needed for linking accountability measures to student outcomes. Policies aimed at promoting student choice for all students can, at least in theory, promote opportunity for traditional and nontraditional students while rewarding institutions for responsible behavior.

Student Choice and Public Accountability

We suggest here a new conceptualization of the linkages between student-choice processes and the outcomes of higher education. After providing an overview of the student-choice sequence, we discuss alternative patterns of student choices, the ways in which "situated" contexts influence choice processes, the outcomes of the choice processes, and how this new construct can inform the refinement of accountability measures.

The Student-Choice Sequence

Higher education opportunities unfold through life experience, a process of developing aspirations and goals, pursuing those goals and aspirations through higher education choices, and changing choices based on new experiences, successes, and failures. Policies and practice aimed at enabling students to make informed choices can, in theory at least, improve educational attainment. We describe each of the steps in the choice sequence and consider their interrelationships and policy linkages.

1. *Formation of higher education and career aspirations.* Aspirations can form in elementary school or earlier, but usually take shape by middle school (Hossler et al., 1999; Hossler & Stage, 1992). Aspirations formed by high school can have long-term effects on educational attainment (St. John, 1991). The formation of aspirations is influenced by educational experiences, family and friends, and information provided by schools, colleges, and educa-

tion agencies (Hossler et al., 1999). Aspirations are among the values and beliefs students consider when they make educational choices.

2. *Opportunity to attend (access).* The decision to attend college is influenced by family background, aspirations, high school experiences, achievement, and affordability (Hossler et al., 1999; Jackson, 1978, St. John & Noell, 1989). The opportunity to attend can be enhanced in several ways: by developing accessible higher education systems, including community colleges and technical programs; by improving the quality of K–12 school systems; by disseminating information on higher education opportunities; and by promoting affordability through appropriate state and federal financing strategies.

3. *Choice of college.* Frequently, college choice is characterized as a sequence of choices involving predisposition, search, and choice from among the colleges to which a student is admitted (Hossler et al., 1999). In addition to factors promoting the predisposition to attend (similar to aspirations and opportunities, as noted above), institutional marketing and student financial aid can influence the search and choice processes, the final stages of the college-choice sequence. Attending higher-quality public colleges and private colleges improves students' learning and earnings (Pascarella & Terenzini, 1991). Thus there are social as well as individual returns from the college-choice process, especially when taking into account the tax revenue returns from improved earnings.

4. *Choice (and change) of major.* The choice of major is influenced by family background (including parents' occupations and aspirations for the child), the student's aspirations and achievement, the college experience, the college's quality and characteristics, and expected earnings and the labor market (Pascarella & Terenzini, 1991; St. John, 1994a; Smart, 1988). Although the choice of major has been viewed primarily as an academic concern, it has historically been important in public policy because of the link between workforce planning and the financing of higher education.

5. *Persistence.* Students' persistence at their chosen college, as aspirations and ability allow, represents progress through and ultimate completion of the undergraduate experience. Persistence is influenced by student and family background, the student's aspirations and commitments, academic and social integration processes in the college, and affordability (Bean, 1990; Pascarella & Terenzini, 1991; St. John et al., 1996; Tinto, 1987).

6. *Graduate education choices.* Choices about graduate education follow the same pattern as for undergraduate education: developing aspirations, having opportunity, deciding on universities and programs, and persisting. Persistence in graduate education is influenced by student background, undergraduate experience, characteristics of the graduate institution, experiences in graduate school, expected earnings, and affordability (Andrieu & St. John, 1993; Pascarella & Terenzini, 1991). Choices about graduate study and professional development are situated in values and beliefs acquired over a student's lifetime.

Gains in each of these student-choice processes result in gains in student *attainment.* A focus on how policy decisions link to these choice processes thus provides a means of building workable linkages between higher education policy and student outcomes (e.g., St. John & Hossler, 1998). The student-choice construct incorporates aspects of both the developmental and the change perspectives and is a reconstruction of the developmental assumptions embedded in the original developmental theories. However, the sequence is more explicitly focused on interactions with the academic environment and employment (see the discussion of outcomes below) and thus more explicitly on policy concerns.

Diverse Patterns of Choice

For the student-choice construct to be useful in rethinking public policy on higher education, it must be applicable to older as well as traditional, college-age students. Indeed, higher education opportunity needs to be expanded beyond the one-third of the population attending college in the last three or four decades. Given that most research on the effects of college on students has focused on traditional-age students (Pascarella & Terenzini, 1991), the student-choice sequence is applicable to these students.

A clear distinction is needed between traditional- and nontraditional-age students. For the first round of educational choices of traditional-age students, the student-choice sequence can be viewed as a lockstep process. (Interestingly, in a recent longitudinal study, Hossler et al., 1999, found that despite the equity in development of aspirations, those with less-advantaged backgrounds were less likely to fulfill their higher education dreams, a finding consonant with recent studies of national longitudinal databases.) However, the proportion of older students attending college has been increasing over the last three decades, indicating the existence of alternative ways through the sequence—that is, students who did not fulfill their higher education aspirations when they first attended or considered attending college may find the opportunity later. Further, many adults change their aspirations and professional interests over time. Thus, when we consider both traditional- and nontraditional-age students, the number of citizens making higher education choices that lead to gains in attainment increases.

There are also racial/ethnic and gender differences in educational choice processes. For example, African Americans are more responsive than whites to tuition and student aid in making decisions about first-time enrollment (St. John & Noell, 1989) and persistence (Kaltenbaugh, St. John, & Starkey, 1999). The current high-tuition, high-loan environment has therefore been detrimental to equal opportunity. A more explicit focus on the differences in choice processes for different groups is essential to a better understanding of how accountability measures and policy influence equal opportunity.

"Situated" Educational Choices

Most theory on student choice, especially that pertaining to college-choice processes, implicitly assumes mobility. However, only a modest percentage of traditional-age students consider attending college away from home (Hossler et al., 1999) and most nontraditional-age students are situated locally. Thus, to expand the opportunity for educational choices, we must keep in mind that many prospective college students reside in the locality of the college or university. Indeed, the recognition in state higher education policy and planning of local high-demand programs—that is, programs for which there is local employment opportunity—is increasingly crucial (St. John & Hossler, 1998). Providing access to a nearby higher education institution may not be sufficient if the programs offered are not those needed by local residents (Grubb, 1996). Clearly, the concept of *congruence* among career interests, education, and employment opportunity provides a way of linking these aspects of student choice to financial and academic policy.

In developing new approaches to public policy in higher education, we must consider racial/ethnic differences in educational attainment, in particular, the need to promote opportunity for African Americans, Latinos, and other groups underrepresented nationally. Analyses of the impact of aid on affordability indicate a great variation in how students of different economic backgrounds view and respond to college prices and subsidies (Heller, 1999; St. John et al., 1996). Thus, if used to focus on promoting choice by formerly excluded populations, the student-choice sequence can be a framework for improving diversity. More research is needed on how public policy decisions influence the integration process and attainment by minority populations

(Allen, Epps, & Haniff, 1991; St. John & Hossler, 1998). Nevertheless, the student-choice construct provides a basis for promoting attainment by diverse populations.

The Outcomes of Student Choice

The student-choice sequence depicts the types of choices students make as they navigate through the educational system. Three outcomes of the choice process could be used as a basis for linking policy decisions about education to the social and economic goal of employability.

First, when students develop and achieve their higher education aspirations, the result is gains in attainment. In the first half of the twentieth century, the opportunity to attain was distributed in several ways:

- Payment of the direct costs of attending college by families who could afford them.
- Subsidies to public institutions, enabling a gradual expansion in opportunity through a low direct cost of attending.
- Student aid, provided by institutions and some states, enabling some high-achieving, low-income students to attend more elite institutions than they could otherwise afford and to maintain continuous enrollment.

In the second half of the twentieth century, the federal government used student aid to promote educational opportunity beyond the population that could afford the direct costs of expensive colleges. However, in the last two decades, a backlash to the growing public expenditures on higher education (in the form of taxpayers' support for institutions and students) caused a shift in the focus of need-based aid from grants to loans, which were less costly to taxpayers. An analysis of this history, along with detailed analyses of affordability (St. John, 1994b), reveals that expanding student aid led to gains in attainment. However, reconstructing the choice sequences alone does not provide a sufficient basis for reconstructing public finance policy.

Second, gains in higher education attainment clearly produce gains in individual earnings (Leslie & Brinkman, 1988; Pascarella & Terenzini, 1991) and tax revenues (at a given rate of taxation). When we consider the tax revenue returns from increased earnings, along with increased individual returns (Bluestone, 1993; St. John & Masten, 1990), the linkage between attainment and earnings provides an improved basis for rethinking public finance strategies. Focusing on the link between tax revenues and investment in higher education also provides another view on the new policy discourse. Given the importance of education to earnings—and tax revenues—why would so many taxpayers want to reduce tax rates rather than support higher education? To address this question, we need to consider the congruence between higher education and employment, an alternative to social development as a policy goal. Social-attainment theory (Alexander & Eckland, 1974, 1977; Blau & Duncan, 1967) has limited utility in this construction of public finance strategy. For example, the status-attainment perspective assigns a higher social value to the more elite professions rather than valuing individuals' attainment of their aspirations. We propose that congruence between an individual's academic preparation, employment opportunities, aspirations, and interests provides a more workable way of viewing the linkage between higher education and employment.

Third, congruence between education and employment also potentially provides an appropriate outcome linking student choice to both social and economic development. Rather than relying on attainment theory, perhaps we should build on the logic of Holland's (1980) vocational types and the related notion of congruence between college major and employment (Smart, 1975, 1985, 1989). The inclusion of aspirations provides, in this construct, a way of linking the sequence of student choices to colleges' academic programs and to later employment opportunities, without assuming one type of employment is inherently more valuable to society than another. Specifically, we should consider whether students have the opportunity to study in their fields of interest and whether graduates find employment related to their fields of study.

Congruence between education and employment thus provides an improved basis for thinking about linkages between the public's financial strategy and educational choices. The congruence of education, employment opportunity, *and* individual interests is an important policy goal that merits further systematic exploration as employability becomes a more central aim of educational and social policy.

Rethinking Public Accountability

While not sanguine about the notion that government agencies should strive to construct tight links between public policy and student outcomes, we think it necessary to provide a better foundation for doing so. We have our doubts about the value of accountability systems because local choices, based on the professional autonomy of faculty, are essential for a healthy system of higher education. However, given the penchant of many policymakers for focusing on accountability, an alternative to the current course of public policy on accountability is essential. In this section we examine how the student-choice perspective might inform a rethinking of public accountability and consider strategies for integrating a concern about accountability with efforts to improve affordability, productivity, and employability.

Improving Affordability

A fundamental problem with many of the current accountability efforts is that they are overly concerned with quality measures and virtually ignore affordability. Ironically, the goal of affordability is a state accountability issue seldom explicitly considered by legislatures or taxpayers. But the combination of student and institutional subsidies is what determines whether a state's system of public higher education is affordable to its residents. The state's responsibility in maintaining affordability can be measured by monitoring two indicators.

First, we need to measure whether state systems are meeting their access and affordability goals. The most direct measure of affordability is the participation rate, adjusted for socioeconomic and racial/ethnic diversity. State agencies can cooperate with schools and colleges in collecting information on the percentage of high school graduates who attend college. Also essential is a consideration of the college participation rates of low-income students (students receiving free and reduced-price lunches in high school) and students of diverse racial/ethnic groups (African Americans, Latinos, and other groups with historically low participation rates).

A second measure is the availability of adequate student aid to equalize the opportunity for students to persist in college. It is possible to collect and maintain information on college students that can be used to assess whether public colleges are affordable, controlling for students' backgrounds and achievement in college (e.g., St. John, 1999; St. John, Hu, & Weber, 1999). This approach clearly identifies and measures the state's responsibility for maintaining affordability, especially if it is linked to consideration of access (i.e., participation rates). It also provides a baseline against which we can realistically assess institutional efforts to improve persistence. If this approach were adopted, measures of persistence could be developed that essentially account for the state's role in promoting affordability. This would involve establishing predicted baseline persistence rates for different cohorts of college students, controlling for age, race/ethnicity, need, and so forth. Only with this analytical base could we assess whether institutional practices and finances improve the chances that admitted students persist in college (e.g., St. John, 1999). This approach could be used to reward institutions for improvements in their persistence rates and diversity by increasing funding when persistence rates are improved after controlling for the entry characteristics of students. Such an approach would be more likely than the use of simple persistence rates to improve diversity. In fact, rewarding institutions simply for higher persistence rates could reduce diversity because it rewards them for selecting students with a greater probability of persisting.

Improving Productivity

The current accountability movement in higher education often ignores taxpayers' concerns about educational costs. States need to consider education and related expenditures per FTE student in the funding and accountability process, and this requires a coordination of finance strategies (Hearn & Anderson, 1989). One method might include the following:

1. Identifying reasonable cost targets (e.g., level of educational expenditures per student, expanding or reducing them as necessary to account for economies of scale).
2. Setting state funding of institutions at a percentage of educational costs per student as agreed upon by institutions and state agencies.
3. Guaranteeing adequate need-based grant aid to ensure affordability.
4. Reducing subsidies further for public institutions that raise tuition above the targeted percentage of costs.

Such an approach would put in place a set of fiscal controls and, more importantly, could create incentives for fiscal accountability and for ensuring access and affordability. This method provides a way of balancing the goals of quality, affordability, and productivity (Hearn & Anderson, 1995). It attempts to balance taxpayers' interests in efficiency, institutions' interests in quality, and students' interests in affordability. It differs from the older approach to subsidizing institutions that lacked both sufficient constraints on escalating costs and revenue maximization by institutions (Bowen, 1980).

With this system of finance, the monitoring of whether public system costs are being appropriately controlled would be relatively easy. Such a method could use routine reports to estimate educational expenditures per FTE student enrolled and could calculate the percentage of costs paid for by tuition and the percentage paid for by state subsidies (e.g., Bowen, 1980; St. John, 1994b). The Integrated Postsecondary Education Data System (managed by the U.S. Department of Education) could be used for this purpose, but states could also develop better methods of measurement.

Improving Employability

The argument that the new call for accountability should be linked to a strategy to improve the employability of college graduates has seldom been seriously considered. A first step would require collecting information from public colleges and universities about the employment of departing students, including the percentage who depart and are employed in a "congruent" position—a field related to the degree or using the knowledge and skills acquired in earning the degree—and the percentage who graduate and enroll in a more advanced program in the same or related field.

Using congruence as an accountability measure would create a new reporting burden on institutions as it involves expanding the current procedures of tracking former students. However, it has the advantage of encouraging colleges and universities to be more responsive to students' and employers' interests. Many high-demand technical programs lose students to employment before they complete their degree programs, because the students can reach their personal goals through employment in a congruent field before graduating. It does not seem reasonable, from either a student or a social perspective, that institutions should be penalized because students drop out or stop out (take off a semester or more from their studies) when they find employment consonant with their educational goals. Using a measure of education-employment congruence as part of an accountability system would help mitigate this unintended consequence of using persistence rates as an outcome measure.

Linking performance funding to evidence of congruence between education and employment would provide financial incentives for public colleges and universities to be more responsive to students and to local labor markets. Without these measures, accountability systems could insulate colleges and universities from labor market forces. By adding congruence to the indicators used in performance funding, a more direct link could be built between student development and economic development. In the short term, states or institutions may need to survey departing students (graduates and dropouts) to establish baseline information on employment. In the longer term, such data could most likely be collected through more routine and systematic means.

Accountability Measures in Selected States

The ongoing battles over state fund allocations, coupled with increasing criticism of college and university performance, have convinced states to examine the productivity and efficiency of state institutions. The Rockefeller Institute of Government (Burke & Serban, 1997) surveyed higher education financial officers in the fifty states, Puerto Rico, and the District of Columbia. Ten states were using performance funding at the time of the survey, and eight states had adopted performance budgeting. Of those institutions surveyed, about two-thirds had either implemented or were planning to adopt programs that use results of accountability measures in their public higher education budgets.

In this section we briefly examine recent attempts to implement accountability measures in two states, then compare the measures to those we suggested above.

Florida's Accountability Measures

Florida is in the process of rewriting its performance indicators, which have been renamed systemwide accountability measures. The Florida legislature mandated the implementation of performance indicators approximately ten years ago. The proposed measures, devised collaboratively by campus leaders and state policymakers, were developed so that the board of regents could demonstrate to the citizens and the state that the state university system (SUS) was fulfilling its responsibilities. The six measures were intended to "accurately and clearly reflect the aggregate performance" of Florida's universities in delivering quality higher educational opportunities and services (Florida Board of Regents, 1998, p. 1):

1. *Meeting the SUS enrollment plan:* a measure expressed as over or under the funded plan.
2. *SUS graduation rate:* a measure of the six-year graduation rate for senior college students and the four-year graduation rate for students transferring into the system from community colleges.
3. *SUS retention rate:* a measure of the extent to which SUS is keeping students on track toward their baccalaureate degrees.
4. *SUS total sponsored research and development expenditures per statefunded research expenditure:* an approximation for the return on state research investment, expressed as National Science Foundation research and development funds received.
5. *Total increase in endowment and total amount of annual giving to SUS institutions:* a measure of annual giving and endowment that provides a good indication of the quality and value of the universities as perceived by their many constituencies.
6. *SUS degrees granted:* a measure including separate totals for baccalaureate, master's, specialist, engineering, first professional, and doctoral degrees granted statewide.

In a sense, this approach to setting accountability measures can be viewed as an attempt to adapt traditional planning approaches to new market concerns. On the one hand, setting numerical goals for enrollment and graduation is consistent with the older approach to master planning. On the other, the focus on generating resources from alternative sources and rewarding higher student persistence rates is consistent with some of the newer, market-oriented approaches to accountability. However, this approach to constructing accountability measures stops short of the balanced approach we recommend above. First, these standards emphasize enrollment goals and persistence rates rather than a balanced approach that addresses affordability and access. Second, they emphasize alternative revenue sources without addressing the state's role in providing an adequate level of support to ensure affordability and improve productivity. Finally, although graduation is addressed, the measures exclude the issue of employability.

New York's Accountability Measures

Performance indicators were first discussed in New York State in 1994 as the result of a plan to develop a vision statement for the State University of New York (SUNY) system as it approached the year 2000. This project was developed as a joint venture between campus constituent groups and SUNY Central, the state's higher education governing board. The planning process that resulted, SUNY 2000: A Vision for the New Century, consisted of two parts: one celebrated and recognized the diversity of the system's sixty-four campuses; the other was an effort to identify common goals shared by all the campuses.

SUNY 2000 was prompted by the reality of shrinking state funding and the demands of state constituents for greater productivity. The combination of increased demands for higher education, stiff competition for state funds, and limited financial growth ultimately brought the appropriate parties to the table. The parties agreed that performance indicators, if developed through a collaborative effort, would indicate to both state constituents and campus personnel whether an institution was effectively achieving its goals. In turn, the parties hoped that these performance reports might increase the likelihood of increased state funds for the colleges and universities, as well as greater autonomy through less state regulation.

The planning committee set out to "identify indicators, which would demonstrate system-wide accountability for common purposes, yet not diminish the autonomy each campus needed to pursue its individual mission" (Burke, 1994). These indicators, along with an annual report describing them, would serve as the basis for SUNY 2000. The proposed performance indicators were based on five central goals developed by the SUNY 2000 planning committee:

1. Provide full access to undergraduate education.
2. Achieve excellence in undergraduate programs and services.
3. Become nationally competitive in graduate studies and research.
4. Meet the state's needs in economic development, environmental conservation, health care, public education, and social services.
5. Enhance management efficiency and effectiveness (Burke, 1994).

The parties to this process lobbied for a distinction between macro-indicators, universal for all institutions, and micro-indicators, designed specifically by and for individual institutions. The SUNY 2000 planning committee laid the groundwork for a single, encompassing report that could be understood by state legislators, citizens, and institutional personnel alike. This endeavor attempted to answer some of the calls for more accountability and productivity within New York colleges and universities. Instead of refuting the criticisms of state policymakers, SUNY sought a possible solution to this complex process.

The next few years brought hard times for the SUNY system. There were several budgetary reductions on state-operated campuses, significantly affecting the morale of faculty and staff. The lack of certainty about the future, along with new leadership, caused much introspection and scrutiny throughout the system. State institutions generally believed they were faced with an increase in workload (due to a reduction in professional positions) while the quality of their teaching and service was being questioned. This volatility led to ongoing discussions among campus presidents, constituents, and state policymakers about the future of public education in New York, resulting in an effort to institutionalize a performance-based funding system that mirrored SUNY's overall mission.

The SUNY system, under new leadership, was interested in integrating a performance review process through collaboration between the campuses and the systemwide leadership of the university. A Resource Allocation Model committee was created and charged with developing a new funding formula, to include a merit-based funding component. The committee asked the SUNY Office of the Provost for assistance with the merit-based funding component, and the office developed a taskforce consisting of campus and systemwide leadership.

The Task Force on Performance Indicators was convened in September 1997. It developed a set of guiding principles and assumptions to serve as a benchmark as SUNY developed its merit-based funding program. Some of these principles/assumptions illustrate a shifting paradigm within state university systems in general:

- The only purpose of measuring performance or basing any funding on performance is to promote improvement and reward excellence.
- Indicators should measure outcomes rather than inputs and processes.
- Wherever possible, measures should use trends over time so that improvement can be rewarded. Multi-year rolling averages are preferable to single-year data.
- Merit-based performance funding should be phased in and will work most effectively with new money.
- Performance measures should do no harm. Wherever possible, they should be used positively and with care for promoting institutional improvement as measured against prior performance rather than for interinstitutional comparison. Campuses in need of improvement in certain areas should not be disadvantaged in such a way as to virtually guarantee the impairment of future performance (SUNY Task Force on Performance Indicators, 1998).

Using the student-choice perspective to review these standards, we see a potential for a balanced approach to accountability. These principles emphasize outcomes rather than inputs or processes, which could move the performance-funding process in the direction outlined earlier. However, the principles do not explicitly consider access, affordability, or diversity and thus may have the same limitations as most other approaches. A phased-in approach to achieving greater efficiency has merit, but it does not appear to coordinate financial strategies (e.g., Hearn & Anderson, 1989). Further, the standards still lack specificity and do not address employability. Thus, although the proposed method has potential, it lacks sufficient specificity to be evaluated using the framework we have outlined.

A Contrast in Approaches

These two state cases present an interesting contrast. In both we find an implicit tension between the older values of equity and the new values of efficiency. In Florida, the accountability measures seem to be an attempt to reconcile the historical values of expanding opportunity with the newer values of efficiency. The New York process seems to make an attempt to step beyond this tension by developing an approach that focuses on student outcomes. This raises the question of whether it is possible to develop approaches to accountability that promote improvement in affordability, productivity, and employability rather than merely maintain the status quo of using accountability to reward elite institutions. However, the accountability process in

New York is still in a formative stage and the actual measures of account-ability have not yet been developed.

Conclusion

The current accountability movement seems caught between two clash-ing forces in the policy arena: a progressive approach that uses direct subsi-dies and values equal opportunity and a market approach that values effi-ciency and uses financial incentives for quality performance. Historically, higher education in the United States has valued the expansion of public sys-tems as a means of promoting equal opportunity. The core public funding strategy (i.e., institutional subsidies per student) is a holdover from this ear-lier period. However, recent market-oriented approaches to the financing of higher education emphasize improving student outcomes but tend to ignore issues of affordability and diversity that are compatible with older beliefs in equal opportunity.

In this chapter we have proposed an alternative way of viewing student outcomes and the role of public accountability. A more explicit focus on un-derlying student-choice processes may help. The proposed approach not only is compatible with a new wave of research on how public policies influ-ence student choices and educational outcomes, but also suggests a new bal-ance between historical concerns about equity and diversity and newer con-cerns about public accountability and the efficient use of public resources. This approach would involve rewarding gains in student attainment as an ap-propriate outcome of student-choice processes. It also suggests the possibil-ity of using public and private resources to optimize gains in these outcomes and using accountability measures to facilitate this process.

We have identified a specific set of measures that states can use to monitor affordability, productivity, and employability as critical outcomes of their public systems of higher education. Such an approach might allow states to develop accountability standards compatible with social (e.g., af-fordability) and economic (e.g., congruent employment) goals and students' interests. Its aims are to hold states responsible for maintaining affordability, to encourage collaboration between states and institutions in maintaining quality and productivity, and to reorient the system as a whole toward a fo-cus on congruence between undergraduate education and the labor market. This approach would require more collaboration between institutions and states than is yet evident in most states.

An examination of the development of accountability standards in two states revealed some differences in approach. In one state, the standards seem to be a mixture of traditional measures related to student opportunity and measures focused on market incentives for generating new revenues. Yet there was little focus on affordability for students or meaningful productivity gains. In the other state, recently developed principles for accountability seem to leave open the possibility of promoting affordability and productivity, but the standards are not yet sufficiently developed to allow a definitive judgment. Neither state addresses the underlying concern about the employability of graduates. Thus, current responses to the call for public accountability (at least as demonstrated by these two examples) fall short of addressing the most critical issues facing students, taxpayers, and academe.

The implications of our analysis are twofold. First, states and public institutions need to share responsibility for affordability. Unfortunately, current efforts to promote accountability essentially ignore this issue. One of the best measures of affordability is the opportunity to persist in college (St. John, 1999), an outcome measure not adequately addressed in the accountability movement for improving students' chances of success. However, this measure needs to be balanced with a routine assessment of higher education participation rates for high school graduates. Performance-funding systems that provide rewards for persistence should adjust for baseline opportunity (i.e., the chances of success before entry).

Second, taxpayers' concerns about efficient use of tax dollars must be addressed as higher education responds to the expansion in demand expected in the near future. More than a little ironic is that current performance-funding measures have reinforced the status quo in research universities (e.g., Weerts, 1999) rather than responded to taxpayers' concerns about efficiency. Marginal gains in efficiency and productivity can most easily be achieved through true improvement in educational outcomes, and more substantial gains in efficiency are possible through a better use of technology. The call for greater efficiency is therefore especially pertinent to efforts to expand public systems in the new century.

Public colleges and universities share responsibility with states for providing quality higher education in an efficient manner. We agree with Hearn and Anderson (1989, 1995) on the importance of establishing targets for expenditures per FTE student and for the percentage of these expenditures that states subsidize. This provides an appropriate system of checks and balances that can encourage quality and affordability within the constraints of the state system of taxation. If new lower-cost, high-technology delivery systems do emerge as a supplement to the current public systems of higher education, these may drive down average costs in the entire system while maintaining a responsible funding approach in the traditional, campus-based delivery system. (See the Conclusion to this volume for more on the cost-savings potential of technology in higher education.)

Finally, while employability has not yet surfaced in the debates on accountability, this outcome should be addressed explicitly if public higher education is to have a realistic hope of regaining taxpayer support in the long term. Specifically, low congruence between undergraduate degrees and employment opportunities is problematic given the high levels of debt borne by undergraduates (Grubb, 1996). Focusing explicitly on strategies for improving employability will necessarily involve faculty in changing their curricula through deeper integration of technology and better linkages with employers. This is not another argument for transforming the liberal arts into technical education, but rather for realizing the hope that a liberal arts education will prepare students for entry-level professional opportunities.

Unfortunately, most states lack a workable set of measures on employability of graduates and students who leave college before graduation to seek employment. Putting systems in place to measure the congruence between education and employment for departing students offers a way of valuing state economic interests more directly within the policy process. It also provides a way of recognizing the added value of technical and academic education for some students who make early departures, an issue especially important in high-technology fields in both community colleges and universities. Greater attention should be given to this issue in the next round of efforts to improve public accountability.

References

Alexander, K. L., & Eckland, B. K. (1974). Sex differences in the educational attainment process. *American Sociological Review, 59,* 668–682.

Alexander, K. L., & Eckland, B. K. (1977). High school context and college selectivity: Institutional constraints in educational stratification. *Social Forces, 56*(1), 166–168.

Allen, W. R., Epps, E. G., & Haniff, N. Z. (Eds.). (1991). *College in black and white: African American students in predominantly white and historically black public universities.* Albany: State University of New York Press.

Andrieu, S. C., & St. John, E. P. (1993). The influence of prices on graduate student persistence. *Research in Higher Education, 34,* 399–418.

Astin, A. W. (1975). *Preventing students from dropping out.* San Francisco: Jossey-Bass.

Astin, A. W. (1993). *Assessments for excellence: The philosophy of assessment and evaluation in higher education.* Phoenix, AZ: Oryx Press.

Banta, T. W., Rudolph, C. B., VanDyke, J., & Fisher, H. S. (1996). Performance funding comes of age in Tennessee. *Journal of Higher Education, 67*(1), 23–45.

Bean, J. P. (1990). Why students leave: Insights from research. In D. Hossler, J. P.
     Bean, & Associates (Eds.), *The strategic management of college enrollments.* San
     Francisco: Jossey-Bass.
Blau, P., & Duncan, O. D. (1967). *The American occupational structure.* New York:
     Wiley.
Bluestone, B. (1993). *An economic impact analysis.* Boston: University of Massachu-
     setts.
Bowen, H. R. (1980). *The costs of higher education: How much do colleges and univer-
     sities spend per student and how much should they spend?* San Francisco: Jossey-
     Bass.
Burke, J. (1994, May/June). The proof is in the performance. *Trusteeship, 4,* 25–29.
Burke, J., & Serban, A. M. (1997). *State performance funding and budgeting for public
     higher education: Current status and future prospects.* Albany: State University
     of New York, Rockefeller Institute of Government.
Chickering, A. W. (1969). *Education and identity.* San Francisco: Jossey-Bass.
Chickering, A. W. (1976). Development as an outcome of education. In M. Keeton
     & Associates (Eds.), *Experiential learning: Rationale, characteristics assessments.*
     San Francisco: Jossey-Bass.
Flint, T. (1997). Predicting student loan defaults. *Journal of Higher Education, 68*(3),
     322–354.
Florida Board of Regents. (1998). *Systemwide accountability measures proposal.* Tal-
     lahassee: Author.
Grubb, W. N. (1996). *Working in the middle.* San Francisco: Jossey-Bass.
Hearn, J. C., & Anderson, M. S. (1989). Integrating post-secondary finance policies:
     The Minnesota model. In R. H. Fenske (Ed.), *Studying the impact of student
     aid on institutions.* San Francisco: Jossey-Bass.
Hearn, J. C., & Anderson, M. S. (1995). The Minnesota financing experiment. In
     E. P. St. John (Ed.), *Rethinking tuition and student aid strategies.* San Francisco:
     Jossey-Bass.
Heller, D. E. (1999). The effects of tuition and state financial aid on public college
     enrollment. *Review of Higher Education, 23*(1), 65–89.
Holland, A. S. B. (1980). *Complex function theory.* New York: Elsevier North Hol-
     land.
Hossler, D. (1984). *Enrollment management: An integrated approach.* New York: Col-
     lege Entrance Examination Board.
Hossler, D., Bean, J. P., & Associates. (1990). *The strategic management of college en-
     rollments.* San Francisco: Jossey-Bass.
Hossler, D., Braxton, J. M., & Coopersmith, G. (1989). Understanding college
     choice. In J. C. Smart (Ed.), *Higher education: Handbook of theory and research.*
     New York: Agathon Press.
Hossler, D., Schmit, J., & Vesper, N. (1999). *Going to college.* Baltimore: Johns Hop-
     kins University Press.
Hossler, D., & Stage, F. K. (1992). Family and high school experience factors influ-

ence on post-secondary plans of ninth grade students. *American Educational Research Journal, 29*(2), 425–447.

Jackson, G. A. (1978). Financial aid and student enrollment. *Journal of Higher Education, 49*(6), 548–574.

Kaltenbaugh, L. S., St. John, E. P., & Starkey, J. B. (1999). What difference does tuition make? An analysis of ethnic differences in persistence. *Journal of Student Financial Aid, 29*(2), 21–32.

Kohlberg, L. (1981). *The philosophy of moral development: Moral stages and the idea of justice.* San Francisco: Harper & Row.

Leslie, L. L., & Brinkman, P. T. (1988). *The economic value of higher education.* New York: Macmillan.

Loevinger, J. (1976). *Ego development: Conceptions and theory.* San Francisco: Jossey-Bass.

Manski, E. F., & Wise, D. A. (1983). *College choice in America.* Cambridge: Harvard University Press.

Pascarella, E. T., & Terenzini, P. T. (1979). Interaction effects in Spardo's and Tinto's conceptual models of college drop-out. *Sociology of Education, 52*(4), 197–210.

Pascarella, E. T., & Terenzini, P. T. (1980). Predicting voluntary freshmen year persistence and withdrawal behavior in a residential university: A part analytic validation of Tinto's model. *Journal of Educational Psychology, 51*(1), 60–71.

Pascarella, E. T., & Terenzini, P. T. (1991). *How college affects students.* San Francisco: Jossey-Bass.

Paulsen, M. B. (1990). *College choice: Understanding student enrollment behavior* (ASHE-ERIC Higher Education Report No. 6). Washington, DC: George Washington University.

Perry, W. (1970). *Forms of intellectual and ethical development in the college years.* New York: Hart, Rinehart & Winston.

St. John, E. P. (1990a). Price response in enrollment decisions: An analysis of the high school and beyond sophomore cohort. *Research in Higher Education, 31*(2), 161–176.

St. John, E. P. (1990b). Price response in persistence decisions: An analysis of the high school and beyond senior cohort. *Research in Higher Education, 31*(4), 387–403.

St. John, E. P. (1991). What really influences minority attendance? Sequential analyses of the high school and beyond sophomore cohort. *Research in Higher Education, 32*(2), 141–158.

St. John, E. P. (1994a). The influence of debt on choice of major. *Journal of Student Financial Aid, 24*(1), 5–12.

St. John, E. P. (1994b). *Prices, productivity and investment: Assessing financial strategies in higher education* (ASHE/ERIC Higher Education Report No. 3). Washington, DC: George Washington University.

St. John, E. P. (1999). Evaluating state grant programs: A case study of Washington's grant program. *Research in Higher Education, 40*(2), 455–480.

St. John, E. P., Andrieu, S. C., Oescher, J., & Starkey, J. B. (1994). The influence of student aid on within-year persistence by traditional college-age students in four-year colleges. *Research in Higher Education, 35*(4), 301–334.

St. John, E. P., & Hossler, D. (1998). Higher education desegregation in the post-Fordice legal environment: A critical-empirical perspective. In R. Fossey (Ed.), *Readings in equal education.* New York: AMS Press.

St. John, E. P., Hu, S., & Weber, J. (1999). *The affordability of public colleges and universities: The influence of student aid on persistence in Indiana public higher education* (Policy Research Report No. 99–2). Bloomington: Indiana Education Policy Center.

St. John, E. P., & Masten, C. L. (1990). Return on the federal investment in student financial aid: An assessment of the high school class of 1972. *Journal of Student Financial Aid, 20*(3), 4–23.

St. John, E. P., & Noell, J. (1989). The effects of student financial aid on access to higher education: An analysis of progress with special consideration of minority enrollment. *Research in Higher Education, 30*(6), 563–581.

St. John, E. P., Paulsen, M. B., & Starkey, J. B. (1996). The nexus between college choice and persistence. *Research in Higher Education, 37*(2), 175–220.

Slaughter, S. (1991). The official ideology of higher education: Ironies and inconsistencies. In W. G. Tierney (Ed.), *Culture and ideology in higher education.* New York: Praeger.

Smart, J. C. (1975). Environments as reinforcer systems in the study of job satisfaction. *Journal of Vocational Behavior, 6*(3), 337–346.

Smart, J. C. (1985). Holland environments as reinforcement systems. *Research in Higher Education, 23,* 279{endash}292.

Smart, J. C. (1988). College influences on graduates' income levels. *Research in Higher Education, 29*(1), 41–59.

Smart, J. C. (1989). Life history influences on Holland vocational type development. *Journal of Vocational Behavior, 34,* 69–87.

State University of New York Task Force on Performance Indicators. (1998, July). *Final report.* Albany, NY: Author.

Terkla, D. G. (1985). Does financial aid enhance undergraduate persistence? *Journal of Student Financial Aid, 15*(3), 11–18.

Tierney, M. L. (1980). The impact of student financial aid on student demand for public/private higher education. *Journal of Higher Education, 51*(5), 527–545.

Tinto, V. (1987). *Leaving college: Rethinking causes and links of student attrition.* Chicago: University of Chicago Press.

Weerts, D. J. (1999, November). *Understanding differences in state support for higher education: A comparative study of state appropriations for Research I universities.* Paper presented at the Annual Meeting of the Association for the Study of Higher Education, San Antonio, TX.

Wilms, W. W., Moore, R. W., & Bolus, R. E. (1987). Whose fault is default? A study of the impact of student characteristics and institutional practices on guaranteed student loan default rates in California. *Educational Evaluation and Policy Analysis, 9*(1), 41–54.

CONCLUSION: Technology and the Future
of Public Higher Education Policy

DONALD E. HELLER

Few topics are more dominant in current discussions of higher education than the role of computers and information technology. Terms such as *distance learning, browsers, virtual education, URLs, asynchronous learning,* and *telephony* are entering the higher education lexicon of students, faculty, administrators, and policymakers alike. Management guru Peter Drucker has claimed that technology will help force such changes on higher education that "thirty years from now the big university campuses will be relics. Universities won't survive. It's as large a change as when we first got the printed book" (quoted in Lenzner & Johnson, 1997, p. 124).

The use of technology in higher education can take many different forms. It can be as simple as a professor's use of electronic mail to communicate with students or faculty colleagues, or use of software to prepare slides for in-class presentations. Technology can involve the development and use of courseware, software designed for specific pedagogical purposes and used in traditional classrooms (such as statistical analysis or simulation of scientific experiments). Perhaps the most integrative and intensive use of technology is in courses delivered entirely electronically, that is, with no face-to-face contact between instructor and student.

The impact of technology cannot be overstated. It is becoming ubiquitous in all aspects of university life: teaching, learning, research, administration, and service. Some claim that the push for the use of technology is driven by higher education's key customers, the students. According to James Duderstadt (1997), former president of the University of Michigan, "Today's students are members of the 'digital generation.' They have spent their early lives surrounded by robust, visual, electronic media—Sesame Street, MTV, home computers, video games, cyberspace networks, MUDs, MOOs, and virtual reality. Unlike those of us who were raised in an era of passive, broadcast media such as radio and television, they expect—indeed demand—interaction. They approach learning as a 'plug-and-play' experience, unaccustomed and unwilling to learn sequentially—to read the manual—and

243

instead inclined to plunge in and learn through participation and experimentation" (p. 7).

Another catalyst for expanded use of technology is the concern about limitations on funds available to support public colleges and universities. As described in Chapters 1 and 2, both demographic and college participation trends point to increasing enrollments in higher education in the future, but there does not appear to be much political will to greatly expand state appropriations for higher education. Roy Romer, former governor of Colorado and one of the founders of the Western Governors University (WGU), an institution that acts as a clearinghouse for distance education courses offered by colleges in the western states, claimed that the WGU "is a revolutionary idea. Many people can't afford the traditional way of getting a higher education degree, which is learning by sitting in the classroom. Technology can be an *effective* and *cheaper* way to help people learn" (quoted in Twigg, 1996, p. 28, emphasis added). As noted by Michael Leavitt, governor of Utah and another founder of the WGU, "This is not a replacement for the existing systems of higher education. It is a new element. It is a supplement. It is a way of creating new choices and new opportunities. But while this is not a replacement, it is an important part of a quality education for everyone. Because this is the way the world is going to work in the future" (quoted in Cushman Jr., 1996, p. A15). Some believe the potential of technology for changing education is limitless. "Some futurists even go so far as to predict the demise of conventional teachers. Joseph Coates, coauthor of '2025: Scenarios of U.S. and Global Society Reshaped by Science and Technology,' envisions a virtual education system from kindergarten to grad school that would eventually dispense altogether with age-based grades and allow pupils to progress independently" (Hamilton & Miller, 1997, p. 12).

The opportunities that technology affords to higher education institutions and students are numerous. Among the potential benefits articulated by various authors are the following:

1. *Overcoming geographic boundaries.* Not all students can afford the time or the expense to travel to a college campus. Technology allows students to take college courses wherever they choose—at home, at the office, or anywhere that is convenient for them.

2. *Overcoming temporal boundaries.* Technology can allow students to "attend" class whenever it is convenient for them, rather than organizing their lives around fixed class schedules offered by colleges and universities. In addition, students can progress at their own pace, rather than being bound by the traditional semester or quarter format still used by most colleges.

3. *Reducing the cost of delivering education.* Most boosters of integrating technology into postsecondary instruction recognize the large up-front costs necessary for converting a traditional class into one delivered electronically. But once those fixed costs are invested, the economies of scale are such that delivering the course to a hundred students or to a thousand students is equally inexpensive.[1] Even traditional classroom-based courses can be delivered less expensively by using technology. Many expensive experiments in laboratory-based science courses can be replaced with computer simulations at much lower cost.

4. *Reducing the cost of libraries.* Much of the cost of libraries goes into acquiring books and journals. As more of these publications are available over the Internet or in other electronic forms, libraries can begin to shift their resources away from acquiring hard-copy materials and toward providing a broader array of resources and better meeting patron needs.

5. *Reducing the barriers to entering the higher education marketplace.* This is perhaps the most revolutionary and threatening aspect of the role of technology in education. Before the ubiquity of technology, starting up a new college or university required a fairly substantial investment in people, buildings, and materials.[2] Technology has helped eliminate these barriers and has opened the door to new providers in the higher education marketplace, many of them for-profit businesses.

> To Wall Street and entrepreneurs-at-large, the postsecondary education and training market looks huge and ripe for the picking . . . an "addressable market opportunity at the dawn of a new paradigm," in the breathless words of Morgan Stanley Dean Witter. In dollar terms, close to $300 billion is spent a year on the function, $635 billion if grades P–12 are added in. Several Wall Street houses have set up "education industry" practices to attract investors. A report from NationsBanc Montgomery Securities characterizes the industry with words such as "inefficient," "cottage industry," "low tech," and "lack of professional management." It claims $1.7 billion has been raised on Wall Street since 1996 to finance new competitive ventures. (Marchese, 1998, p. 5)

6. *Improving the quality of education.* Technology has the potential to make the educational process more effective, interesting, and challenging for students. Gerald Van Dusen (1997) believes that "although technology is essentially neutral with respect to learning, the new campus environment made possible by technological innovation creates almost unlimited educational opportunities for students, even those constrained by time and distance factors; and well established methods of instruction—demonstration,

simulation, and visualization, for example—may be enhanced by newly available technologies" (p. 39).

While technology may hold great promise, many observers are more skeptical about the extent of its transformational power. According to Terry Hartle, vice president of the American Council on Education, "The question is whether you can deliver quality higher education on a massive scale using existing technology. High quality higher education is hard enough to do when you have people on campuses and in classrooms. Whether or not you can do it successfully at distances and at a large scale we do not know" (quoted in Cushman Jr., 1996, p. A15). Robert Mendenhall (personal communication, November 9, 1999), president of the WGU, has acknowledged that the colleges, universities, and other organizations delivering the courses for the WGU are finding that the economies of scale thought to occur in distance education simply do not exist yet. Faculty who teach distance courses, especially courses involving intensive use of technology, indicate that the instruction requires *more* of their time than classroom teaching. They insist that distance courses be capped at twenty to twenty-five students, the same size as their "bricks and mortar" courses.

Two recent reports have questioned assumptions about both the cost and the quality of virtual education and distance learning.[3] Lawrence Gladieux and Scott Swail (1999) point out that "most educational technology introduced over the past fifty years has supplemented and often enhanced— not supplanted—traditional classroom instruction, thus adding to its cost, not reducing it" (p. 15). The Institute for Higher Education Policy (1999b), in a review of research on the effectiveness of distance learning courses,[4] concludes that although most studies find equivalent levels of student satisfaction and learning outcomes in traditional (classroom-based) and distance education, "the overall quality of the original research is questionable and thereby renders many of the findings inconclusive" (p. 3). The report also finds that "technology cannot replace the human factor in higher education. Faculty involved in distance education find themselves being a combination of content experts, learning process design experts, process implementation managers, motivators, mentors, and interpreters . . . many of the results seem to indicate that technology is not nearly as important as other factors, such as learning tasks, learner characteristics, student motivation, and the instructor" (p. 8).

Technology and the Shaping of Higher Education Policy

What impact has technology had on affordability, access, and accountability in public higher education, and how will it affect these issues in the future? Answering these questions is difficult. Part of the difficulty is the lack of research into how pervasive virtual education and distance learning have become in recent years. The National Center for Education Statistics, the arm of the U.S. Department of Education responsible for collecting and disseminating data about all levels of education, surveyed institutions about distance learning during the 1997–98 academic year (Lewis, Snow, Farris, & Levin 1999). That year, approximately 1.4 million students, or 10 percent of all college students, were enrolled in some form of distance learning. This represented a doubling of the 5 percent of all college students enrolled in at least one distance-learning course in 1995 (Lewis, Alexander, & Farris, 1998). The pace of technological change in recent years is indicated by data on the mode of delivery used by most institutions in the survey: Nineteen percent of the institutions in the later period used the Internet to deliver synchronous computer-based courses (in which communication between parties occurs in real time, as in a telephone conversation) and 58 percent delivered asynchronous courses over the Internet. This represented a substantial increase from the 14 percent of institutions reporting use of either synchronous or asynchronous computer-based instruction in 1995.

The research on virtual learning falls into two categories: (1) small-scale studies of student cognitive outcomes or satisfaction (or both) in distance learning environments, often compared with data for similar students in traditional classrooms (much of this literature was reviewed by the Institute for Higher Education Policy, 1999b); and (2) case-study analyses of how technology is used to facilitate learning at a single site. Few well-designed research studies are available on the use of technology across a broad range of institutions, types of classes, and types of students that would allow any generalization to a broader audience of institutions and students.

Affordability

Contrary to the pronouncements of Roy Romer (noted above), we know little today about whether technology will help hold down instruction costs in colleges and universities, translating into lower tuition prices for students and their families. The cynic might say that computer technology, widely available at the desktop level for more than a dozen years, did little to rein in the tuition increases of the late 1980s and 1990s. A more optimistic viewpoint may be that because institutions are only now beginning to implement wide-scale virtual education programs, it is too early to say what role technology will play in the affordability of higher education. Another problem is the methodologies researchers use to measure the cost of postsecondary instruction. Such studies usually track only the direct tuition (and room and board) costs, neglecting such factors as the time students spend commuting to campus or arranging their schedules around existing class offerings. (See Chapter 1 for more on different measures of the price of attending college.) If distance learning does lower these hidden costs, then studies that ignore them will tend to overestimate the cost of virtual education.

Economic studies of higher education's production function, which examine the costs to institutions of educating students, tend to focus only on operating expenditures with little attention to capital expenses. When capital costs are included, providing traditional "bricks and mortar" higher education can become much more expensive than originally estimated.[5] Governor Leavitt of Utah has used the high cost of building campuses as a rationale for the founding of the WGU. One projection indicates that increasing population and increasing higher education participation rates will double public college and university enrollments in Utah by 2015. While this projection may be overly optimistic, Leavitt estimates that it would cost $3 billion to build the nine new campuses required to accommodate the increased demand (Hamilton & Miller, 1997). Including the cost of capital is also important when calculating the cost of virtual education. Video production studios, high-bandwidth computer networking infrastructure, and Internet-based web servers can greatly add to the direct costs of preparing a computer-based course. The challenge of funding these technology costs cannot be overstated; Molly Broad, president of the University of North Carolina system, outlined this challenge. "If you look at American business, you find there has been a dramatic shift in the share of resources allocated for information technology, both in corporate operating budgets and in capital budgets. We [higher education institutions] are far, far behind. The way we have to invest is a combination of student participation, increased support from the state, uses of partnerships with business and industry, more effective creative financing strategies, and also reallocation of existing resources. We cannot achieve the necessary investment solely by add-ons. At some point those resources will have to come out of internal reallocations" ("Preparing for a Very Different Future," 1999).

Much of the ostensible cost savings in distance education depend upon achieving certain economies of scale. The few studies that have examined these costs recognize that the up-front, fixed costs of developing a technology-laden course likely exceed those of traditional courses (Green, 1997; Massy & Wilger, 1998; Massy & Zemsky, 1996). The potential cost savings come in the delivery of the course: variable costs can be minimized by substituting capital (technology) for labor (faculty). Few have been able to demonstrate true cost savings through application of this model. "The skeptics are right when they say that few extant technology applications have saved money . . . Based on the evidence to date, one cannot be sanguine about the prospect that institutions will voluntarily 'do more with less' through the use of technology" (Massy & Wilger, 1998, p. 51). This view, and that of Gladieux and Swail (1999) described above, was echoed by David Breneman (1995) when he examined potential solutions to accommodating the additional four hundred thousand college students that California is expected to enroll in the next decade. "While higher education is a relatively capital-intense enterprise, it has not benefited from cost savings through the substitution of capital for labor, the route to enhanced productivity in industry. Instead, as new technological capabilities arise, they are typically added to the existing mix of teaching methods, enhancing the quality of education provided, but raising, not lowering, the cost. As a consequence, I am not as optimistic as some about the potential cost savings to be found along the information highway" (pp. 15–16).

The reality may be that it is simply too early in the virtual learning revolution to determine whether technology will help hold down or will increase the price of higher education, or have no impact whatsoever. We need more experience with the use of technology in distance education and better research to measure the efficiency and quality of those experiences to determine whether technology can live up to the cost-savings potential many have predicted.

Access

Even if technology cannot help control increases in the price of higher education, can it at least be used to expand access? This would seem to be the promise subscribed to by the founders of the Western Governors University. The evolving forms of virtual learning, which use the Internet and personal computers to expand and improve on the more traditional forms of distance education (television, videotape, mail), may hold great potential for expanding access to higher education to those students who cannot make their way to a college campus for any reason—time or schedule commitments, family responsibilities, or geographic or physical barriers.

The major providers of virtual learning courses (including traditional colleges and universities now in the virtual learning business) have only just begun their efforts to use the Internet, and they enroll a small number of the almost fifteen million students enrolled in higher education nationwide. The WGU, which perhaps has garnered as much publicity as any virtual learning institution, was founded in 1996 and began enrolling its first students in the fall of 1998. While initial projections were that it would enroll up to 5,000 students in its first year and almost 100,000 by its eighth year, it had only 150 degree-seeking students in the fall of 1999 (Blumenstyk, 1998b, 1998c; R. Mendenhall, personal communication, November 9, 1999; Young, 1999). The California Virtual University, founded in 1997 and championed by California's former governor Pete Wilson as an alternative to the WGU, ceased operations in early 1999 after it depleted its initial funding and could not raise more from private, state, or institutional sources (Blumenstyk, 1999a). North Carolina, which faces a large projected growth in enrollments in the first decade of the new century, expects to count on distance education to serve less than 2 percent of its college students by 2010 (Selingo, 1999b).

Other virtual learning efforts appear to be off to a more promising start. The Southern Regional Education Board estimated in 1998 that institutions in its sixteen member states enrolled twenty thousand students in distance education courses, though it did not distinguish between traditional correspondence courses (using print, broadcast, or video materials) and Internet-based courses ("Enrollment Figures Spur Optimism," 1998). Many of these students enrolled in courses through the Southern Regional Electronic Campus, a broker of virtual learning courses offered by institutions in the sixteen member states. In 1999, Kentucky began the Kentucky Commonwealth Virtual University with $8 million in start-up funds from the legislature (a funding commitment that will help it overcome the obstacle faced by the California Virtual University). The University of Maine System Network for Education and Technology Services (UNET, originally founded as the Education Network of Maine) has operated for ten years and enrolls more than three thousand students, or 10 percent of the total public enrollment in the state (University of Maine System, 1999). While its course offerings have been delivered primarily through one-way television links to remote sites (with some courses offered via cable television), UNET has begun to offer courses over the Internet. The Open University in Great Britain, widely recognized as the largest and most successful distance learning institution in the world, enrolls more than 150,000 students annually and has awarded 227,000 degrees since it began in 1971 (Blumenstyk, 1999b). It too has begun to make more use of the Internet in recent years to expand on the more traditional forms of distance education offered since its founding.

A key question about the impact of distance education on access is, access to what? The Institute for Higher Education Policy (1999b) raised a number of related questions in its review of research on the efficacy of distance learning. "Questions that need to be asked include the following: What is the 'quality' of the access? Does the student have the necessary skills to use the technology? What are the best ways to participate in asynchronous communication? Is there adequate technical support? Perhaps the most important, will the cost of purchasing a computer and maintaining software be prohibitive for a substantial number of students?" (p. 30). We know that access to traditional "bricks and mortar" higher education is not the same at all institutions; the education a student receives at a community college is different from that at a large research university. So why shouldn't virtual learning be considered just one more access point for students seeking a postsecondary education?

In the words of WGU cofounder Mike Leavitt, the WGU "isn't something that we're inventing. The market is driving it. People are demanding it" (quoted in Blumenstyk, 1998a, p. A23). The concern of many, however, is that a computer-based education will become the only entry point to college for some students and that technology will be used to supplant the choice of traditional institutions available under the current higher education policy structure. Almost all students must have a high school diploma or General Educational Development credential before entering a postsecondary degree or certificate program, but a virtual education also requires students either to have or to develop particular computer skills. A recent study by the National Telecommunications and Information Administration (1999) found that computer ownership and network access are strongly correlated with income and race. In 1998, 80 percent of families with annual incomes above $75,000 owned a personal computer, but less than 25 percent of those with incomes below $25,000. In the same year, almost 50 percent of white families owned a computer, but only a quarter of African American and Hispanic families. Similar gaps occurred in access to electronic mail and the Internet. Computer skills are important to students pursuing any form of postsecondary education, but they are most critical to students participating in an entirely or largely virtual-based educational experience.

Another barrier to wide-scale implementation of virtual education is the current structure of the financial aid programs in the United States. Title IV of the Higher Education Act, which authorizes the majority of federal student aid programs, restricts access by institutions that enroll more than half their students or offer more than half their courses in distance education. In addition, the regulations stipulate an academic year of at least thirty weeks for students to be eligible for the maximum amount of federal grants and loans, and no aid to distance education students for computers or living expenses (Selingo, 1998a; van der Werf, 1999). Recognizing the key role of financial aid in determining access to college, in the 1998 reauthorization of the Higher Education Act the U.S. Congress mandated that the Department of Education create a pilot project that waives these regulations for some institutions and students.[6] In July 1999 the department announced the first fifteen institutions to participate in the pilot.

In response to the pilot project, a coalition of colleges and universities in Colorado organized a roundtable discussion of key issues on financial aid for distance-education students (Institute for Higher Education Policy, 1999a). The discussions, involving institutional leaders and policymakers from around the nation, focused on three primary questions about financial aid policy and distance education: Where are we now? Where do we want to go? What do we need to change to get there? The group developed six principles for future policy development:

1. Student aid should be available without regard to mode of instructional delivery.
2. Delivery of student aid should be learner-centered, with aid following the student through the academic program.
3. Aid should be awarded only to those in accredited programs of study that confer a recognized credential, such as a degree or certificate.
4. The awarding of student aid should be tied primarily to standards of academic progress and not arbitrary measures of time.
5. Regulations should give institutions flexibility in determining how to calculate eligibility for aid to pay for direct ("tuition") and indirect ("living expenses") costs of attendance.
6. Aid amounts and limits should be focused more on lifetime standards than on annual or institutional maximums (pp. 21–23).

The participants believed these principles could ensure that financial aid would continue to assist in providing both access to and choice of higher education programs and institutions in an era of continuing expansion of virtual learning.

Accountability

Little has been written about the expanding role of technology in the accountability movement in U.S. public higher education. The biggest link to the accountability movement is the way in which technology is changing the structure of higher education. A number of authors (Blustain, Goldstein, & Lozier, 1998; Duderstadt, 1998; Marchese, 1998) have described how technology is opening up higher education to new competitors, many of which are in the business sector and see an opportunity for profit through the delivery of postsecondary education. This increasing level of competition among postsecondary institutions (expanded beyond the existing mix of public and private, not-for-profit institutions) may add a new type of accountability to public higher education: accountability to the marketplace.[7]

In 1999, Jones International University (JIU) became the first entirely virtual university to become an accredited institution, an action that drew fire from many in higher education. JIU is a subsidiary of Jones International, a conglomerate that includes the Knowledge TV cable television channel. A letter from the American Association of University Professors (1999) to the executive director of the North Central Association of Colleges and Schools (the body that accredited JIU) expressed "shock and dismay at the reported action of . . . accrediting Jones International University . . . By all public accounts, this virtual institution presents a very weak case for accreditation. Indeed it embodies most of our major worries about the denigration of quality that could follow this apparently inexorable march toward on-line education." The accreditation of JIU raised the stakes in the higher education marketplace.

In 1998, the University of Phoenix applied for a license to operate a campus in New Jersey, its first in the eastern United States. The application attracted notice and concern from both public and private institutions in New Jersey. While most responses were critical, some community colleges welcomed Phoenix because of past difficulties in establishing transfer agreements with four-year colleges and universities (Selingo, 1998b). The community colleges thought Phoenix was more willing to accept transfers into its baccalaureate programs and thus would improve the marketability of a community college as the starting point for a degree program.

Nine months after filing its application, and before a detailed review could be completed by the New Jersey Commission on Higher Education, Phoenix withdrew its request. It instead chose Pennsylvania as the site for its first programs in the east and was quickly granted approval by that state's Secretary of Education (Selingo, 1999a). A vice-president of a private college in the Pittsburgh area, where the first Phoenix campus would be developed, recognized the potential impact the new competitor would have on the existing institutions in that area. "It has already forced some four-year institutions to develop articulation agreements with community colleges. Institutions that are flexible and innovative are going to survive. Phoenix appeals to adults who know what they want and how they want to get it" (quoted in Selingo, 1999a, p. A43).

Public and nonprofit institutions now must compete for students not only with each other (in traditional and virtual classes) and with new virtual learning brokers such as the Western Governors University and Southern Regional Electronic Campus, but also with new, for-profit entities such as JIU that will deliver their own virtual education courses. Observers of the higher education market believe this new competition is akin to the charter school movement in K–12 education. Charter schools, by offering a low- or zero-cost alternative to public schools, provide an incentive for public schools to improve in order to compete for students. Public schools are forced to be more accountable to students and their parents, rather than answering only to school boards, teachers' unions, and state education bureaucracies. In the same manner, for-profit, accredited postsecondary institutions will provide a new alternative to traditional higher education. As the market is still evolving and responding to the changes enabled by technology and virtual learning, the basis on which these new challengers will compete—price, convenience, quality, or other criteria—remains to be seen.

The entry of new players in the postsecondary education marketplace may induce legislatures, governors, and state coordinating boards to place more pressure on public colleges and universities to change how they educate their students. If adoption of technology into the college curriculum is seen as a means of controlling the costs or improving the quality of instruction or improving access to college, policymakers are likely to accept it as a yardstick with which to measure the performance of public institutions. As described in Chapter 7, a number of states that have initiated performance-based funding schemes have included measures of the use of technology and distance learning in the criteria used to assess public colleges and universities. A 1998 survey conducted by the State Higher Education Executive Officers found that ten states have included standards on funding for distance and virtual education initiatives in their higher education appropriations process (Epper, 1999). As the use of technology in instruction expands, we can expect more states to jump on the bandwagon and establish specific performance and funding goals in this area.

Conclusion

Technology is not the only force that will help shape the future of public higher education policy, but it is one that has garnered much attention and is likely to continue to do so. Although technology holds great promise, we have yet to see whether its impact on public colleges and universities will be evolutionary or revolutionary. The evolutionists envision a scenario in which institutions slowly adapt and change to take advantage of the power of computers, networks, and other forms of technology to integrate them more fully into the existing postsecondary educational paradigm. Technological revolutionaries believe that computers will radically reshape higher education, replacing not just the current modes of instruction but also the existing organizational structures.

Policymakers and institutional leaders need to be proactive in encouraging the implementation and use of technology in higher education. Used appropriately, computers and other types of technology may be critical tools for addressing the societal demands on public higher education institutions. More research is needed, however, to determine how best to use technology. Technological innovation and adoption for its own sake will not serve the public interest. What we need at the start of the new millennium is to make the best use of technology to achieve our existing goals for more affordable, accessible, and accountable public institutions of higher education.

Notes

1. This claim by the backers of virtual learning is somewhat overstated. Some support costs, in the form of faculty or other instructional personnel, will increase with the number of students enrolled in a virtual learning course. But these costs would conceivably be less (and grow less quickly as the number of students increased) than in a traditional classroom.

2. For more than a century, numerous correspondence schools in the United States have offered postsecondary education at a distance, with few or no physical facilities. Many are not accredited, however, and therefore occupy a different market niche than traditional (accredited) institutions. Those that are accredited have generally focused their efforts on small sectors of the market and have enrolled a very small percentage of all college students.

3. *Virtual education* and *distance learning* are used interchangeably here to describe the use of technology to facilitate learning outside the traditional classroom.

4. Some of the research reviewed by the institute involved less technology-intensive forms of distance learning, including correspondence courses and television-based courses.

5. Gordon Winston of Williams College has written on the importance of including capital expenditures when calculating higher education production functions (Winston, 1992, 1993, 1999; Winston & Lewis, 1997).

6. The prominence of the WGU was solidified during the reauthorization as it was the only institution mandated to be included in the first phase of the pilot project.

7. Higher education has long been the subject of competition from proprietary (for-profit) trade schools. Most of these institutions, however, occupy a particular niche of the postsecondary market, offering only programs below the associate degree level. A handful of for-profit institutions, including the University of Phoenix (a subsidiary of the Apollo Group, Inc.), ITT Educational Services, Inc.,

and DeVry, Inc., offer accredited bachelor's and master's degrees (Strosnider, 1998). Most students at these institutions are still enrolled in traditional, classroom-based courses, however.

References

American Association of University Professors. (1999, March). Letter from Dr. James Perley, AAUP, to Dr. Steven D. Crow, North Central Association of Colleges and Schools [On-line]. Washington, DC: Author. Available: http://www.aaup.org/319let.htm

Blumenstyk, G. (1998a, February 6). Utah's governor enjoys role as a leading proponent of distance learning. *Chronicle of Higher Education*, pp. A23–A24.

Blumenstyk, G. (1998b, February 6). Western Governors U. takes shape as a new model for higher education. *Chronicle of Higher Education*, pp. A21–A23.

Blumenstyk, G. (1998c, September 25). Few students enroll at Western Governors U. *Chronicle of Higher Education*, p. A35.

Blumenstyk, G. (1999a, April 2). California Virtual University will end most of its operations. *Chronicle of Higher Education*, p. A30.

Blumenstyk, G. (1999b, July 23). Distance learning at the Open University. *Chronicle of Higher Education*, p. A35.

Blustain, H., Goldstein, P., & Lozier, G. (1998). Assessing the new competitive landscape. *CAUSE/EFFECT, 21*(3), 19–27.

Breneman, D. W. (1995). *A state of emergency? Higher education in California*. San Jose: California Higher Education Policy Center.

Cushman, J. H., Jr. (1996, June 25). Virtual university will offer authentic degrees by e-mail. *New York Times*, p. A15.

Duderstadt, J. J. (1997, August). *The challenges and opportunities of the digital age for higher education*. Paper presented at the Seminars on Academic Computing, Snowmass, CO.

Duderstadt, J. J. (1998, February). *The 21st century university: A tale of two futures*. Paper presented at the NACUBO Financial Executives Symposium, Washington, DC.

Enrollment figures spur optimism at virtual universities. (1998, November 27). *Chronicle of Higher Education*, p. A21.

Epper, R. M. (1999). *State policies for distance education: A survey of the states*. Denver, CO: State Higher Education Executive Officers.

Gladieux, L. E., & Swail, W. S. (1999). *The virtual university and educational opportunity*. Washington, DC: College Board.

Green, K. C. (1997). Money, technology, and distance education. *On the Horizon, 5*(6), 3–7.

Hamilton, K., & Miller, S. (1997, March 10). Internet U—No ivy, no walls, no keg parties. *Newsweek*, p. 12.

Institute for Higher Education Policy. (1999a). *Student aid for distance learners: Charting a new course*. Washington, DC: Author.

Institute for Higher Education Policy. (1999b). *What's the difference? A review of contemporary research on the effectiveness of distance learning in higher education*. Washington, DC: Author.

Lenzner, R., & Johnson, S. S. (1997, March 10). Seeing things as they really are. *Forbes, 159*(5), 122–128.

Lewis, L., Alexander, D., & Farris, E. (1998). *Distance education in higher education institutions*. Washington, DC: National Center for Education Statistics.

Lewis, L., Snow, K., Farris, E., & Levin, D. (1999). *Distance education at postsecondary education institutions: 1997–98*. Washington, DC: National Center for Education Statistics.

Marchese, T. (1998, May). Not-so-distant competitors: How new providers are remaking the postsecondary marketplace. *AAHE Bulletin, 50*, 3–9.

Massy, W. F., & Wilger, A. K. (1998). Technology's contribution to higher education productivity. In J. Groccia & J. Miller (Eds.), *Enhancing productivity: Administrative, instructional, and technological strategies*. San Francisco: Jossey-Bass.

Massy, W. F., & Zemsky, R. (1996). Information technology and academic productivity. *Educom Review, 31*(1), 12–14.

National Telecommunications and Information Administration. (1999). *Falling through the net: Defining the digital divide*. Washington, DC: U.S. Department of Commerce.

Preparing for a very different future: An interview with Molly Broad. (1999). [Online]. *CAUSE/EFFECT* 22(1). Available: http://www.educause.edu/pub/ce/cem99/cem991.html

Selingo, J. (1998a, June 5). Congress moves cautiously on aid for students in distance education. *Chronicle of Higher Education*, pp. A30–A31.

Selingo, J. (1998b, October 23). U. of Phoenix picks New Jersey for its first foray in eastern U.S. *Chronicle of Higher Education*, pp. A28–A30.

Selingo, J. (1999a, March 26). Pennsylvania surprises colleges by letting U. of Phoenix open campuses in state. *Chronicle of Higher Education*, p. A43.

Selingo, J. (1999b, July 9). Several fast-growing states prepare for projected enrollment increases. *Chronicle of Higher Education*, pp. A36–A37.

Strosnider, K. (1998, January 23). For-profit higher education sees booming enrollments and revenues. *Chronicle of Higher Education*, pp. A36–A37.

Twigg, C. A. (1996). Is technology a silver bullet? *Educom Review, 31*(2), 28–29.

University of Maine System. (1999). *University of Maine system profile* [On-line]. Bangor: Author. Available: http://www.maine.edu/profile.html

Van der Werf, M. (1999, July 9). Colleges picked for project on aid to distance-learning students. *Chronicle of Higher Education*, p. A34.

Van Dusen, G. (1997). *The virtual campus: Technology and reform in higher education* (ASHE-ERIC Higher Education Report Vol. 25, No. 5). Washington, DC: George Washington University,

Winston, G. C. (1992). The necessary revolution in financial accounting. *Planning for Higher Education, 20*(4), 1–16.

Winston, G. C. (1993). Why are capital costs ignored by nonprofit organizations and what are the prospects for change? In M. S. McPherson, M. O. Schapiro, & G. C. Winston, *Paying the piper: Productivity, incentives, and financing in U.S. higher education*. Ann Arbor: University of Michigan Press.

Winston, G. C. (1999). Subsidies, hierarchy and peers: The awkward economics of higher education. *Journal of Economic Perspectives, 13*(1), 13–36.

Winston, G. C., & Lewis, E. G. (1997). Physical capital and capital service costs in U.S. colleges and universities: 1993. *Eastern Economic Journal, 23*(2), 165–189.

Young, J. R. (1999, May 7). A virtual student teaches himself. *Chronicle of Higher Education*, pp. A31–A34.

Contributors

ERIC H. ASKER is a doctoral candidate in the School of Education, Indiana University. His research focuses on issues of graduate student persistence.

DAVID W. BRENEMAN is University Professor and Dean of the Curry School of Education, University of Virginia. From 1990 to 1995 he was a visiting professor at the Harvard Graduate School of Education. As a visiting fellow at the Brookings Institution, Breneman conducted research for *Liberal Arts Colleges: Thriving, Surviving, or Endangered?*. He formerly served as president of Kalamazoo College.

PATRICK M. CALLAN is president of the National Center for Public Policy and Higher Education in San Jose, California. He has served as executive director of the California Higher Education Policy Center, the California Postsecondary Education Commission, the Washington State Council on Postsecondary Education, and the Montana Commission on Postsecondary Education, and as vice president of the Education Commission of the States.

JOHN COLE is a Spencer Foundation Fellow and doctoral candidate in the Center for the Study of Higher and Postsecondary Education and a research assistant at the National Center for Postsecondary Improvement, University of Michigan. His chief research interests include assessment, federal higher education policy, and international and comparative higher education.

ARTHUR M. HAUPTMAN is an independent public policy consultant and author, writing on issues relating to student aid, college costs, and higher education finance. His most recent book, *The College Aid Quandary*, coauthored with Lawrence Gladieux, examines the federal role in helping students pay for college. Over the past two decades Hauptman has been a consultant to the federal government, state agencies, and dozens of colleges and universities on issues of higher education finance.

DONALD E. HELLER is an assistant professor at the Center for the Study of Higher and Postsecondary Education, University of Michigan. He teaches and conducts research on issues relating to higher education economics, public policy, and finance, as well as academic and administrative uses of technology in higher education. He has been a consultant on higher education policy issues to university systems and policymaking organizations in several states.

SYLVIA HURTADO is an associate professor at the Center for the Study of Higher and Postsecondary Education, University of Michigan. Her book *Enacting Diverse Learning Environments* focuses on the research, practice, and access policies that promote better campus climates for the success of diverse college students.

KIMBERLY A. KLINE is a graduate student in the Department of Educational Leadership and Policy Studies, Indiana University. Her research interests include higher education policy, adventure-based education, and organizational cultures.

MICHAEL MUMPER is a professor and chairman of the Department of Political Science, Ohio University. His teaching and research interests are in the politics of higher education, social welfare, and economic policy. His most recent book is *Removing College Price Barriers: What Government Has Done and Why It Hasn't Worked.*

MICHAEL NETTLES is a professor at the Center for the Study of Higher and Postsecondary Education, University of Michigan. He was formerly assistant director for academic affairs at the Tennessee Higher Education Commission, senior research scientist in the Education Policy Research Division at the Educational Testing Service, and vice president for assessment for the University of Tennessee system.

BRIAN PUSSER is an assistant professor in the Department of Leadership, Foundations and Policy and an affiliate in the Center for the Study of Higher Education at the Curry School of Education, University of Virginia. His research addresses higher education organization and governance, including studies of the political context shaping access and admissions, the dynamics of governing board appointments, and the influence of interest groups on higher education policymaking.

EDWARD P. ST. JOHN is a professor in the Department of Educational Leadership and Policy Studies, chairman of the Higher Education Program, and director of the Indiana Education Policy Center, Indiana University. His research considers higher education finance and a range of policy issues in both elementary/secondary and higher education. His most recent book, coauthored with Alison I. Griffith and Leetta Allen-Haynes, is *Families in Schools: A Chorus of Voices in Restructuring.*

HEATHER WATHINGTON CADE is a doctoral student and research assistant in the Center for the Study of Higher and Postsecondary Education, University of Michigan. Her research interests include diversity in higher education, affirmative action policy, and the postgraduate outcomes of students who attended minority-serving institutions.

WILLIAM ZUMETA is a professor at the Daniel J. Evans School of Public Affairs and the College of Education, University of Washington, where he teaches public budgeting, policy analysis, and higher education policy and finance. He is the author of *Extending the Educational Ladder: The Changing Quality and Value of Postdoctoral Education in the United States.* Zumeta has served on the editorial boards of *Review of Higher Education* and *Journal of Public Administration Research and Theory.* He is a member of the Policy Council (national board) of the Association for Public Policy Analysis and Management.

Index